Julia Georger,
May, 1916.

PSYCHOTHERAPY

PSYCHOTHERAPY

BY

HUGO MÜNSTERBERG

M.D., PH.D., LITT.D., LL.D.

PROFESSOR OF PSYCHOLOGY IN HARVARD UNIVERSITY

NEW YORK

MOFFAT, YARD AND COMPANY

1913

TO

MY FRIEND AND COLLEAGUE

DR. FRANZ PFAFF

PROFESSOR OF THERAPEUTICS IN
HARVARD UNIVERSITY

PREFACE

THIS volume on psychotherapy belongs to a series of books which I am writing to discuss for a wider public the practical applications of modern psychology. The first book, called "On the Witness Stand," studied the relations of scientific psychology to crime and the law courts. This new book deals with the relations of psychology to medicine. Others discussing its relations to education, to social problems, to commerce and industry will follow soon.

For popular treatment I divide applied psychology into such various, separated books because they naturally address very different audiences. That which interests the lawyer does not concern the physician, and again the school-teacher has his own sphere of interests. Moreover the different subjects demand a different treatment. The problems of psychology and law were almost entirely neglected. I was anxious to draw wide attention to this promising field and therefore I chose the form of loose popular essays without any aim towards systematic presentation of the subject. As to psychology and medicine almost the opposite situation prevails. There is perhaps too much talk afloat about psychotherapy, the widest circles cultivate the discussion, the magazines overflow with it. The duty of the scientific psychologist is accordingly not to stir up interest in this topic but to help in bringing this interest from mere gossip, vague mysticism, and medical amateurishness to a clear understanding of principles. What is needed in this time of faith cures of a hundred types is to deal with the whole circle of problems in a serious, systematic way and to emphasize the aspect of scientific psychological theory.

Hence the whole first part of this book is an abstract discussion and its first chapters have not even any direct relation to disease. I am convinced that both physicians and ministers and all who are in practical contact with these important questions ought to be brought to such painstaking and perhaps fatiguing inquiry into principles before the facts are reached. To those who seek a discussion of life facts alone, the whole first part will of course appear to be a tedious way around; they may turn directly to the second and third parts.

One word for my personal right to deal with these questions, as too much illegitimate psychotherapeutics is heard to-day. For me, the relation between psychology and medicine is not a chance chapter of my science to which I have turned simply in following up the various sides of applied psychology. And still less have I turned to it because it has become the fashion in recent years. On the contrary, it has been an important factor in all my work since my student days. I have been through five years of regular medical studies, three years in Leipzig and two years in Heidelberg; I have an M.D. degree from the University of Heidelberg. In my first year as docent in a German university twenty years ago, I gave throughout the winter semester before several hundred students a course in hypnotism and its medical application. It was probably the first university course on hypnotism given anywhere. Since that time I have never ceased to work psychotherapeutically in the psychological laboratory. Yet that must not be misunderstood. I have no clinic, and while by principle I have never hypnotized anyone for mere experiment's sake but always only for medical purposes, yet I adjust my practical work entirely to the interests of my scientific study. The limitations of my time force me to refuse the psychotherapeutic treatment of any case which has not a certain scientific interest for me, and of the many hundreds whom I have helped in the laboratory, no one ever had to pay anything. Thus my practical work has strictly the character of laboratory research.

The chief aim of this book is twofold. It is a negative one: I want to counteract the misunderstandings which overflood the whole field, especially by the careless mixing of mental and moral influence. And a positive one: I want to strengthen the public feeling that the time has come when every physician should systematically study psychology, the normal in the college years and the abnormal in the medical school. This demand of medical education cannot be postponed any longer. The aim of the book is not to fight the Emmanuel Church Movement, or

even Christian Science or any other psychotherapeutic
tendency outside of the field of scientific medicine.   I
see the element of truth in all of them, but they ought
to be symptoms of transition.   Scientific medicine
should take hold of psychotherapeutics now or a most
deplorable disorganization will set in, the symptoms
of which no one ought to overlook to-day.

HUGO MUNSTERBERG.

HARVARD UNIVERSITY, March 20, 1909.

CONTENTS

I

INTRODUCTION

PSYCHOTHERAPY is the practice of treating the sick by influencing the mental life. It stands at the side of physicotherapy, which attempts to cure the sick by influencing the body, perhaps with drugs and medicines, or with electricity or baths or diet.

Psychotherapy is sharply to be separated from psychiatry, the treatment of mental diseases. Of course to a certain degree, mental illness too, is open to mental treatment; but certainly many diseases of the mind lie entirely beyond the reach of psychotherapy, and on the other hand psychotherapy may be applied also to diseases which are not mental at all. That which binds all psychotherapeutic efforts together into unity is the method of treatment. The psychotherapist must always somehow set levers of the mind in motion and work through them towards the removal of the sufferer's ailment; but the disturbances to be treated may show the greatest possible variety and may belong to mind or body.

Treatment of diseases by influence on the mind is as old as human history, but it has attained at various times very different degrees of importance. There is no lack of evidence that we have entered into a period in which an especial emphasis will be laid on the too long neglected psychical factor. This new movement is probably only in its beginning and the loudness with which it presents itself to-day is one of the many indications of its immaturity. Whether it will be a blessing or a danger, whether it will really lead forward in a lasting way, or whether it will soon demand a reaction, will probably depend in the first place on the soberness and thoroughness of the discussion. If the movement is carried on under the control of science, it may yield lasting results. If it keeps the features of dilettanteism and prefers association with the antiscientific tendencies, it is predestined to have a spasmodic character and ultimately to be harmful.

The chaotic character of psychotherapy in this first decade of the twentieth century can be easily understood. It results from the fact that in our period one great wave of civilization is sinking and a new wave rising, while the one has not entirely disappeared and the other is still far from its height. The history of civilization has shown at all times a wavelike alternation between realism and idealism, that is, between an interest in that which is, and an interest in that which ought to be. In the realistic periods, the study of facts, especially of the facts of nature, is prevalent; in idealistic periods, history and literature appeal to the world. In realistic periods, technique enjoys its triumphs; in idealistic periods, art and religion prevail. Such a realistic movement lies behind us. It began with the incomparable development of physics, chemistry, and biology, in the middle of the last century, and it brought with it the achievements of modern engineering and medicine. We are still fully under the influence of this gigantic movement and its real achievements will never leave us; and yet this realistic wave is ebbing to-day and a new period of idealism is rising. If the signs are not deceitful, this new movement may reach its historical climax a few decades hence, when new leaders may give to the idealistic view of the world the same classical expression which Darwin and others gave to the receding naturalistic age. The signs are clear indeed that the days of idealistic philosophy and of art, and of religion, are approaching; that the world is tired of merely connecting facts without asking what their ultimate meaning is. The world dimly feels again that technical civilization alone cannot make life more worth living. The aim of the last generation was to explain the world; the aim of the next generation will be to interpret the world; the one was seeking laws, the other will seek ideals.

Psychotherapy stands in the service of both; it is the last word of the passing naturalistic movement, and yet in another way it tries to be the first word of the coming idealistic movement; and because it is under the influence of both, it speaks sometimes the language of the one, and sometimes the language of the other. That brings about a confusion and a disorder which must be detrimental. To transform this vagueness into clear, distinct relations is the immediate duty of science.

Indeed it may be said that psychotherapy is the last word of a naturalistic age, because psychotherapy finds its real stronghold in a systematic study of the mental laws, and such study of mental laws, psychology, must indeed be the ultimate outcome of a naturalistic view of the world. Realism begins with the analysis of lifeless nature, begins with the study of the stars and the stones, of masses and of atoms. At a higher level, it turns then to the living organism, studies plants and animals and even brings the human organism entirely under the point of view of natural law. When science has thus mastered the whole physical universe, it finally brings even the mental life of man under the naturalistic point of view, treats his inner experiences like any outer objects, tears them in pieces, analyzes them, and studies them as functions of the nervous system. A scientific psychology is thus reached which is the climax of realism, because it means that even the ideas and emotions and volitions of man are treated as natural phenomena, that their causes are sought and that their effects are determined, that their laws are found out. To apply this realistic knowledge of the mind in the interest of therapy is merely to use it in the same way in which the engineer uses his knowledge of physics, when he wants to harness outer nature. As that is possible only when theoretical science has reached a certain height of development, it can indeed be said that practical psychotherapy on a scientific basis can be considered almost as the ultimate point of a realistic movement; it cannot set in until psychology has reached high development, and psychology cannot set in unless biology has preceded it.

There is no doubt that we are still far from this last phase of the realistic period. The practical application of scientific psychology is still a new problem. Experimental psychology began about twenty-five years ago; at that time there existed one psychological laboratory. To-day there is no university in the world which does not have a psychological workshop. But laboratories for applied psychology are only arising in these present days, and the systematic application of scientific psychology to education and law and industry and social life and medicine is almost at its beginning. While the height of the last realistic wave was in the period of the sixties, seventies, and eighties, of the last century, its last phase, the practical application of physiological psychology, including psychotherapy, is only at its commencement.

But while this last great movement has not yet reached its end, the new idealistic movement to come has not yet reached a clear self-expression. A general philosophical interest can be felt, but a great philosophical synthesis seems still lacking. A new sense of duty can vaguely be felt, but great new tasks have not yet found common acknowledgment. Above all, the unshaped emotionalism of the masses has not yet been brought into any real contact with the new idealism which grows up on the higher level of scholarly thought. But it is evident, if a new great mood of idealism is to come, one of its popular forerunners must be the demand that the spirit is real in a higher sense than matter, that the mind controls the body, that faith can cure. In such unphilosophic crudeness, no definite thought is expressed, as everything would depend on the definition of spirit, of faith, of mind, of reality. Moreover, every inquiry would prove that the idealistic value of such statements as are afloat among the masses to-day is reached only by a juggling with words. That faith can cure appears to point towards the higher world, as the word faith has there the connotation of the faith in a religious sense; and yet the faith which really cures a digestive trouble, for instance, is the faith in the final overcoming of the intestinal disturbance, an idea which belongs evidently in the region of physiological psychology, but not in the region of the church. Yet, however clumsy such statements may be, they are surely controlled by the instinctive desire for a new idealistic order of our life, and the time will come when their unreasoning and unreasonable wisdom will be transformed into sound philosophy without losing its deepest impulse. The realistic conviction that even the mind is completely controlled by natural laws and the idealistic inspiration that the mind of man has in its freedom mastery over the body, are thus most curiously mixed in the popular psychotherapy of the day, and too few recognize that the real meaning of mind is an entirely different one in these two propositions.

Of course the one or the other of these two elements prevails in the systematic treatises on the sub-

ject; the realistic one in those written by the psychiatrists, the idealistic one in those written by clergy-
men or Christian Scientists. The literature indeed is
almost entirely supplied from these two quarters: and
yet it is evident that neither the one nor the other
party can give to the problem its most natural setting.
The student of mental diseases naturally emphasizes
the abnormal features of the situation, and thus
brings the psychotherapeutic process too much into
the neighborhood of pathology. Psychotherapy became in such hands essentially a study of hypnotism,
with especial interest in its relation to hysteria and
similar diseases. The much more essential relation
of psychotherapy to the normal mental life, the relation of suggestion and hypnotism to the normal
functions seemed too often neglected. Whoever
wants to influence the mind in the interest of the
patient, must in the first place be in intimate contact
with psychology. On the other hand, the minister's
spiritual interest brings the facts nearer to religion
than they really are. That a suggestion to get rid
of toothache, or to sleep the next night, is given by a
minister, does not constitute it as a religious suggestion. If the belief in religion simply lies alongside of the belief in most trivial effects, and both are
applied in the same way for curing the sick, it is evident that not the spiritual meaning of religion is
responsible for the cure, but the psychological process
of believing. But if that is the case, it is clear that
here again the psychologist, and not the moralist, will
give the correct account of the real process involved.

In short, it is psychology, psychology in its scientific modern form, which has to furnish the basis for a full understanding of psychotherapy. From psychology it cannot be difficult to bridge over to the medical interests, on the one side, to the idealistic ones on the other side.

Our task here is, therefore, to lay a broad psychological foundation. We must carefully inquire how the modern psychologist looks on mental life and how the inner experiences appear from such a psychological standpoint. The first chapters of this volume may appear like a long, tiresome way around before we come to our goal, the study of the psychotherapeutic agencies. And yet it is the only possible way to overcome the superficiality with which the discussion is too often carried on; we must understand exactly how the psychological analysis and explanation of the scientist differ from the popular point of view. After studying in this spirit the foundation of psychotherapy, we shall carefully examine the practical work, its methods and its results, its possibilities and its limitations. We shall inquire finally into the place which it has to take, looking back upon its history, criticising the present status and outlining the development which has to set in for the future, if a haphazard zigzag movement is not to destroy this great agency for human welfare by transforming it into a source of superstition and bodily danger.

PART I

THE PSYCHOLOGICAL BASIS OF PSYCHO-
THERAPY

II

THE AIM OF PSYCHOLOGY

THE only safe basis of psychotherapy is a thorough psychological knowledge of the human personality. Yet such a claim has no value until it is entirely clear what is meant by psychological knowledge. We can know man in many ways. Not every study of man's inner life is psychology and the careless mixing of different ways of dealing with man's inner life is largely responsible for the vagueness which characterizes the popular literature of psychotherapy. It is not enough to say that a statement is true or not true. It may be true under one aspect and entirely meaningless under another. For instance, a minister's discussion of man's energies may be full of deep truth and may be inspiring; and yet it may not contain the slightest contribution to a really psychological knowledge of those energies, and would mislead entirely the physician were he to base his treatment of human energies on such a religious interpretation.

Can we not look from different standpoints even

on any part of the outer world? I see before me the ocean with its excited waves splashing against the rocks and shore, I see the boats tossed on the stormy sea and I am fascinated by the new and ever new impulses of the tumultuous waves. The whole appears to me like one gigantic energy, like one great emotional expression, and I feel deeply how I understand this beautiful scenery in appreciating its unity and its meaning. Yet would I ever think that it is the only way to understand this turmoil of the waters before me? I know there is no unity and no emotion in the excited sea; each wave is composed of hundreds of thousands of single drops of water, and each drop composed of billions of atoms, and every movement results from mechanical laws under the influence of the pressing water and air. There is hydrogen and there is oxygen, and there is chloride of sodium, and the dark blue color is nothing but the reflection of billions of ether vibrations. But have I really to choose between two statements concerning the waves, one of which is valuable and the other not? On the contrary, both have fundamental value. If I take the attitude of appreciation, it would be absurd to say that this wave is composed of chemical elements which I do not see; and if I take the attitude of physical explanation, it would be equally absurd to deny that such elements are all of which the wave is made. From the one standpoint, the ocean is really excited; from the other standpoint, the molecules are moving according to the laws of hydrodynamics. If I want to understand the meaning of this scene every reminiscence of physics will lead me astray; if I want to calculate the movement of my boat, physics alone can help me.

As long as we deal with outer nature, there is hardly a fear of confusing the various attitudes; but it becomes by far more complex when we deal with man and his inner life. We might abstract entirely from æsthetic appreciation or from moral valuation, we might take man just as an object of knowledge; and yet what we know about him may be entirely different in accordance with our special attitude. Each kind of knowledge may be entirely true, and yet true only from the particular standpoint. Let us consider two extremes. If I meet a friend and we enter into a talk, I try to understand his thoughts and to share his views. I agree or disagree with him; I sympathize with his feelings, I estimate his purposes. In short, he is for me a center of aims and intentions which I interpret: he comes in question for me as a self which has its meaning and has its unity. The more I am interested in his opinions, the more I feel in every utterance, in every gesture, the expression of his will and his purposes; their whole reality for me lies in the fact that they point to something which the speaker intends; his personality lies in his attitude towards the surroundings, towards the world. Yet I may take an entirely different relation to the same man. I may ask myself what processes are going on in his mind, what are the real contents of his consciousness, that is, what perceptions and memory pictures and imaginative ideas and feelings and emotions and judgments and volitions are really present in his consciousness. I watch him to find out, I observe his mental states, I do not ask whether I agree or disagree; his will is for me now not something which has a meaning, but simply something which occurs in his inner experience; his ideas now have for me no reference to something in the world, but they are simply contents of his consciousness; his memories now are for me not symbols of a past to which he refers, but they are present pictures in his mind; in short, what I now find is not a self which shows itself in its aims and purposes and attitudes, but a complex content of consciousness which is composed of numberless elements. I might say in the first place that my friend was to me a subject whom I tried to understand by interpreting his meaning, and in the second case, an object which I understand by describing its structure, its elements, and their connections.

Both ways of looking on man are constantly needed. We might alternate between them in any experience. In the heat of argument, my friend will certainly be for me the subject with whose meanings I try to agree or disagree, whose emotions carry me away, whose ideas open the world to me. Yet in the next moment, I may notice that his ideas were shaped and determined by certain earlier experiences; that they linked themselves in memory according to certain laws of mental flow; that the vividness of his ideas made him overlook certain impressions of the surroundings; and that may turn my attention to an entirely different aspect of his inner life. His feelings and emotions, his volitions and judgments now have for me simply the character of processes which go on and which are observed, which coincide and which succeed each other, which fuse and overlap, and which are composed of smaller parts. My interest is now no longer in the meaning and intentions of this self, but it belongs to the structure and the connections in this system of mental facts. At first, I wanted to understand him by living with him, by participating in his attitudes, and by feeling with his will; now I want to understand him by examining all the processes which go on in his consciousness, by studying their make-up and their behavior, their elements and their laws. In one case I wanted to interpret the man, and finally to appreciate him; in the other case I wanted to describe his inner life, and finally to explain it. The man whose inner life I want to share I treat as a subject, the man whose inner life I want to describe and explain I treat as an object.

I might express these two standpoints still otherwise. If my neighbor is to me a subject, for instance, in the midst of an ordinary conversation, he comes in question only with reference to his aims and meanings: whatever he utters has a purpose and end. I understand his inner life by taking a purposive point of view. On the other hand, the man whose inner life is to me an object can satisfy my interest only if I understand every particular happening in his mind from its preceding causes. I transform his whole life into a chain of causes and effects. My standpoint is thus a causal one. No doubt in our daily life, our purposive interest and our causal interest may intertwine at any moment. I may sympathize with the hopes and fears of my neighbor in a purposive way, and may yet in the next moment consider from a causal standpoint how these emotions of his are perhaps affected by his fatigue or by some glasses of wine, or by a hereditary disposition, or by a suggestion; in short, at one time I look out for the meaning of the emotion as a part of the expression of a self, and at another time for the structure and appearance of the emotion as a part of a causal chain of events. In both directions I can go on with entire consistency, and there cannot be any part of inner experience which cannot be fully brought under either point of view. How far we have a right to mix the two standpoints in practical life, we shall carefully examine; but it is clear that if we want to understand the true meaning of the study of inner life, we have no longer any right carelessly to mix the two standpoints without being conscious of their fundamental difference. We must understand exactly what the aim of the one and of the other is, and where each has its particular value; science certainly has no right to throw together such different views of life. And now this may be said at once: the causal view only is the view of psychology; the purposive view lies outside of psychology.

Such a separation does not at all aim to indicate that the one view is more important than the other,

or that the one has more scientific dignity than the
other; both yield us truth, and both may be carried
from the simplest and most trivial observations of
daily life to the highest elaborations of scholarship.
To those who are inclined to give all value and all
credit only to the strictly psychological view, it may
be replied at once that surely our most immediate life
experience is carried on by the non-psychological attitude. If we love our family and like our friends,
and deal with the man of the street, we are certainly
moving in a world of purposive reality. We try to
understand each other, to agree and to disagree, to be
in sympathy and antipathy, without asking how those
volitions and feelings and ideas of other people are
built as mental structures, and from what causes they
arose; we are satisfied to understand what they mean.
In the same way with ourselves. We live our lives
by hinging them on our aims and purposes and ideas,
and do not ask ourselves what are the causes of our
attitudes and of our thoughts.

This purposive view has in no respect to disappear
if we move on from our personal intercourse to a
scholarly study of reality. The historian, for instance, who tries to understand the will relations of
humanity, is the more the true historian the more he
sticks to this purposive view of man. The truth
which he seeks is to interpret the personalities, to
understand them through their attitudes, to make
their will living once more, and to link it by agreement and disagreement, by love and hate, with the
will of friends and enemies, groups and parties,

nations and mankind. It is only a loose popular way of speaking, if this purposive analysis of a character is often called psychological. In a stricter sense of the word, it is not psychological. If the historian really were to take the psychological attitude, he would make of history simply a social psychology, seeking the laws of the social mind, and treating the individual, the hero, and the leader, merely as the crossing-point of psychological law. For such a psychological view the mental life of the hero would not be more important or more interesting than the mental life of a scoundrel, and the psychology of the king would not draw his interest more than the psychology of the beggar. The historian has to shape all that from an entirely different standpoint: his scientific interest depends upon the importance of men's attitudes and actions, and such importance refers to the world of purposes.

In the same way, we have to stick to the non-psychological point of view whenever man's life, his thoughts and feelings and volitions, are to be measured with reference to ideals; that is in ethics and æsthetics and logic, sciences which ask whether the volitions are good or bad, whether the feelings are valuable or worthless, whether the thoughts are true or false. The psychologist does not care; just as the botanist is interested in the weed as much as in the flower, the pychologist is interested in the causal connections of the most heinous crime not less than in those of the noblest deed, in the structure of the most absurd error not less than in that of the maturest wisdom. Truth, beauty, and morality are thus expressions of the self in its purposive aspect.

We can go one step further. Those who narrowly seek every truth only in the scientific understanding, ought to be reminded that this seeking for causal connections is itself, after all, only a life experience which as such is not of causal but of purposive character. " Life is bigger than thought." In the immediate reality of our purposive life we aim towards mastering the world by a causal understanding, and for this end we create science; but this aim itself is then a purpose and not an object. The first act is thus for us, the thinkers, not a part of the causal events, but a purposive intention towards an ideal. Therefore, our purposes have the first right; they represent the fundamental reality; the value of causal connections and thus of all scientific and psychological explanation, depends on the value of the purpose. Causal truth can be only the second word; the first word remains to purposive truth. From this point of view we may understand why there is no conflict between the most consistent causal explanation of mental life on the one side, and an idealistic view of life on the other side; yes, we can see that the fullest emphasis on a scientific psychology—which is necessarily realistic and, to a certain degree, materialistic—is fully embedded in an idealistic philosophy of life, and that without conflict. And we shall see how this consistency in sharply separating the psychological view from the non-psychological, secures much greater safety for true idealism than the inconsistent popular mixing of the two principles, where scientific psychology is constantly encroached upon by demands of faith and religion, and where faith and religion seem constantly in danger of being overturned by new discoveries in physiological psychology. We may, indeed, remove from the start the mistaken fear that a consistent causal aspect of life leads to injustice to the higher aims and ideal purposes of mankind. If we want to have psychology,—and that means if we want to consider the mental life in a system of causes and effects,—we must proceed without prejudices, and without side-thoughts.

From a psychological standpoint our own mental life and that of our neighbor, that of the man and that of the child, that of the normal and that of the insane, that of the human being and that of the animal, are to be considered as a series of mental objects. They are to be analyzed, and to be described, and to be classified and to be explained, just as we deal with the physical objects in the outer world. How are these objects of the psychologist different from the objects of the physicist, from the pebbles on the way and the stars in the sky? There is only one fundamental difference and all other differences result from it. Those outer objects which we call physical, are objects for everybody. The star which I see is conceived as the same star which you see, the table which I touch is the table which you may grasp, too. But every psychical object is an object for one particular person only. My visual impression of the star, that is, my optical perception, is a content of my own consciousness only, and your impression of the star can be a content of your consciousness only. We both may mean the same by our ideas, but I can never have your perception and you can never have my perception. My ideas are enclosed in my mind. I may awaken in your mind ideas which have the same purpose and meaning, but they are new copies in your mind. We both may be angry, but your anger can never be my anger, and your volitions can never enter my mind. Every possible psychical fact thus exists in one consciousness only, while every physical fact exists for every possible consciousness.

The psychologist's final task is to explain the appearance and disappearance, the connections and sequences of these mental objects, the contents of consciousness. But before he can start on explanation of the facts, he has to describe them, and describing means analyzing them into their elements and fixating those elements and their combinations for an exact report. Such descriptive work is in a way preparatory for the further task of real explanation; yet it is in itself important, complicated, and difficult. Of course, it may be easy to separate the complex content into some big groups of facts, to point out that this is a memory idea and this an imaginative idea and the other an abstract idea, and this a perception and that a feeling, this an emotion and that a volition. But such clumsy first discrimination does not go further, perhaps, than does the naturalist's, who tells us that this is a mountain and that a tree, this a pond and that a bird. The real description would demand, of course,

an exact measurement of the height of the mountain
and the geological analysis of its structure, or an
exact classification of the tree and the bird, with a
complete description of their organs, and in each
organ the various tissues have to be described, and in
each tissue the various cells, and the microscopist goes
further and describes the structure of the cell. Certainly in the same way the psychologist has to go on
to resolve every one of those complex structures;
he has to examine the mental tissues and the mental
cells of which a volition or a memory idea or a perception are composed. And while he cannot use a
microscope for these mental elements, yet his studies
may cause elements to appear which the naïve observation remains entirely unaware of.

Perhaps he finds in his consciousness the perception
of the table before him which lingers for a little while
in his mind. He finds no difficulty in analyzing it
into color sensations and tactual sensations; and yet
he is aware of so much more in it. The table, for
instance, has form for him and he may find that these
form perceptions involve the sensations of the eye
movements which he makes from one corner of the
table to the other; he may find that if the idea lasts
in him, he becomes aware of the time by sensations of
tension; he finds that in his perception of the table
lies an idea of its use, and he discovers that that is
made up of elements which are partly memory repro-
ductions of earlier impressions, partly sensations of
movement impulses; he also finds that the table feels
smooth, and he discovers by his analysis that this im-

pression of smoothness results from a special combination of tactual sensations and movement sensations; and again those movement sensations he analyzes further into sensations of muscle contraction and sensations of pressure in the joints and sensations of tension in the tendons. Before a zoölogist has completed his description of a bird in the landscape, he has given account of hundreds of thousands of things; but before the psychologist would complete the enumeration of the mental elements which enter into the seeing of the table, he would have to give account of by far more psychical elements. Every point in the surface of the table has its own light value, perhaps different in its quality and intensity and saturation, in its hue and tint and shade from the next one, and at whatever point of the table's edge our attention is directed, each one involves numberless shades in the vividness of all the other points and numberless mental relations of space perception among the various parts of the table. In the thorough analysis of the describing psychologist, every single idea, and in the same way, every single emotion or feeling or judgment becomes complex like a living organism, an aggregate of thousands of mental tissues, and yet made up from " the stuff that dreams are made of."

But there is one particular difficulty which makes the psychological description so much harder than that of the physicist, and which gives rise to many disagreements and discussions in psychological literature. The psychologist has not only to tear the complex into pieces and thus to seek the elements, but he has to

fixate those elements for the purpose of communication, as, of course, a scientific description demands
that he be able to give account to others of what he
experiences. The physicist has no difficulty whatever in that line because, as we saw, the world of
physical things is the world which all men are sharing
together. Every element which I find in it, I can
show to every other person, and if I cannot show that
particular thing, because I cannot yet carry the mountain to another place, then I can at least measure it,
as we share those standards of space. Thus natural
science has in its objective measurements the possibility of describing every part of the physical world.
The psychical world, on the other hand, is as we saw,
the world which is private property. Every effort
at description is thus entirely in vain as long as our
mental facts cannot somehow be linked with physical
happenings. If I say that I have in my mind sweetness or sourness, or bitterness or saltness, I cannot
carry any understanding to anyone else and therefore cannot give any description until I have agreed
that I mean by sweetness the sensation which sugar
gives me, and by saltness the sensation of salt. The
sugar and salt I can point out to my neighbor and
only in that way I understand what he means if he
says that he tastes salt and sweet; otherwise I should
have no means whatever to discriminate whether that
which he calls a sweet taste sensation is not just what
I call headache. Where no such direct relation for
a physical thing is known, description of the mental
element would remain impossible. Of course, every

perception of the outer world, all our seeing and hearing, and touching and tasting, offers us at once such
definite connection between the inner experience and
a piece of the physical universe. Our own organism is
also such a piece of physical nature: just as I describe
my tasting or touching, I may describe the perception
of my arms and legs or my inner organs. Thus everything which is material of perception gives us a
handle for a real psychological description. Psychology usually calls the elements of these perceptions sensations. Whatever is composed of sensations is thus describable.

On the other hand, no other way of description is
open. If there were mental states which are composed of other elements than sensations, they would
necessarily remain indescribable; we could not grasp
them because they would not have any definite relation to the common physical world. We might
say, for instance, that our mental content is made up
of sensations and feelings, but if such feelings were
really entirely different from sensations, they would
have to remain for all time mysterious and unknown.
We could not compare notes. The feeling which I
call joy may feel just like the one which you call
despair. The consistent development of modern psychology and its emancipation from vagueness and
superficial analysis became possible only through the
fact that such recourse to indescribable elements has
become unnecessary. Modern psychology has been
able to demonstrate more and more that the same
elements which constitute our perceptions are also the

elements of the other contents of consciousness. In other words modern psychology has recognized that the volitions and emotions and feelings and judgments, and the whole stream of inner life, are made up of sensations. Millions of sensations in all degrees of vividness and clearness, of intensity and fusion, in endless manifoldness of rhythms and relations constitute their whole content. It is a discovery quite similar to the one which chemistry made when it found that the same elements which are part of the inorganic substances are also the only possible elements of the organic world.

From a strictly psychological standpoint, the ideas and the not-ideas contain thus nothing but sensations. Their grouping, their shading, their combination, their succession decide whether we have before us a perception or an imagination, a volition or an emotion. What are we ourselves then for the psychologist? Evidently we ourselves belong also to the inner experiences which we know; and psychology has succeeded in analyzing this idea of our own self just in the same way as it analyzes our idea of the moon. In this analysis, psychology finds its idea of the self as a content of consciousness crystallized about the sensations from the body. Every one of our bodily activities is represented in our consciousness by movement sensations, and these sensations form the core of the complex aggregate which develops into the idea of ourselves. Organic sensations from our inner organs, pain sensations and pleasure sensations fuse with the movement sensations, and the whole complex shapes itself slowly into the idea of the personality of the self in contrast to the idea of other personalities. We ourselves are for ourselves a complex combination of sensations; and yet all our feelings and emotions and volitions are only a part of it. Psychology thus necessarily considers those experiences of feeling and will and character simply as changes in the midst of that central experience of personality which is itself made up of bodily sensations. Each bit of will and emotion must be decomposed into its finest elements. There is no passing mood, and no floating half-thought in our mind, no dream and no intuition, no slightest change of attention, no instinct and desire which cannot be analyzed thus into its sensation elements or rather which must not be analyzed, if we are to describe it at all, and that means if we are to give a psychological account. Psychology is endlessly far from this ideal to-day. It has been claimed, not without justice, that psychology has reached to-day only the level which physics attained in the seventeenth century; but psychology must insist that its ideal lies in this direction. No one takes a real psychological view of the human mind who does not understand this endless complexity of the material, and who does not see that even the simplest mental state practically presents a most complex problem to scientific analysis. The physician who really aims towards scientifically exact influence on the human mind has reached the first step of his preparation as soon as he understands that the content of consciousness is composed of hundreds of thousands of elements. To treat the mind as if there were only a few large pieces, one thing called memory and one thing called will and one called emotion and so on, is as if a surgeon were to perform an operation, knowing that there are arms and legs, but not knowing the ramifications of the nerves and blood-vessels which his knife may injure. Yet the description of these complex facts is only the beginning of psychology. We saw that the real aim is their explanation.

III

MIND AND BRAIN

THE central aim of the psychologist must be to explain the mental facts. It is not sufficient to describe the procession of mental experiences in us, we must understand the causes which determine that now this and now that appears and disappears, and appears just in this combination of elements. The astronomer is not satisfied with describing the stars, he wants to explain their movements and to determine which movements are to be expected. The psychologist, like the naturalist, aims towards explanation, and it is this demand which forces him to look from the psychical facts to the physical ones, from the mind to the brain. He is under an illusion if he fancies that he can explain mental facts by themselves. The purposive mind has its connection in itself, the causal psychological mind demands for its connection the body. To understand this necessity is the first step towards understanding the relation of mind and brain.

The psychologist's problem of explanation is in one way entirely different from that of the physicist. The physicist finds a world of an unlimited number of atoms which are ultimately conceived as all alike,

but each one in a different place, and all the changes
in the universe, the movements of the stars, the waves
of the ocean, are to be explained by the causal connections of the movements of these atoms.   The
psychologist, on the other hand, finds an endless manifoldness of elements which are not in space, and
which have no space form whatever.   My will is
neither triangular nor oval; my emotion is neither
shorter than five feet nor longer; my memory image
of a melody has no thickness and no tallness; my
contents of consciousness are as such not in space;
their elements cannot pass through any space movements like the atoms of the physicist.   Instead of it,
the psychical atoms, the sensations, have different
qualities, are blue and green, and cold and warm, and
sweet and sour, and toothache and headache.   The
changes which go on in such a system are thus not
changes of position and movements, but changes in
kind and strength and vividness and fusion; and
exactly such changes are the processes which the psychologist wants to explain.   He wants to make us
understand why this idea grows up and the other
fades away, why this impression stands out with clearness as an attended object while the other lacks vividness and disappears, why this volition grows out of
that emotion, why this feeling leads to this imaginative thought.

The first step towards such explanation is, of
course, in psychology, as in all other sciences, the
careful observation of regularities.   It quickly leads
us to formulate some general laws.   Psychology has

known, for instance, for two thousand years, that if we have perceived two things together, and later we see the one again, the new perception brings us a memory image of the other thing. If we saw a man's face and heard at the same time his name, seeing his face may later awaken in us the memory of his name, or the hearing of his name may later awaken in us a reproduced memory image of his face. On such a basis, for instance, we formulate some general laws of association of ideas, and as soon as we have such laws laid down, we consider the appearance of such a memory image by association as sufficiently explained. We feel that it gives us sufficient basis to predict that in the future this idea will stir up in us the other idea. Psychology has formulated plenty of such general statements, and they serve well for a first orientation.

Yet can this ever be considered as a last word of scientific explanation of psychical facts? Can psychology really in this way reach an ideal similar to that of scientific astronomy or chemistry? Would the scientist of nature ever be satisfied with this kind of explanation, which is nothing but generalization of certain sequences? Does not the explanation of the naturalist contain an entirely different element? He does not merely want to say that this effect has sometimes been observed and that there is thus probability that it will come again, when similar causes are given. No, the physicist wants to understand those connections of cause and effect as necessary ones. He tries to find sequences which cannot be otherwise because they cannot be thought in any other way. Therefore he is not satisfied with complex regularities, but analyzes them until he can bring them down to simple physical connections, and these physical connections finally to mechanical processes, which realize for us logical necessities. That matter lasts and cannot disappear is such a presupposition, which comes to us with the necessity of logical thinking. We simply cannot think it otherwise. And the whole idea of natural science is to conceive the physical universe in such a way that all changes in the outer world can be understood as the movements of its parts in accordance with such necessary physical axioms. If we knew all the atoms of the present status of the universe, and we knew every present movement of every atom, we should be able to foresee the position of every atom in the next moment and in the following moment and in all following moments, and all that by the necessary continuation of the substance and its energies. That alone is the background of all special physical inquiry, and we rely on the special laws of physics and chemistry, because we trust that this universe, as a whole, could be ultimately understood as such a system of necessary changes in the positions of the lasting atoms.

For the psychologist there is no hope of finding such necessity in the mental processes. The point is not that psychology is to-day too far removed from the fulfillment of such an ideal, the point is rather that such an ideal would be meaningless for the psychologist. His materials, the psychical contents of consciousness, are by their nature unfit to enter into such necessary connections; they cannot do it because they cannot last. The physical object, we saw, is the object which is common property, which we all feel in common, which must thus exist for all time. The things in nature may burn down or decay, but no atom of them can ever disappear from the universe, each must enter into new and ever new combinations and last through all changes. The psychical thing, on the other hand, can exist only for the one immediate experience. Every sensation which enters into my ideas or volitions or emotions is a new creation of the instant which cannot last; each one flashes up and is lost with the moment's experience. My will to-day may have the same aim as my will of yesterday, but as psychical object, my will to-day is a new will, is a new creation in every pulse beat of my life. I must will it again, I cannot store it up. And my joy of to-day can never be as psychical fact the same joy which I may have to-morrow. Mental objects as such, as psychological material, are not destined to last. It has no meaning whatever to think of their being kept over until another time. It is a coarse materialism to conceive the mental contents like pebbles which may remain on the road from one day to another. Our ideas and feelings are mental appearances which have their existence in the act of the one experience; each new experience must be an entirely new creation.

If I remember my last year's perception, I do not dig it out from an under-mind, in which it was stored up and buried, but I create an entirely new memory picture, just as I may make to-day a speech which says the same thing which I said last year, and yet my action of speaking is not last year's speech movement. It is a new action, and the movement did not lie over somewhere during the interval. Mental life is produced anew in every moment. When the first experience is gone and the second comes, nothing of the stuff from which the first was made still has existence in the content of consciousness. By this fact it becomes entirely impossible ever to conceive necessary connections in the sense of physical necessity in the world of consciousness. The one idea may bring to me another idea by association, but as long as I consider both strictly as mental facts, I can never understand why this association happens, I can never grasp the real mechanism of the connection, I can never see necessity between the disappearance of the one and the appearance of the other. It remains a mystery which does not justify any expectation that the same sequence will result again. Whatever belongs to the psychical world can never be linked by a real insight into necessity. Causality there remains an empty name without promise of a real explanation.

Only when we have recognized this fundamental difficulty in the efforts for psychological explanation, can we understand the way which modern psychology has taken most successfully. The end of this way is simply this: every psychical fact is to be thought of as an accompaniment of a physical process and the necessary connections of these physical processes determine, then, the connections of the mental facts. Indeed this has become the method of modern psychology. It has brought about the intimate relation between psychology and the physiology of the brain, and has given us, as foundation, the theory of psychophysical parallelism; the theory that there is no psychical process without a parallel brain process. But the real center of the theory lies indeed in the fact which we discussed; it lies in the fact that we cannot have any explanation of mental states as such at all, if we do not link them with physical processes.

Is it necessary to express again the assurance that such statements of a parallelism between mind and brain in no way interfere with an idealistic view of inner life? Have we not seen clearly enough that these mental facts which are conceived parallel to physiological brain processes do not represent the immediate reality of our inner life, that our life reality is purposive and as such outside of all causal explanation, and that we have to take a special, almost artificial, point of view to consider inner life at all as objects, as contents of consciousness, and thus as psychological material? But since we have seen that for certain purposes such a point of view is necessary, as soon as we have taken it we must be consistent. Our inner life in its purposive reality has therefore nothing to do with brain processes, but if we are on the psychological track and consider man as a system of psychological phenomena, then to be sure, we must see that our only possible interest lies in the finding of necessary causal connections. But these cannot be found otherwise than by linking the mental facts with the physical ones, the psychological material with the processes of the brain.

Of course, that mental experience stands in intimate relations to the body is a knowledge which does not wait for such philosophical arguments. That mind and body come in contact is a conviction which goes with every single sense perception. I see and hear because light and sound stimulate my sense organs, and the sense organs stimulate my brain. The explanation of perception through causes in the physical system seems the more natural as it is evident that in such cases there are no psychical causes which might have brought forward the perception. If I suddenly hear bells ringing, there was on the mental side nothing preceding which could be responsible for my sound perception. And the same holds true if the physical source lies in my own body, if perhaps my tooth begins to ache, although no expectation preceded it.

In the same way it seems a matter of course that mind and body are connected wherever an action is performed. I have the will to grasp for the book before me, and obediently my arm performs the movement; the muscles contract themselves, the whole physical apparatus comes into motion through the preceding mental fact. The same holds true where no special will act arouses the muscles. If a · thought is in my mind and it discharges itself in appropriate words, those words are after all as physical facts the movements of lips and tongue and vocal cords and chest; in short, a whole system of physical responses has set in through a mental experience. But the same thought may be the starting-point for many other bodily changes; it may make me blush, and that means that large groups of blood-vessels become dilated; or I may get pale, the blood-vessels are contracted. Or I may cry, the lachrymal gland is working; or it may spoil my appetite, the membranes of my stomach cease to produce; or my muscles may tremble, or my skin may perspire; in short, my whole organism may resound with mental excitement which some words may set up.

But it is not only the impression of outer stimuli and the expression of inner thoughts in which mind and body come together. Daily life teaches us, for instance, how our mental states are dependent upon most various bodily influences. If the temperature of the blood is raised in fever, the mental processes may go over into far-reaching confusion; if hashish is smoked, the mind wanders to paradise, and a few glasses of wine may give a new mental optimism and exuberance; a cup of tea may make us sociable, a dose of bromide may annihilate the irritation of our mind, and when we inhale ether, the whole content of consciousness fades away. In every one of these cases, the body received the chemical substance, the blood absorbed and carried it to the brain, and the change in the brain was accompanied by a change in the mental behavior. Even ordinary sleep at night presents itself surely as a bodily state—the fatigued brain cells demand their rest, and yet at the same time the whole mental life becomes entirely changed. It is not difficult to carry over such observations of daily life to the more exact studies of the psychological laboratory and to examine with the subtle means of the psychological experiment the mental variations which occur with changes of physical conditions. We might feel, without instruments, that our ideas pass on more easily after a few cups of strong coffee, but the laboratory may measure that with its exact methods and study in thousandth parts of a second, the quickening or retarding in the flow of ideas. Every subjective illusion is then excluded, our electrical clocks, which measure the rapidity of mental action and of thought association, will show then beyond doubt how every change in the organism influences the processes of the mind. Bodily fatigue and indigestion, physical health and blood circulation, everything, influence our mental make-up. In the same way it is the laboratory experiment which shows by the subtlest means that every mental state produces bodily effects where we ordinarily ignore them. As soon as we apply the equipment of the psychological workshop, it is easy to show that even the slightest feeling may have its influence on the pulse and the respiration, on the blood circulation and on the glands; or, that our thoughts give impulse to our muscles and move our organs when we ourselves are entirely unaware of it.

Again we may turn in another direction. Pathology shows us how every physical disablement of

the brain is accompanied by mental processes. If
the blood supply to the brain is cut off, we faint; a
blow on the head may wipe out the memory of the
preceding hours, and a hemorrhage in the brain,
the bursting of a blood vessel which destroys groups
of brain cells, produces serious defects in the mental
content. A tumor in the brain may completely
change the personality; the bodily disease of certain
convolutions in the brain brings with it the loss of
the power of speech; paralysis of the brain dissolves
the whole mental personality. Physical inhibition in
the growth of the brain involves, on the mental side,
feeble-mindedness and idiocy. Of course, all this is
not sufficient to bring out a definite parallelism between special mental functions and special physical
processes, as the phenomena are extremely complex.
If a patient who has suffered from a mental disturbance dies, and his brain is examined, there is no
simple correlation before us. It may be difficult to
diagnose exactly the mental symptoms. If we have
heard that the man was unable to read, we do not
know from that what really happened in his brain.
He may not have read because he did not see the
words, or because the letters were confusing, or because he had lost memory for the meaning, or because he had lost the impulse to speak the words, or
because he felt unable to turn his attention, or because the impulse to read aloud was not carried out
by his organism, or because an inner voice told him
that it is a sin to read, or for many similar reasons;
and yet each one represents psychologically an en-

tirely different situation. On the other hand, on the physical side, the destruction is probably not confined to one particular spot. Complications have crept over to other places or the disturbance in one part works as inhibitory influence on other brain parts, or a tumor may press on a far-removed part, or the disturbance may be one which cannot be examined with our present microscopic means. In short, we have always a complex mental situation and a complex physical one, and to find definite correlations may be possible only by the comparison of very many cases.

Other methods, however, may supplement the pathological one. The comparative anatomist shows us that the development of the central nervous system in the kingdom of animals goes parallel to the development of the mental functions, and that it is not only a question of progress along all lines. Any special function of the mind may have in certain animal groups an especially high development, and we see certain parts correspondingly developed. The dog has certainly a keener sense of smell than the man—the part of the brain which is in direct connection with the olfactory nerve is correspondingly much bulkier in the dog's brain than in the human organism. Here too, of course, research may be carried to the subtlest details and the microscope has to tell the full story. Not the differences in the big structure, but the microscopical differences in the brain cells of special parts are to be held responsible. But comparison may not be confined to the various species of animals; it may refer not less to the various stages of man. The genetic psychologist knows how the child's mind develops in a regular rhythm, one mental function after another, how the first days and first weeks and first months in the infant's life have their characteristic mental possibilities, and no mental function can be anticipated there. The new-born child can taste milk, but cannot hear music. The anatomist shows us that correspondingly only certain nervous tracts have the anatomical equipment by which they become ready for functioning. Most of the tracts at first lack the so-called medullar sheath, and from month to month new paths are provided with this physical equipment.

Finally we have the experiment of the physiologist. His vivisectional experiments, for instance, demonstrate that the electrical stimulation of a definite spot on the surface of a dog's brain produces movements which we should ordinarily take as expressions of mental states, movements of the front legs or of the tail, movements of barking or whining. On the other hand, the dog becomes unable to fulfill the mental impulses if certain definite parts of his brain are destroyed. The physiologist may show from the monkey down to the pigeon, to the frog, to the ant, to the worm, how the behavior of animals is changed as soon as certain groups of nervous elements are extirpated. It is the mental emotional character of the pigeon which is changed when the physiologist cuts off parts of his brain. In short, stimulation and destruction demonstrate, by experiments which supplement each other, that mental functions correspond to brain functions.

There is thus no lack of demonstration from all quarters that mental facts and brain processes belong together; and yet, however much we may cumulate such popular and scientific observations, they would never by themselves admit of the sweeping generalization that there cannot be any mental state which is not accompanied by a process in the central nervous system. Someone might say, to be sure, the perceptions and memory images, the volitions and instincts and impulses, have their physiological basis, but there remain after all acts of attention, or decisions, or subtle feelings, or flights of imagination, which are independent of any brain action. Here, indeed, observation cannot settle such a general principle. Its real hold lies in the fact with which we started: there is no causal connection in the mental states as such. If we want to understand mental facts as such in a chain of causal events, we have first to conceive them as parallel to physical events. The principle of psychophysical parallelism, that is, the principle that every psychical process accompanies a physiological change is thus not a mere result of observation. It is simply a postulate. Every science begins with postulates and only that which fulfills such postulates has the dignity of truth in the midst of that scientific realm. The astronomer cannot find by observation that there is no star the movements of which are not the effects of foregoing causes. He knows it beforehand, he demands it, he does not recognize any movement as understood until he has found the causes, he presupposes that such causes exist, that no star moves simply by a magic power, and that nowhere in the astronomical universe is the chain of causality broken. He postulates it, and where he does not discover the causes, he is sure that he has not solved the real problem.

In the same way the psychologist who aims towards explanation of mental facts must postulate that there cannot be any mental state which is not an accompaniment of a physical brain process, and is as such connected through physical means with the preceding and the following events in the psychophysical system. Only when such a general framework of theory is built up by a logical postulate, is the way open to make use of all those observations of the laboratory and of the clinic, of the zoölogist and of the anatomist. It is the theory which has to give the right setting to those scattered observations. However far we may be from being able to point to the special brain process which lies at the bottom of the higher mental state, we know beforehand that there is no shadow of an idea, no fringe of a feeling, no suggestion of a desire which does not correspond to definite processes in the brain. The details may and must be material for diverging theories, but the conflict of such hypothetical opinions has nothing to do with the certainty of the underlying conviction that if we knew the whole truth, we should recognize every single mental happening as parallel to physical processes in the nervous system. To explain mental facts means to think them as parallel to the brain processes which have their own causal connections in the physical world.

We started, for instance, from the old observation that two impressions which come to our mind at the same time have a tendency to reawaken one another; and we saw that psychology was well able to formulate these facts in general statements of the association of ideas. But we realized that that in itself is not really explanation. If the odor which we smell awakes in us the name of a chemical substance, and if we now bring this under the general heading of association of ideas, an explanation is not really given by it. That smell sensation itself is not really understood as a cause of those sound sensations of the word. We have no insight into the connection of those two happenings. But the situation is entirely changed, if we consider the smell effect from the point of view of the parallelistic theory. Now the association of facts would indicate that we got the first two impressions together, because two brain processes were going on at the same time. My nose brought me the smell stimulus, my ear gave me the sound stimulus, each going on in a particular center, or, to express it in a simplified schematic way, each reaching particular brain cells, and the excitement of these brain cells being accompanied by the particular sensations. The physiologist has many possibilities of conceiving the further stages of the process, in order to satisfy the demand of explanation. He may say the excitement of each of these two brain cells, the one in the olfactory center, the other in the auditory center, irradiates in all directions through the fine branches of the brain fibers. Each cell has relations to every other cell in the brain; thus there is also one connecting path between those two cells which were stimulated at once. Now if the two ends of an anatomical path are excited at the same time, the path itself becomes changed. The connecting way becomes a path of least resistance, and that means that if, in future, one of the two brain cells becomes excited again, the overflow of the nervous excitement will not now go on easily in all directions, but only just along that one channel which leads to that other brain cell. A theory like this explains in real explanatory terms, in ways which physics and chemistry can demonstrate as necessary, that any excitement of the odor cell runs over into the sound cell and vice versa. In short, the psychological association of ideas, which we should simply have to accept as inexplainable fact, is thus transformed into a connection which we understand as necessary; and the fact is really explained.

This simple scheme of the physiology of association for a hundred years has given a most decided impulse to the progress of psychology. As the association process can so easily be expressed in physiological terms, the aim was prevalent to understand the interplay of mental life more and more as the result of association. The underlying thought of this whole association psychology was thus a conviction that whenever two mental experiences occur

together, either of them keeps the tendency to reawaken the other at a later time. Through the endless combination which life's impressions awaken in
the mind from the first hour after birth, the whole
stream of memory images and thoughts and aims
and imaginations is thus to be explained.

The whole theory of physiological associationism
works evidently with two factors. First, there are
millions of brain cells of which each one may have its
particular quality of sensation, and second, each brain
cell may work with any degree of energy, to which
the intensity of the sensation would correspond. If
I distinguish ten thousand different pitches of tone,
they would be located in ten thousand different cell
groups, each one connected through a special fiber
with a special string in the ear. And each of these
tones may be loud or faint, corresponding to the
amount of excitement in the particular cell group.
Every other variation must then result from the millionfold connections between these brain cells. Indeed, the brain furnishes all possibilities for such a
theory. We know how every brain cell resolves
itself into tree-like branch systems which can take up
excitements from all sides, and how it can carry its
own excitement through long connecting fibers to distant places, and how the endings of these fibers clasp
into the branches of the next cell, allowing the propagation of excitement from cell to cell. We know further how large spheres of the brain are confined to
cells of particular function, that for instance cells
which serve visual sensations are in the rear part of

the brain hemispheres, and so on. Finally we know how millions of connecting fibers represent paths in all directions, allowing very well a coöperation by association between the most distant parts of the brain. The theories found their richest development, when it was recognized that large spheres of our brain centers evidently do not serve at all merely sensory states, but that their cells have as their function only the intermediating between different sensory centers. Such so-called association centers are thus like complex switchboards between the various mental centers. Their own activity is not accompanied by any mental content, but has only the function of regulating transmission of the excitement from the one to the other. Above all their operation would make it possible that through associative processes, the wonderful complexity of our trains of thought may be reached.

Yet even the highest development of the association theories did not seem to do justice to the whole richness of the inner life. We may well understand through those association processes that a rich supply of memory pictures is at our disposal, that ideas stream plentifully to our minds and enter into new and ever new combinations. But that alone is not an account of our inner experience. If there is anything essential for inner life, it is the attention which gives emphasis to certain states and neglects others. And that means that certain mental contents are growing not only in strength but in vividness and clearness, and that others are losing their vividness, are inhibited and suppressed. Here were always the real difficulties of the association theories; they seemed so entirely unable to explain from their own means why certain states become foremost in our minds and others fade away, why some have the power to grow and others are neglected. These facts of attention and vividness, inhibition and fading, worked almost as a temptation to give up the physiological explanation altogether and to rely on some mystical power, some mental influence which could pull and push the ideas without any interference and help from the side of the brain. Yet since we have seen that the truth of psychophysical parallelism has the meaning of a postulate which we cannot escape unless we want to give up explanation altogether, it is evident that such falling back into unphysiological agencies would be just as inconsistent as if the naturalist should posit miracles in the midst of chemistry or astronomy. If the facts which cluster about attention cannot be understood by the simple scheme of associationism, the demand must be for a better physiological theory.

The development of physiological psychology in recent years has indeed shown the way to such a wider theory, which furnishes the physiological accompaniment also for those experiences of attention and vividness which form the weakness of associationism. This new development has come up with the growing insight that the brain's mental functions are related not only to the sensory impressions, but at the same time to the motor expressions. The older

view, still prevalent to-day in popular writings, made
the brain the reservoir of physical stimuli, which
come from the sense organs to the cortex of the brain
hemispheres.   There the perceptions arose and
through associative interplay the memory pictures
and the ideas of action and the feelings arose, and the
whole inner life was thus bound up with the processes
in these sensorial spheres.   When the mind had done
its work, finally an impulse was sent to some motor
apparatus in the brain which then sent off the impulse to some acting muscles.   That whole motor
part was thus a kind of appendix to the brain process.
The psychical life had nothing to do with it but to
give the command for its action.   The process in the
motor part thus began when the mental proceeding
was completed.   But it became clear that this view
was only the outgrowth of the strong interest which
physiology took in the sense processes.   If a neutral
fair account of the brain actions is attempted, there
can hardly be doubt that this whole sensorial view
of the brain is only half of the story and that the
motor half has exactly the same right to consideration.   The cortex of the brain, the functions of
which are accompanied by mental processes, is always
and everywhere not only the recipient of sensory
stimuli but at the same time the starting point of
motor impulses.   That which is centripetal, leading
to the cortex, is therefore not more important for the
central process than that which is centrifugal, leading
from the cortex.   The cortex is the apparatus of
transmission between the incoming and the outgoing

currents, between the excitements which run to the brain and the discharges which go from the brain, and the mental accompaniments are thus accompaniments of these transmission processes. If the channels of discharge are closed and the transmission is thus impossible, a blockade must result at the central station and the accompanying mental processes must be entirely different from those which happen there when the channels of discharge are wide open. Here too all the special theories are still in the midst of tumultuous discord. Yet this new emphasis on the motor side of the psychical process seems to influence modern psychology more and more.

Nobody can deny that first of all this is the necessary outcome of a biological view of the brain. What else can be the brain's function in the midst of nature than the transforming of impressions into expressions, stimuli into actions? It is the great apparatus by which the organism steadily adjusts itself to the surroundings. There would be no use whatever biologically in a brain which had connections with the sense organs, but which had no connections with the muscular system, and on the other hand, a brain which had motor nerves and muscular adjustment would be entirely useless if it had not sensory nerves and sense organs connected with it. In the one case the world would be experienced, but no response would be possible; in the other case, the means for response would be given, but no adjustment could set in because no experience of the surroundings would be possible. Adjustment every

moment demands the relation of the brain in both
directions. Through the sensory nerves the brain
receives; through the motor nerves the brain directs,
and this whole arc from the sense organs through the
sensory nerves, through the brain, through the motor
nerves and finally to the muscles, is one unified apparatus of which no part can be thought away. The
brain in itself would be just as useless for the organism as the heart would be without the arteries and
veins.

We must keep this intimate and necessary relation
between the sensory and motor parts constantly in
view, and must understand that there cannot be any
sensory process which does not go over into motor
response. Then only the ways are open to develop
physiological views which give a physical basis to the
processes of attention and vividness and inhibition,
just as well as to the processes of memory and association. Such motor theories take many forms.
Perhaps we shall most quickly bring the most essential factors together, if we say that full vividness
belongs only to those sensations for which the channels of motor discharge are open, while those are inhibited for which the channels of discharge are
closed; and any channel of discharge is closed, if
action is proceeding in the opposite channel. If I
open my hand, the motor paths which lead to closing
my fist are blocked; and if I close my fist, the channels
which lead to the opening of the hand are closed.
Now if only those ideas are vivid which find the
channels open, it is clear that all the ideas which

would lead to the opposite action have no chance for development; they remain inhibited, and just this relation between the vividness of certain ideas and inhibition for those ideas which lead to the opposite action is the characteristic of the process of attention.

From such a point of view, the total mental life can be brought into the psychophysical scheme. We now have not two variable factors, but three, namely, the qualities of the elements, the intensities of the elements, and, as a third, the vividness of the elements. The quality corresponds, as we saw in the association theory, to the local position and connection of the brain cells; the intensity corresponds to the energy of the excitement; and the vividness, we may add now, corresponds to the relation to motor channels. The whole mental life thus becomes the accompaniment of a steady process of transmitting impressions and memories into reactions. That every experience involves millions of such elements we saw when we spoke of the description of mental life. The effort to explain mental life shows us now that this million-fold manifoldness belongs to a system of reactions of which all parts are in steady correlation: a moving equilibrium of unlimited complexity. Surely no one can reduce this wonderful manifoldness to those clumsy concepts with which popular psychology is reporting the story of the mind and its relations to the brain.

It may seem that such a psychological view of inner life annihilates that which we feel as the most essential characteristic of our inner experience, its unity and its freedom. In one sense that is certainly true. In the real life which we live and fight through, where our duties and our happiness lie, we know a unity and freedom of our personality which psychology must destroy. Of course that does not mean that psychology denies the truth of that freedom and unity. Moreover it would condemn itself if it were to deny that which gives meaning to the endeavors of our life and thus also to every search for truth. Psychology claims only that we must abstract from it, when we take the psychological standpoint towards life. Freedom of our real life means that we must know ourselves in the midst of our life work as guided by aims and obligations, and that in this purposive existence of ourselves we do not feel ourselves as determined by causes. I will the fulfillment of my ideals only because I will them. That this will itself may be the effect of foregoing causes is an aspect which does not belong to my naïve experience. Our freedom means that in our real life our will is not related to causes, that the point of view of causality is thus meaningless for the value of our achievements. And the other man's will too comes in question for us as something to be interpreted and to be appreciated, but not to be explained by connection with causes. As long as we move in this sphere of purposive interest, we are free and deal with free selves; but if in the midst of these free aims, the will arises to consider the actions of others and of ourselves from the standpoint of causality, then we have ourselves decided to enter a new sphere in which it would be meaningless to seek for any will which is not determined by causes. As soon as we have chosen the psychological standpoint and are in the midst of the work of causal reconstruction, any will which is not understood as determined by causes is simply an unsolved problem. In the midst of a causal construction, absence of causes would never mean real freedom.

In that purposive world of immediate life experience, we also are unities inasmuch as we ourselves know us as the same in every new will of ours. We remain identical with ourselves because every purpose is posited in the midst of, and bound up with, the general purpose of ourselves. And in this internal unity of meaning, nothing breaks ourselves into pieces, and the whole manifold of experience is thus expressed by a personality which knows itself in its purposive unity. But this unity again is denied by our own intention as soon as we decide to take the causal view of inner life. The purposive unity must now transform itself into an endless complexity, and our own self becomes a composite of hundreds of thousands of elements.

On the other hand, all this does not mean that psychology cannot have its own consistent conception of the mind's unity and freedom. Our psychological mind is a unity because its manifold is a system in which all parts hang together. A change in any one part involves changes in the whole system. The interrelation, to be sure, is not a strictly psychical one, for we have seen that the causal connection as such appears at the physical side. But, inasmuch as there is no psychical process which does not belong to a physiological one, the interconnection of the mental facts is complete and involves the totality of neural processes of which after all a small part only has its psychological record. We might compare those hundreds of millions of neurons in each brain with the hundreds of millions of individuals who make up the population of the nations, and the psychical accompaniment we might compare with the written historical record of mankind. The written records themselves have no direct interconnection, they are only accompaniments of what happens in these millions of men. And again only the higher layer of the neurons in the population sees its doings recorded in the annals of history; and yet whatever those leaders of action and thought and emotion may achieve is dependent upon and working on the actions of those millions of subcortical population neurons. The historical record has its unity through the interrelation of all parts of historical mankind.

But after all the psychologist has no less a right to speak of freedom. Of course his freedom cannot mean exemption from causality. Whatever happens in the psychological system must be perfectly determined by the foregoing causes. But the psychologist has good reason to discriminate between those actions which result from the normal psychophysical factors and such actions as result from broken machinery. If the brain is poisoned by alcohol or in fever, if an infectious disease has destroyed the brain cells, action is no longer the outcome of the normal coöperation of the organs, and even those clusters of neural activities which are accompanied by the consciousness of the own personality lose their control of the motor outcome. The man in delirium or paralysis acts without causal connection with his past; the action is, therefore, not the product of his whole personality, and the psychologist is justified in calling the man unfree. But, whenever the motor response results from the undisturbed coöperation of the normal brain parts, then the inherited equipment and the whole experience and the whole training, the acquired habits and the acquired inhibitions will count in bringing about the reaction. This is the psychological freedom of man. The unity of an interconnected composite and the freedom of causal determination through normal coöperation of all its parts characterize the only personality which the psychologist has to recognize.

IV

PSYCHOLOGY AND MEDICINE

WE are now ready to take the first step towards an examination of the problem of curing suffering mankind. So far we have spoken only of the meaning of psychology, of its principles and of its fundamental theories as to mind and brain. We have moved in an entirely theoretical sphere. Now we approach a field in which everything is controlled by a practical aim, the treatment of the sick. Yet our discussion of psychology should have brought us much nearer to the point where we can enter this realm of medicine. Everything depends on the right point of entrance. That an influence on the inner life of man may be beneficial for his health is a commonplace truth to-day for everybody. Every serious discussion of the question has to consider which influences are appropriate, and in which cases of illness the influence on inner life is advisable. The popular treatises usually start this chapter by speaking of the "mental and moral" factors; and this coupling of mental influences and moral influences characterizes large parts of the discussions of the Christian Scientists and the Christian half-scientists. Yet we must insist that the right entrance to psychotherapy is missed if the difference between morality and mentality is not clearly recognized from the beginning. The confusion of the two harms every statement. To avoid such a fundamental mistake, we had to take the long way around and to examine carefully what psychology really means and what it does not mean.

We know now that inner life can be looked on from two entirely different standpoints: a purposive one and a causal one, and we have seen that these two ways of looking on inner life bring about entirely different aspects of man's inner experience, serve different aims, and stand in different relations to the immediate needs of our real life. We know that the one, the causal aspect, belongs to psychology, while the non-psychological, the purposive aspect, belongs to our immediate mutual understanding in the walks of life. If the physician is to make use of inner experience in the interests of overcoming sickness, he must first decide whether to take the causal or the purposive point of view in dealing with the patient's mind. This problem is too carelessly ignored and through that neglect arises much of the popular confusion. Of course just this carelessness becomes in some ways the ground for apparent strength for many a superstition and prejudice. If the doors of the causal mind and of the purposive mind are both open, and the spectator does not notice that there are two, any trick on thought and reason can easily be played. Whatever cannot pass through

the causal door slips in through the other, and whatever does not go in through the door of purpose
marches through the entrance of causality. With
such methods anything can be proved, and the most
unscrupulous doctrines can be nicely demonstrated.
If we are to avoid such logical smuggling, we must
see clearly which attitude towards mental life belongs
properly to the domain of psychotherapy.

But what we have discussed now leaves little doubt
as to the necessary decision. The physician is interested in the mental life with the aim of producing a
certain effect, namely, that of health. Thus the mental life of the whole personality comes in question
for him as belonging to a chain of causes and effects;
whichever levers he may move, everything is to be a
cause which, in accordance with causal laws, is to
produce a certain change. Inner life is thus, in the
interests of medical treatment, necessarily a part of a
causal system. This means the standpoint of scientific psychology is the only adequate one. The purposive view of inner life ought not to be in question
when the patient enters the doctor's office.

To characterize the difference, it may be said at
once that it is a purposive view which belongs to the
minister. If the minister says to his despairing
parishioner, "Be courageous, my friend, and be
faithful," nothing but a strictly purposive view gives
meaning to the situation. The word friend indicates
it, that one subject of will approaches another subject
of will, with the intention of sympathy and understanding of the attitude of the other; and the advice

to be courageous and faithful means an appeal which
has its whole meaning in the relation to aims and
ends.   The speaker and the hearer are both moving
in a sphere of will relations, purposes and ideals, sin
and virtue, hope and belief.   To take the other extreme: if the neurasthenic in his state of depression
and in his feeling of inability seeks relief from the
nerve specialist, he too may say: " My friend, be
courageous and faithful," yet his words have an entirely different purpose.   They are not appeals to a
common interest of belief; they are subtle tools with
which to touch and to change certain psychophysical
processes, certain states in mind and brain; there
each word is a sound which awakens certain mental
associations, and these associations are expected to be
causes of certain effects and these effects are to inhibit
those disturbing states of emotional depression.   If
a few grains of sodium bromide were to produce the
same effect, they would be just as welcome.   The
whole consideration moves in a sphere in which only
physiological and psychological processes are happening.   Thus the physician may work with the ideas of
religious belief, but those ideas are then no longer
religious values but natural psychophysical material,
which is to be applied whenever it appears as the
right means to secure a certain effect.

On the other hand the minister also knows, of
course, that every word which he speaks has its psychological effect, but he abstracts from that entirely,
as his belief should appeal directly to the struggling
will of the man.   As minister, he is thus not a psy-

chologist.   He works with moral means; the physician, with causal means.   The view which the doctor has to take of the man before him is therefore
thoroughly psychological; whereas that of the religious friend is thoroughly unpsychological, or better,
apsychological.   Indeed it is misleading, or at least
demands a special kind of definition, if people say
that the minister has to be a good psychologist.   It
is just as misleading as the claim, which we hear so
often, that for instance Shakespeare was a great psychologist.   No, the poet deals with human beings
from the purposive standpoint of life and the mere
resolving of complex purposes into parts of purposes
is not psychology in the technical sense of the term.
The poet makes us understand the inner life, but he
does not describe or explain it; he makes us feel with
other people, but he does not make those feelings
causally understood.   The realistic novelists sometimes undertake this psychological task, but they are
then on the borderland of literature, the analysis of
their heroes becomes then a psychological one.
Shakespeare understood human beings better than
anyone and therefore the men and women whom his
imagination created are so fully lifelike that the psychologist may feel justified in using them as material
for his psychological analysis, but Shakespeare himself did not enter into that psychological dissection;
he kept the purposive point of view.   In the same
way certainly the minister—the same holds true for
the lawyer or the tradesman or anyone who enters
into practical dealings with his neighbor—may

resolve complex attitudes of will into their components, but each part still remains a will attitude which
has to be understood and to be interpreted and to
be appreciated, while the psychologist would take
every one of those parts as a conscious content to be
described and to be explained. But here we abstract
from the purposive relations. Our attention belongs
now to the doctor's dealing with man; for him cause
and effect are the only vehicles of connection. Thus
he has to exclude the purposive interpretation of
inner life and has to understand every factor involved
from a psychological point of view: his psychotherapy must be thoroughly applied psychology.

The day of applied psychology is only dawning.
The situation is indeed surprising. The last three
or four decades have given to the world at last a
really scientific study of psychology, a study not un-
worthy of being compared with that of physics or
chemistry or biology. In the center of the whole
movement stood the psychological laboratory with its
equipment for the most subtle analysis and explanatory investigation of mental phenomena. The first
psychological laboratory was created in Leipzig,
Germany, in 1878. It became the parent institution for laboratories in all countries. At present,
America alone has more than fifty psychological
laboratories, many of them large institutions equipped
with precious instruments for the study of ideas and
emotions, memories and feelings, sensations and
actions. Still more rapid than this external growth
of the laboratory psychology was the inner growth

of the experimental method.   It began with simple experiments on sensations and impulses, and it seemed as if it would remain impossible to attack with the experimental scheme the higher and more complex psychical structures.   But just as in physics and chemistry the triumphal march of the experimental method could not be stopped, one part of the psychological field after another was conquered.   Attention and memory, association and inhibition, emotion and volition, judgment and feeling all became subjected to the scientific scheme of experiment.   And that was all supplemented by the progress of physiological psychology, pathological psychology, child psychology, animal psychology.   In this way the last decades created a science which of course was by principle a continuation of the old psychology, but yet which had good reason to designate itself as a "new" psychology.

But in this whole development, until yesterday, the curious fact remained that it was going on without any narrow contact with practical life; it was a science for the scientist and measured by its practical achievements in daily life, it seemed barren and unproductive.   Psychology was studied as palæontology and Sanscrit were studied, without any direct relation to the life which surrounds us.   And yet after all it deals with the mental facts which have to enter into every one of our practical deeds, if we are to consider mental life from a psychological point of view.   The psychologists were certainly not to be blamed for sticking to their theoretical interests.

More than that, they were certainly justified in their reluctance, as everything was in the making, and incomplete theories can easily do more harm than good. But slowly a certain consolidation has set in; large sets of facts have been secured, and psychology seems better prepared to become serviceable to the practical tasks. On the other hand, it has been noticeable for some time that not a few of the psychological results have gone over into unprofessional hands and have been thrown on the market places and have been brought into many a home where no one knew how to deal with them rightly. Thus the need seems urgent that the psychologists give up their over-reserved attitude and recognize it as their duty to serve the needs of the community.

It is not sufficient for that end, simply to take odds and ends of psychology and to hand them over to anyone who can see some use for them. We must have a systematic scientific work done for the special purpose of adjusting psychological knowledge to the definite practical tasks and of examining the psychological facts with that practical end in view. A science must be developed which is related to psychology as engineering is related to physics and chemistry. Just as the technological laboratories of the engineer bring out many new problems which the physicist would never have approached, in the same way we may expect that special institutions for applied psychology will shape the psychological inquiry in a new way.

Such a new science of applied psychology of course

has before it a field just as large and manifold as the field of technology, where physical engineering, chemical engineering, mechanical engineering, and electrical engineering and so on are separated. Such / a future psychological technology would deal, for instance, with psychopedagogical problems. There belongs everything which refers to the psychology of memory or attention, of discipline, of fatigue, of habit, of imitation or effort; in short, all those mental factors which have to be considered whenever the schoolchild is looked on from a causal point of view. Further there is the psycholegal field where the memory and the perceptions, the suggestibility and the emotions of the witness are to be studied, where the psychological conditions which lead to crime, the means to tap the hidden thoughts of the criminal, the inhibitions for the prevention of crime, the mental effects of punishment and similar causal processes must be determined. There are the psychoscientific problems referring to psychological influences on the observations and judgments and discriminations of the scholar who watches the stars or who translates an inscription. There are the psychoæsthetic problems where the task is to examine causally the factors which lead to the agreeable effects of beautiful surroundings, and from the height of the psychology of æsthetics in painting and sculpture, the inquiry may go to the psychology of the pleasant effects in dressmaking or cooking. There are the large groups of psychotechnical problems where the effort refers to the application of psychology in securing the best conditions for labor and industry and commerce. It leads from the mental effects of signals or the mental fatigue in mills to the secrets of advertisements and salesmanship. There are especially important psychodiagnostical studies where the aim is to determine the individual differences of man by experimental methods and to make use of them for the selection of the right man for the right place. There are psychosocial problems where we examine the psychological factors which have to enter into public movements, into social reforms, into legislation and into politics. In this way new and ever new groups may be added; every time the central thought is: how far can causal psychological knowledge help us to reach a certain end? Together with these forms of applied psychology, we find the psychomedical problems; here belongs everything which allows the application of causal psychology in the interests of health.

It might be answered that this demand for a strictly causal point of view can hardly be fulfilled, because, if I am acting,—it may be in the interest of education or law or technique or medicine,—I must always have an end in view and to select such an end belongs after all to my system of purposes. If I am a teacher and have to deal with children, then it may be said that after all, my knowledge of causal psychology cannot help me if I am uncertain for which ideals I want to educate these children. Psychology can tell me that I need these means, if I want to reach certain effects, but I cannot find out by psychology which effects are desirable. Psychology may tell me

how to make a good business man or a good scholar
or a good soldier out of my boy, but whether I want
him to become a soldier or a merchant I must decide for myself with reference to general aims, and
that leads me back to the purposive view of life.
Such argument is entirely correct. Yes, it is evident
that it is in full harmony with our whole understanding of the purpose of psychology. We saw that psychology with its causal treatment of man's mind does
not express the immediate reality, but is a certain reconstruction which allows a calculation of certain effects.
Thus it is itself a system existing for a subject who
has certain ends in view. The whole causal view of
man is thus a tool in the service of the purposive man.
This is the reason why it is indeed utterly absurd to
think that psychology can ever help us to determine
which end we ought to reach.

In education, for instance, very many different ends
might be reached; psychology cannot decide anything. The decision as to the aims of education
must be made by ethics, which indeed takes not a
causal but a purposive attitude. Only after ethics
has selected the aim, psychology can teach us how to
reach it. Of course this principle must hold for the
physician too. All his causal dealing with the mind
presupposes that he has selected a certain end in
harmony with his purpose. The only difference is
that, in the case of the physician, there can be no
possible doubt as to the desirable end; what he aims
at is a matter of course, namely, the health of the
patient. To desire the health of the sufferer is thus

itself a function which belongs entirely to the purposive view of the world, and only in the interest of this purpose does the physician apply his knowledge of psychology or of the causal sciences of physics, physiology, and chemistry. Indeed only with this limitation have we the right to say that the psychotherapist takes the causal,—and that means the psychological,—view of his patient. As far as he decides to take care of the health of his patient, this decision itself belongs to the purposive world and to his moral system. The physician is thus ultimately just like the minister and just like anyone who deals with his neighbor, a purposive worker; but while the minister, for instance, remains on this purposive track, the physician puts a causal system into the service of his purpose. He knows the end, and his whole aim is to apply his causal knowledge of the physical and psychical world to the one accepted end of restoring the health of the patient. He has to ask thus in general: what has psychology to-day to offer which can be applied in the interests of medicine?

It would be an inexcusable narrowness to confine that chapter of applied psychology which is to deal with the psychomedical problems to the work of psychotherapy. Medicine involves diagnosis of illness as well as therapeutics. Between the recognition and the treatment of the illness lies the observation of its development and all this is preceded by steps towards the prevention of illness. In every one of these regions, psychology may be serviceable. Psychotherapy is thus only one special part of psychomedicine. But the situation becomes still more complex by the fact that the illness to be treated or the disturbance to be removed may stand in different relations to the psychophysical processes. The illness may be a disturbance in the psychophysical brain parts, or it may belong to other brain parts which are only in an indirect way under the influence of mental states or which are themselves indirectly producing changes in the mental life. And finally the disturbance may exist outside of the brain in any part of the body, and yet again through the medium of brain and nervous system it may produce effects in the mind or be open to the influence of the mind. Thus we have entirely different groups of medical interests and it would be superficial to ignore the differences.

Both psychodiagnostic and psychotherapeutic studies must be devoted to cases in which the mind itself is abnormal, further to cases in which the normal minds registers the abnormalities in other parts of the body, and finally to cases in which the normal mind influences abnormal processes in the body. These latter two cases have to be subdivided into those where the bodily disturbance still lies in the brain parts and those where it lies outside of the brain. But the situation becomes still more complex by the mutual relations of those various processes. The impulse to take morphine injections may have reached the character of a mental obsession and thus represent an abnormality of the mind, but yielding to it produces at the same time disturbances in the whole body which thus become again external sources for abnormal experiences in otherwise normal layers of the mind.

Of course the interest of the psychologist as such remains always related to the psychological factor, but the relation of the psychological factor itself to the total disturbance may be of most different character. If I diagnose or treat the fixed idea of a psychasthenic, the psychological factor itself represents the disturbance. On the other hand, if I study the pain sensations of a patient who suffers from a disease of the spinal cord, then the sensations themselves, the only psychological factor in the case, are only indications of a disease which belongs to an entirely different physical region; the mind itself is normal. Or, on the other hand, if I try to educate a sufferer from locomotor ataxia to develop his walking by building up in his mind new motor ideas to regulate his coördinated movements, the mind again is entirely normal but the physician needs his psychology on account of the influence which the mind has on the bodily system. Again, we must insist that psychomedicine covers this whole ground. Wherever a psychical factor enters into the calculations of the physician either by reason of its own abnormality or by its relation as effect or as cause to a diseased part of the body in the brain or without, there we have a psychomedical task, and as far as it is therapeutic, we have psychotherapy.

The psychodiagnostic research lies outside of the compass of our book, but we cannot emphasize suffi-

ciently the great importance which belongs to that
work.   Moreover, just in the field of psychodiagnos-
tics, the methods of the modern experimental psychological laboratory are most promising and successful.
Let us not forget that we deal with such psychological factors even when we test the functions of eye
and ear and skin and nose by examining the sensations and perceptions.   The oculist who analyzes the
color sensations of a patient and the aurist who finds
defects in the hearing of the musical scale and discovers that certain pitches cannot be discriminated,
is certainly dealing, for diagnostic purposes, with the
material that the psychological laboratory has sifted
and studied.   Even that sensation symptom which
enters into so many diseases, the sensation of pain,
belongs certainly within the compass of the psychologist and it is only to be regretted that the systematic
study of the pain sensations, mostly for evident practical reasons, has been much neglected in the psychological laboratory.

The psychologists have been at work all the more
eagerly in the fields of association and memory, attention and emotion, habit and volition, distraction and
fatigue.   Here subtle methods have been elaborated,
methods which surely common sense cannot supply,
and which showed differences of mental behavior
with the exactitude with which the microscope reveals
the hidden differences of form.   If physicians are
slow in accepting the help which the psychological
laboratory can furnish, it may be in good harmony
with the desirable conservative policy in medicine, but

finally the time must come when this instinctive
resistance against new methods will be overcome.
The recent attachment of psychological laboratories
to certain leading psychiatric clinics is a most promising symptom. Yet the diagnostic studies with the
means of the psychological laboratory cannot be confined to the cases of mental disease. The mild abnormalities of the mind, and especially the nervous
disturbances which exist outside the field of insanity,
demand this support of psychology much more. And
even the normal personality will be more safely protected from disease and from social dangers for its
mental constitution if the resources of experimental
psychology are employed. The more we know of
the psychological constitution of the individual, the
more we can foresee the development which is to be
hoped for or feared and which may be encouraged
or retarded.

The psychologist may determine, for instance, the
degree of attention with its resistance against distracting stimuli, the power of memory under various
conditions and on various material, the mental excitability and power of discrimination, the quickness
and correctness of perception, the chains of associations, the rapidity of the associative process for
various groups, the types of reaction, the forming of
habits and their persistence, the conditions of fatigue
and of exhaustion, the emotional expressions and the
emotional stability, the time needed for recreation
and the resistance against drugs, the degree of suggestibility and the power of inhibition: and every re-

sult in any of these lines may contribute to the diagnosis and prognosis of cases. The chronoscope here measures the reaction times and association times in thousandths of a second; the kymograph, by the help of the sphygmograph, writes the record of the pulse and its changes in emotional states, while the pneumograph records the variations of breathing, and the plethysmograph shows the changes in the filling of blood vessels in the limbs which is immediately related to the blood supply of the brain. Here belongs also the ergograph, which gives the exact record of muscular work with all the influences of will and attention and fatigue, the automatograph which writes the involuntary movements, especially also the galvanoscope which may register the influence of ideas and emotions on the glands of the skin, and thus lead to an analysis of repressed mental states, and hundreds of other instruments which are used in the psychological laboratory.

Yet it would be misleading to think only of complex apparatus when experimental psychology is in question. An experiment is given whenever the observation is made under conditions which are artificially introduced for the purpose of the observation. Thus there is no need of the physical instrument. If I bring a spoonful of soup to my mouth at dinner and I become interested in the combination of warmth sensation and touch sensation and taste sensation and smell sensation, then I have performed an experiment if I take one more spoonful of soup just for the purpose of the observation. The physician too may carry out important psychological experiments, without needing the outfit of a real laboratory. Association experiments, for instance, promise to become of steadily growing importance. To make them serviceable to the problems of his office, nothing but a subtle psychological understanding is needed, inasmuch as any routine work schematically applied to every case alike would be utterly useless. Give your man perhaps a hundred words and let him speak the very first word which comes to his mind when he hears the given ones. You call rose, and he may say red or flower or lily or thorn; you call frog and he may answer pond or turtle or green or jump, and if you choose your hundred words with psychological insight, his hundred answers will allow a full view of his mental makeup. This is an experiment which does not require any instruments at all but a man's subtle analysis of the replies. That is not seldom sufficient to secure the diagnosis of complex mental variations. The method yields still more if the time for such a reply is measured, but there again not the costly chronoscope of the laboratory is indispensable; a simple stop watch which gives the fifths of a second would be fully sufficient for all practical purposes. From such simple facts of the mental inventory the association experiments may lead to complex questions which slowly may disentangle the confused ideas, for instance, of a dementia præcox, and thus lead to subtle differential diagnosis.

The psychological laboratory alone can also elaborate the methods of studying, for instance, the feeble-

minded with all the individual variations. New and
ever new methods have been tried; the memory was
tested by reading and repeating figures or letters, or
colored papers were shown or cardboards of different
forms or nonsense syllables, and the powers of
remembering were studied. Or the accuracy of arm
movements was examined, or the quickness of understanding associated words, or the success in planning
a complex movement like throwing a ball at a target,
or the tapping of a key in the rhythm of a metronome, or the discrimination and recognition of the
pieces in the game of dominoes and many another
scheme. The laboratory has to analyze the conditions for such methods and the psychologist has to
prepare the means for the use of the physician, just as
the chemist has to prepare the sleeping powders. In
a similar way the laboratory may furnish means to
analyze the mental disturbances by a comparison with
the experimental results of artificial influences, for instance, of over-fatigue or half-sleep, of drugs or alcohol, of poisons and emotional excitements. The psychological resolving of the mental symptoms may of
course, in the same way, furnish the diagnosis where
the mental variation is only a distant effect of a bodily
ailment. The changes in the emotions, for instance,
may lead to the recognition of a heart disease; lack
of attention may be a hint of the overgrowth of the
adenoids; irritability or apathy or delirious character
of the mental behavior may indicate whether
uræmic acid is in the system or an infectious disease:
anæmia and undernutrition may be diagnosed and the

psychology of fever demands too a much closer analysis with the means of the psychological laboratory than it has received so far.

We have not spoken as yet about those psychological methods which themselves introduce abnormal mental states like hypnotism, and which also not seldom are only means for diagnostic purposes. The hypnotic state may bring to memory forgotten experiences of which the physiological effects may have lasted in the brain and which may have brought injury to the psychophysical system. Hypnotic inquiry can thus lead to the recognition of the first causes in many hysterical states and where hypnotism is not the best adjusted tool, a certain dreamlike staring may be more effective. We have to return to much of that later in full detail because just for instance in hysteria, the clear recognition of the sources and of the character of the disease may at the same time prove to be in itself the right starting point for curative treatment.

We have spoken so far only about the relations of psychology and medicine from the point of view of diagnosis; the relations from the point of view of therapy will make up the second part of this book. We shall describe the methods and the results, the possibilities and the limitations with manifold detail. That is the chief topic of this volume. All that is needed to prepare for this principal problem is on the one side a preparatory clearing up of some fundamental conceptions, especially of those two which have played the chief rôle in the whole discussion, namely the subconscious and suggestion. And on the other side, we may consider at first some fundamental discriminations which steadily influence the inquiries and controversies in the field. I think of the difference between normal and abnormal mental states, between psychical and physical facts in psychotherapy, between functional and organic diseases, and to return to our starting point, between mental and moral influences.

Every curative effort presupposes that the normal state of health has been lost and that a diseased state has set in. Yet the mental analysis suggests still less than the bodily inquiry, just where the normal functioning is really lost. It would be easy to draw a demarcation line if the pathology of the mind introduced any mental features which are unknown in our normal existence, but the opposite is true. No mental disease introduces elements which do not occur in the sphere of health. A degenerated brain cell looks differently under the microscope from a normal one, but the ideas of a paranoiac, the emotion of a maniac, the volition of a hysteric, the memory idea of a paralytic is each in its own structure not different from such elements in any one of us. The total change lies thus only in the proportion; there is too much or too little of it. The pathological mental life is like a caricature of a face—each feature is contained, as in the ordinary portrait, but the proportion is distorted, there is too much or too little of chin or of nose. But who can indicate exactly the point where the distortion of the features constitutes a caricature?

Every grotesque change in the relations ruins the
healthy state: what makes us sure that the harmony
of health is spoiled?

Certainly we cannot settle it by mere statistics.
The norm never means merely a majority. Even if
the overwhelmingly larger part of mankind suffered
from phthisis, the few who were free from it would
be recognized as well and all the others would be
considered ill. In mental life still more, no one ought
to propose that the exceptional function is the
symptom of disease. The few persons who never
had a dream in their lives differ much in their mental
experience from the large majority and yet their
peculiarity is certainly not a symptom which needs
curative treatment. The only real test of health is
the serviceableness to the needs of life. We have an
unhealthy state of the personality before us wherever
the equilibrium of the human functions is disturbed
in a way which diminishes the chances of existence,
and the seriousness of the ailment depends upon the
degree of this diminishing power. Seen from a
strictly psychological point of view, we must expect
thus a broad borderland region between the entirely
normal well-balanced mental life and that unbalanced
disorder of functions which really interferes with
the chance for self-protection and effectiveness. That
the melancholic who declines to take any nourishment,
or the paranoiac who misjudges his surroundings,
is unable to secure by his own energies the safety of
his life cannot be doubted. The balance is completely destroyed and the will and the intellect of the

physician and of the nurse must be substituted for his own mental powers, if his life is to be prolonged at all. But the misjudgment and the depression of the insane are only an exaggeration of that which may occur in any man.

There are therefore thousands of steps which lead from the normal error or regret to the destructive disturbance. Everyone knows persons whose pessimistic temperament makes them inclined to an over-frequent depression, or others whose silly disposition brings out constantly those emotional tendencies which the maniac shows in an exaggerated degree. The stupid mind shows those lacks of association and connection which reach their maximum degree in the mind of the idiot. We know from daily life the timid, undecided man who cannot come to a will impulse; the hasty man who rushes towards decisions; the inattentive man who can never focus his consciousness; and the overattentive man who can never dismiss any subject; the indifferent man on whom nothing produces evident impression and feeling; the oversensitive man who reacts on slight impressions with exaggerated emotion; and yet every one of such and a thousand similar variations, needs only the projection on a larger scale to demonstrate a mental life which is self-destructive. The silly girl and the stupid boy, the man who has the blues and the reckless creature, are certainly worse equipped for the struggles of existence than those who are intellectually and emotionally and volitionally well-balanced. They will take wrong steps in life, they may be unsuccessful, their stupidity may lead them to the poorhouse, their recklessness may lead them to the penitentiary. And yet we do not speak of them as patients because their disproportionate mental features may be sufficiently corrected by other mental states which are perhaps more strongly developed.

Further, inasmuch as human life just in its mental functions is related to its social surroundings, much must depend on the external conditions, whether the disproportion and abnormality has to be treated as pathological. The mind which may find perhaps its way under the most simple rural conditions would be unable to protect life under the complex conditions of a great city. The man who in certain surroundings may appear a crank has to be treated as a patient in a different set of life conditions. Wherever psychotherapeutic work is in question, perhaps nothing is more important than to keep steadily in mind this continuity between normal and abnormal mental features. The mental disturbance must constantly be looked upon as a change of proportions between functions which, as such, belong to every normal life. We have to train and to develop, and thus to reenforce, that which is too weak, and we have to drain off and to suppress and to inhibit that which is too strong.

Yet just this functional view of disease must remind us strongly from the beginning that it would be utterly in vain to draw any demarcation line between psychical disturbances and physical ones. We have seen from the start that from the point of view of physiological psychology, there can be no psychical process without an accompanying physiological process in the brain. Every disturbance in mental actions is thus at the same time a disturbance in the equilibrium of nervous functions. Yet that alone would not exclude the possibility of considering some diseases, for instance, exclusively from the mental side, and we should be justified in doing so if those parts of the brain which are the seat of the mental processes could remain in the diseased state without influence on other parts of the nervous system and of the whole body. In such a case it would indeed be sufficient to consider the psychophysical disturbance from the psychological point of view only, that is, to speak of the disease as a disorder of intellect, of emotion or will, without thinking of changes in the brain cells. But such isolation does not exist in nature. Not only the bodily factors like nutrition and circulation and sexual functions have a thousandfold influence on the psychophysical processes, and these in turn change the vegetative functions of the body, but especially the other parts of the brain and nervous system can be affected in most different ways. If we want to consider whether a certain variation of the personality demands curative treatment, we certainly cannot confine ourselves to the mental variations. They are after all only parts of the whole group of changes in the organism and are thus symptoms of a disease which has to be studied in its totality. The mental symptoms alone may be relatively slight variations, which in themselves

might be sufficiently balanced not to disturb the
equilibrium of life, and yet they may be symptoms of
a brain disturbance which as a whole must interfere
with the safety of life. On the other hand, mental
life may appear like a chaos and yet the disturbance
may be the symptom of merely a slight brain affection
and the treatment of the mental symptoms in their
apparent severity would be a useless effort. The
mental disturbance, for instance, of the intoxicated
or the hashish smoker, even the delirium of the
feverish, does not suggest a fight against the mental
symptoms during the attack.

On the whole, there is a far-reaching independence
between the apparent mental variations and the
seriousness of the brain affection. Light hysteric
states may produce a strong absenting of the mind
while severe epileptic conditions of the brain may
be accompanied by very slight mental changes.
Every neurasthenic state may play havoc with mental
life, while grave brain destructions may only shade
slightly the character or the intellect. To deal with
the mental changes as if they belonged to a sphere by
itself, to the soul which is well or ill through its own
independent alterations without steadily relating the
changes to the total organism, leads therefore necessarily to failure. The mind reflects only symptoms
of the disease; the disease itself belongs always to
the organism. Psychotherapy has suffered too much
from the belief that the removal of mental symptoms
is a cure of disease.

Certainly the psychophysical symptoms may often

stand in the foreground of the disease, and in that case it may be left to the special needs whether we deal with them as psychical or as physical changes. Even the patient may be made to see them in one or the other way in accordance with his special needs. To tell him that his brain cells are in disorder and that they can be cured will be the right thing for him who takes only the introspective view of his suffering and is in despair because his own will seems powerless to overcome those mental changes. For the next patient, the opposite may be wiser. The belief that his brain is ill may have induced him to give up effort of the will instead of helping along by steady self-suggestion. He will be helped more if he understands that his mind is working wrongly. But the full truth is that both mind and body are in disorder; the function of the disturbed brain cells accompanies the ineffective will, and to reënforce the will means to bring into equilibrium again the disturbed brain cells. For the psychotherapist the temptation of giving the attention to the mental symptoms only is strong. The more firmly the physician sticks to the standpoint of psychophysiology, the better he will see ailment and cure in their right proportion.

This demand for the consideration of the whole personality, mind and body, ought not to be influenced by the popular separation between organic and functional diseases. If we call organic diseases of the mind those in which the mental disturbance is the accompaniment of a brain disturbance, and functional those in which no brain disturbance exists, we leave entirely the ground of modern psychology. As soon as we believe that the mind can be disturbed without a change in the functions of the brain, we give away all that which has brought scientific order into the study of psychological existence. Every mental disturbance corresponds to a disorder in the brain's functions. But there cannot be a change in the functions of the brain without a change in its structure. Thus we must claim that all those so-called functional disturbances like neurasthenia and hysteria, fixed ideas and obsessions, phobias and dissociations of the personality, as well as the typical insane states of the maniac or paranoiac have their basis in a pathological change of the anatomical structure of the brain. This postulate cannot be influenced by the fact that the microscope has been unable to detect the character of most of these changes.

Of course all this does not exclude its being perfectly justifiable to separate those diseases for which a definite destruction of the brain parts can be detected, as in paralysis of the brain, from those where that is impossible. We may also expect that those disturbances in the brain which we cannot as yet make visible, may allow more easily an organic repair and thus a restoration to the normal functions. Just as a disjointed arm may be brought to function quickly again, a broken arm slowly, an amputated arm never, each brain cell too may suffer lesions which are reparable in different degrees. But it is evident that it remains then an entirely empirical question whether the invisible damage allows repair or not. We have no right to say that where the destruction cannot be seen under the microscope there is no organic change and the disturbance is therefore only a psychical one and can be removed by mental means. All changes are physical and experience has to decide whether they are accessible to psychological influences or not. States like epilepsy may not allow any recognition of definite brain destruction and are yet on the whole inaccessible to mental influence, while many a brain disturbance with visible alterations, resulting perhaps from anæmia or hyperæmia, may be caused to disappear. If on the other hand we say that we can cure with psychotherapeutic means only the functional brain diseases and define as functional simply those diseases which can be cured by such means, we move, of course, in the most obvious circle and yet just that is the too frequent fate of the discussions in certain quarters.

Every psychical disturbance is organic inasmuch as it is based on a molecular change which deranges the function. Some of these changes are beyond restitution; some can be brought back to a well-working structure by strictly physical agencies like drugs or electricity; others can be repaired by physiological stimuli which reach directly the higher brain cells through the sense organs and which we call psychical under one aspect, but which certainly remain physiological influences from another aspect. And these psychophysiological influences of the spoken words or similar agencies are thus indeed for therapeutic effect entirely coördinated with the douche and the bath and the electric current and the opiate. It is a stimulation of certain brain cells, an inhibition of certain others: a subtle apparatus which must be handled with careful calculation of its microscopical causes and effects. That these words from an entirely different point of view may mean a moral appeal and have ethical value, point to moral and religious ideas and reënforce the spiritual personality, lies entirely outside of the psychotherapeutic calculation. As long as the curing of the patient is the aim, the faith in God is not more valuable than the faith in the physician and the moral appeal of no higher order than the influence through the galvanic current. They come in question only as means to an end and they are valuable only in so far as they reach the end. That they can be related to an entirely different series of purposes, to the system of our moral ideas, ought not to withdraw the attention of the psychotherapist from his only aim, to cure the patient. The highest moral appeal may be even a most unfit method of treatment and the religious emotion may just as well do harm as good from the point of view of the physician. Psychotherapy has suffered too much from the usual confusion of standpoints.

V

SUGGESTION AND HYPNOTISM

PSYCHOTHERAPY has now become for us the effort to repair the disturbed equilibrium of human functions by influencing the mental life. It is acknowledged on all sides that the most powerful of these influences is that of suggestion. This is an influence which is most easily misunderstood and which has most often become the starting point for misleading theories. Before we enter into the study of the practical effects of suggestion and the psychotherapeutic results, we must examine this tool in the hand of the psychotherapist from a purely psychological viewpoint. The patient may perhaps sometimes profit from suggestion the more, the less he understands about its nature, but the physician will always secure the better results, the more clearly he apprehends the working of this subtle tool. Of course, that does not mean that any psychology is able to explain the process of suggestion to a point where all difficulties are removed, but at least the mysteries can be removed and the effects can be linked with other well-known processes.

Let us be clear from the start that suggestion is

certainly nothing abnormal and exceptional, nothing which leads us away from our ordinary life, nothing which brings us nearer to the great riddles of the universe. There is no human life into which suggestion does not enter in a hundred forms. Family life and education, law and business, public life and politics, art and religion are carried by suggestion. A suggestion is, we might say at first, an idea which has a power in our mind to suppress the opposite idea. A suggestion is an idea which in itself is not different from other ideas, but the way in which it takes possession of the mind reduces the chances of any opposite ideas; it inhibits them. It is indeed the best result of any successful education, that the teachings have taken hold of the mind of the young in such a way that all the opposite tendencies and impulses and wishes do not come to development. The well-educated person does not need to participate in a struggle between good and bad motives, for that which has been impressed upon his mind does not allow the other side to come up at all. Our life would be crowded with inner conflicts if education had not secured for us from the start preponderance for the suggestions of our educators.

The love of family and friends, of our country and our party are in the same way such suggestions. We may hear arguments for the other side, arguments which easily convince the man of the other party, but they do not appeal to us: they are emasculated before they enter our minds; they have no chance to overcome the resistance because suggestions stand in their way.   No argument will overwhelm the suggestion which religion has settled in our inner life, and from this strongest suggestion which can stand against any temptation of life small psychological steps lead down to the little bits of suggestion with which our daily chance life is over-flooded.   Every advertisement in the newspaper, every display in the shop-window, every warm intonation in the voice of our neighbor has its suggestive power, that is, it brings its content in such a way to our minds that the desire to do the opposite is weakened.   We do buy the object that we do not need, and we do follow the advice which we ought to have reconsidered.   And what would remain of art if it had not this power of suggestion by which it comes to us and wins the victory over every opposing idea?   We believe the painter and we believe the novelist, if their technique is good. We do not remember that the inventions of their genius are contrary to our life experience; we feel sympathy with the hero and do not care in the least that he has no real life.   The suggestion of art has inhibited in us every contrary idea.

Such daily experience shows us that suggestive power may belong to different men in different degree.   There are lawyers whose arguments and whose presentation open our mind, it seems, to any suggestion: while others leave us indifferent; we understand their idea, we follow their thoughts, and yet we remain accessible to opposite influences. There are teachers whose authority gives to every word such an impressiveness and dignity that every opposite thought disappears, while others throw out words which are forgotten. On the other hand, the readiness to accept suggestions is evidently also quite different with different individuals. From the most credulous to the stubborn, we have every degree of suggestibility, the one impressed by the suggestive power of any idea which is brought to his mind, the other always inclined to distrust and to look over to the opposite argument. Such a stubborn mind is indeed not only without inclination for suggestions, but it may develop even a negative suggestibility; whatever it receives awakens an instinctive impulse towards the opposite. Moreover we are all in different degrees suggestible at different times and under various conditions. Emotions reënforce our readiness to accept suggestions. Hope and fear, love and jealousy give to the impression and the idea a power to overwhelm the opposite idea, which otherwise might have influenced our deliberation. Fatigue and intoxicants increase suggestibility very strongly. To look out on a wider perspective, we may add at once that an artificial increase of suggestibility is all which constitutes the state of hypnotism.

At first, however, we want to understand the ordinary process of suggestion in that normal form in which it enters into every hour of our life and into every relation of our social intercourse. But if we begin to examine the structure of the process, we can no longer be satisfied with the vague reference to ideas and their opposites. What does it mean after all if we speak of opposite ideas? Can we not en-

tertain any ideas peacefully together in our consciousness? From a logical standpoint, ideas may contradict each other, but that refers to their meaning.
As mere bits of psychological experience, I may have
any ideas together in my consciousness. I can think
summer and winter or day and night or right and
left or black and white or love and hate in one em-
bracing thought. As mere mental stuff, the one idea
does not interfere with the other. On the other
hand, this is evident: I cannot will to turn to the
right and to turn to the left at the same time. There
may be a wrangling between those two impulses, but
as soon as my will stands for the one, the other is
really excluded. Any action which I am starting to
do thus crowds out the impulse to the opposed action.

In the sphere of psychological facts, we have here
indeed the only relation between two happenings
which necessarily involves an opposition. We could
never understand why one brain cell might not work
together with any other brain cell, but we do understand that nature must provide for an apparatus by
which the impulse to one action makes the impulse to
the opposite action ineffective. There is no action
which has not its definite opposite. The carrying
out of any impulse involves the suppression of the
contrary impulse, and the impulse not to do an action
involves the suppression of the impulse to do it.
When we spoke of the relations of mind and brain,
we mentioned that such a corelation of mental
centers indeed exists. Physiological experiments
have demonstrated that the activity of those centers

which stimulate a certain action reduce the excitability of those brain parts which awaken the antagonistic action. As far as the world of actions is concerned, the mechanism of the process of suggestion thus seems not inaccessible to a physiological understanding.

Various ideas of movements to be carried out are struggling for control in the cortex of the brain. That is the normal status which precedes any decision. The channels of motor discharge are open for both possibilities; we may turn to the right or to the left. Then the play of associations begins. A larger and larger circle of ideas surrounds the idea of the one and of the other goal. Those ideas awaken emotions. On the one side may call our duty and on the other side our pleasure. Larger and larger parts of the central content of our consciousness, of our own personality, become involved; our principles and maxims, our memories, our hopes and fears, enter into the battle until deeper strata of the idea of ourselves enter into a firm association with the one side, reënforcing, perhaps, the idea of the goal at the right. This opens wide the channels of discharge for the movement to the right and inhibits thereby the excitability of the center which leads to the opposite action. The channel of discharge to the movement towards the left becomes closed, the idea of that movement fades away and becomes inhibited: we are moving towards the right. The outcome was the product of our total personality.

But this result would have been different, if from

the start the channels of discharge had not been
equally open for both possible movements, and if
thus the relative resistance to the impulse had not
been equal on both sides. If, for instance, we had
gone from the given point frequently to the left, as a
result of the habit and training, the impulse to the
left would have found less nervous resistance. The
channels would have become widened by the repetition and the opposite channels would have been somewhat closed by the lack of use. Or if instead of such
previous habit, we should see at the decisive moment
others turning to the left, the impression would have
become the starting point for a reaction of mere instinctive imitation. While we might not have followed that imitative impulse at once, yet the channels
would have been widened, the discharge in the direction would have been prepared by it, the resistance
would have been lowered and the chances for the
opposite movement would have been decreased.
Those people who moved to the left gave us by their
action the same kind of an impulse which they would
have furnished if they had begged us with words, or
if they had ordered us to follow them with authoritative firmness. In each of these cases, the influence
would have amounted to a suggestion. Whether we
watched the movements of other people or whether
their words made an impression on us, in either case
the way became prepared for a certain line of action
and therefore the way for the opposite action became
blocked. The final outcome was thus no longer an
entirely free play of motor ideas, but there was a little

inequality in play. The one had from the start a better chance, the other was from the start laboring under difficulties. The suggestion of actions is thus nothing but making use of the antagonistic character in the nervous paths which start from the motor centers. That all such phrases as the opening and the closing, the widening and blocking, of channels of discharge are only metaphors hardly needs special emphasis. Instead of such comparisons, we ought rather to think of chemical processes which offer various degrees of resistance to the propagation of the nervous excitement.

We see from here the direction in which many psychotherapeutic efforts must lie, efforts which are entirely within the limits of the daily normal experience and belong to the medical practice of every physician, yes, to the helpful influence of every man in practical life. The intemperate man may suffer from his inability to resist his desire for whiskey. The idea of his visit to the saloon finds the channels of discharge open. We argue with him, we tempt him by attractions which lead to other ways, we suggest to him that he spend those evening hours perhaps with friends or with books for which we awaken his interest; we do it as impressively as we can, we appeal to his friendly feeling for us; and if again the hour comes in which the desire for the artificial stimulation sets in with a motor impulse towards the bottle, the channels for discharge have now been blocked. The idea of the opposite action arises, it associates itself with the emotions which we stirred up in his mind, it associates itself with the respect for the adviser, and thus new clusters of thought reënforce that idea of action which we suggested, and this opposite line of action now finds a minimum resistance because our appeal has opened beforehand the gate. The desire for the book works itself out into action while the desire for the cup finds increased resistance.

Just this is the kind of suggestion with which we correct faulty action everywhere in our social circle; and yet small steps lead on from here to the case where perhaps the desire for alcohol has reached that pathological intensity in which the equilibrium is entirely disturbed and cannot be repaired without suggestions of a much more powerful character, given in a state of artificially increased suggestibility—in hypnotism. The principle of opening certain channels of discharge for the purpose of closing the opposite channels remains in the extreme case the same as in the more ordinary cases. The impulse to drink is a positive one, but the principle is not different where the impulse is negative. A friend who comes from the quiet country may feel unable to pass the busy square of the city. The fear of an accident holds back his steps, he cannot give the impulse to walk through the crowded rush of vehicles. Now either by words of advice, by persuasion or by showing the way, we may apply our suggestion, we open the channels of discharge for the necessary movements and thus decrease the excitability of those centers in which nervous fear was playing. And again small steps lead from here to the case of the psychasthenic sufferer whose phobia does not allow him to cross any square and where reënforced suggestion has to break open the ways for the walking movement when the square is reached.

Thus we are not far from a causal understanding of suggestive influences wherever actions are concerned, where movements are to be reënforced or to be suppressed and where antagonism of the motor paths is involved. But that does not seem to lead us nearer to the much larger group of states in which the whole suggestive process concerns apparently the interplay of ideas alone, where not actions but impressions are controlled by suggestion, where not impulses but thoughts are strengthened or inhibited. Here lies the real psychophysical problem which has been by far too much neglected in scientific psychology and has almost been hidden and made to disappear in the wonderful accounts of the hypnotists. But all those mysterious stories as to the achievements of suggestion cannot help so long as we do not understand the working of the process, and we shall have the better chance to understand it the more we keep away from the uncanny and mysterious results which refer to the most complex conditions, and rather seek to analyze the state in its simplest forms and compare it with other simple mental processes. The psychology of suggestion has suffered too much by the fascination which its most complex forms exert on a trivial curiosity.

Yet the problem of suggestion in the field of ideas stands after all not isolated. Instead of connecting

it with the weird reports of mystic influence from
man to man, let us rather link it with the simple experience of attention. There is no pulse-beat of our
life in which attention does not play its little rôle.
But does not attention share with suggestion the
characteristic feature that some contents of consciousness are reënforced and others are suppressed? This
negative, this suppressing character of attention is
not a chance by-product, it is most essential. There
is no attention without it. If I am studying, I do
not hear the conversation around me, and if I listen
to the conversation, my studies in hand become inhibited. If I enjoy the play on the stage and give
to it my full attention, my memories of the day's
work are suppressed; if I think of the happenings of
the day, I am not attentive to the play and hardly
notice what is going on. The inhibited impression
may often disappear entirely. While I am reading
I am not at all aware of the tactual and muscular
sensations in my legs, and if I am completely absorbed
by my book, I may not even notice that the bell
rings. In short, we have here as the most characteristic relation, just as in suggestion, the fact that one
mental state becomes vivid, and that others are losing
ground, become less vivid, are inhibited and perhaps
disappear entirely.

Of course, to point to the similarity between suggestion and attention is not a real explanation. It
may be answered that attention simply offers the same
difficulties once more. How can we explain in the
attention process the fact that one idea, the one

attended to, becomes vivid and that others evaporate? The difficulty evidently cannot be removed by simply saying that only one sensorial process can be developed in the brain at one time. The popular descriptions of attention easily make it appear as if such were the solution of the problem. If one sensorial brain part is intensely engaged, the remainder of the brain is condemned to a kind of inactivity. Yet such a dogma is hardly better than the old-fashioned one that the soul can have only one idea at a time. We know too well now that the psychophysical system is an extremely complex equilibrium of millions of elements. Thus every change must be explained with reference to this complex manifold. Above all, the facts simply contradict such an over-simple explanation, inasmuch as it is not at all true that only one content of consciousness can become vivid. Our attention does not focus upon one point at all but may illuminate a large field and thus give vividness to various complex groups. If I am thinking about a scientific problem, an abundance of reminiscences of previous reading and imaginative ideas of possible solutions, associative thoughts and conclusions are with equal vividness before my mind and the forthcoming thought may be influenced by this total combination. I have no right whatever to say that the idea of a certain solution excludes there in my mind the consideration of the books which I have read and of the discussions which I have heard. Emotions may be superadded. In short, a world of mental states may be held together by one act of attention. And new and ever new thoughts are shooting in, and all still find place there in the field attended to, while on the other hand my slight headache is inhibited and an appointment is forgotten. At a gay banquet, my attention may be given to the whole hall with all its color effects and its flowers, and to all that the table offers and to the music from the orchestra and to the jokes of my neighbors. It is not true that any one of those parts suppresses the vividness of the others, they seem rather to maintain and to help one another; and yet in the next moment, my neighbor may bring me news which absorbs my mind entirely and leaves no room for the flowers and the music and the meal. How far can psychology do justice to these characteristics of attention?

There seems to be but one way. The attended-to idea does not exclude every other idea, but it does exclude the opposite idea, and opposite to each other is here again that pair of ideas which lead to opposite actions, to opposite psychophysical attitudes. We must remember here the psychomotor character of our brain processes which we so fully discussed. We recognized the fundamental truth that there is no sensorial state which is not at the same time the starting-point for motor reaction. We recognized that the brain is by its whole psychological development a great switchboard which transfers incoming currents into outgoing ones and that its biological meaning lies in the fact that it is the center piece of an arc which leads from the sense organs to the muscles. We cannot conceive of those relations as complex enough; we know, of course, that millions of nerve fibers lead from the periphery to the highest psychophysical apparatus in the cortex of the brain and that millions of fibers bring about the interrelation between these central stations, but we must never forget that millions of fibers also represent the outgoing paths and that they too lead down to lower central motor instruments which are again in numberless corelations. Any impression is thus a starting point for attitudes and reactions and it is an empty abstraction to consider it otherwise. An idea is never, psychophysically considered, the end of the process, it is always also a beginning. No external action may follow, but the mental impulse to such is nevertheless starting in the highest center.

If we look at the landscape, every single spot of color, reaching a nerve fiber in our eye and finally a sensory cell in our brain, is there the starting point for an impulse to make an eye movement in the direction of the seen point. The eye may remain entirely quiet as the impulse to move to the right and to the left, to move up and to move down, may be equally strong, but those thousands of impulses work in the motor paths and only their equilibrium results in the suppression of the outer movement. With such motor scheme, we begin to understand the selective process in attention. An impression may be accompanied by other stimuli and associations, by thoughts and ideas, and thousands of sensory excitements may thus arise in the cortex, but only those have a chance for full vividness of development which cooperate in the motor action already started. Those impressions which would lead to the opposite actions have no chance because their motor paths are blocked and their own full development is dependent upon their possibility of expression. To close the path means to inhibit the idea which demands such action. We can attend to a hundred thoughts together, if they all lead to the same attitude and deed. We can look at the opera, can see every singer and every singer's gown, can listen to every word, can have the whole plot in mind, can hear the thousands of tones which come from the orchestra; and yet combine all that in one act of attention, because it all belongs to the same setting of our reactive apparatus. Whatever the one wants is wanted by the others. But if at the same time our neighbor speaks to us, we do not notice it; his words work as a stimulus which demands an entirely different motor setting as answer. Therefore the words remain unvivid and unnoticed.

To attend means therefore to bring about a motor setting by which the object of attention finds open channels for discharge in action. Which particular action is needed in the state of attention cannot be doubtful. Attention demands those motor responses and those inner steps by which the object of attention shows itself more fully and more clearly. When we give attention to the picture we want to see more details, when we give attention to the problem we want to recognize more of the factors involved, when we give attention to the banquet we want to grasp more of the pleasurable features. This aim of attention

involves that, as part of such reactions, the sense
organs become adjusted; we fixate the eyeball, we
listen, and in consequence the object itself becomes
clearer, and through the easy passage into the motor
channels the whole impression becomes vivid. At
the same time, all those associations must be reënforced and become vivid too which lead to the same
action. On the other hand, the opening of the one
passageway closes the path to the opposite action and
inhibits the impressions which would interfere with
our interest. Every act of attention becomes, therefore, a complex distribution in the reënforcement and
inhibition of mental states.

Now let us come back to suggestion. It shares, we
said, with attention, the power to reënforce and to
inhibit. But if we examine what is involved in the
suggestion of an idea, we find surely more than a
mere turning of the attention towards one idea and
turning the attention away from another idea. That
which characterizes and constitutes suggestion is a
belief in the idea, an acceptance of the idea as real
and the dismissal of the opposite idea as unreal.
Yes, we may say directly that it is meaningless to
speak of suggesting an idea; we suggest either an
action or, if no action is concerned, we suggest belief
in an idea. If I suggest to the fearful man at twilight that the willow-tree trunk by the wayside is a
man with a gun, I do not turn his attention to an
abstract idea of a robber nor do I simply awaken
the visual impression of one, but I make him believe
that such an idea is there realized, that he really sees

the person. If I suggest to him that he hears distant bells ringing or that he feels a slight headache, he may not be suggestible enough to accept it, but if he accepts it he is not simply attending to the idea which I propose but he is convinced of its real existence. The same holds true with the negative; if I suggest to him that the slight headache of which he complained has disappeared or that the smell which he noticed has stopped, I do not simply invite him to think of the absence of such sensations. It becomes for him a suggestion only if he becomes convinced that these disturbances have now become unreal. The same holds true for all those suggestions of ideas which belong to our practical life, the suggestions which art imprints on our minds, or which politics and religion impart. As long as we are under the suggestion of the novelist, we really believe in the existence of the heroine; we really believe in the validity of the political party principle; it is not an argument to which we simply give our attention, it becomes a suggestion only when the belief in its objective existence controls our minds. We may say in general that suggestions which are not suggestions of actions are without exception suggestions of belief. Actions and beliefs are the only possible material of any suggestion.

Yet what else is a belief than a preparation for action? I may think of an object without preparing myself for any particular line of behavior. Here in the room I may think of rain or sunshine on the street as a mere idea, but to know that it now really

rains or shines means something entirely different.
It means a completely new setting in my present attitude, a setting by which I am prepared to act along
the one or the other line, to take an umbrella or to
take a straw hat, when I am to leave the house. I
may think of the door of this room as locked or un-
locked without transcending the mere sphere of
imagination, but to believe that it is the one or the
other means a new setting in my motor adjustments. If
it is locked I know that I cannot leave the room without a key. Every belief means the preparation for a
definite line of action and a new motor adjustment in
the whole system of motor paths, an adjustment by
which my actions in future will be switched off at once
into particular paths. And there is theoretically no
difference whether my belief refers to the proposition
that the door is locked or that a God exists in Heaven.

But if every belief is such a new motor setting, then
we are evidently brought back to the mechanism
which was essential for every suggestion of action
on the one side and for every process of attention on
the other side, namely, the mechanism of antagonistic
movements. To prepare ourselves for one line of
action means to close beforehand the channels of discharge for the opposite. The suggestible mind sees
the man with a gun on the wayside because he is
preparing himself in his expectation for the appropriate action; he is ready for the fight or ready to
run away, and every line of the tree trunk is apper-
ceived with reference to this motor setting. The
smell, on the other hand, has disappeared under the

influence of the suggestion because a new motor adjustment has set in, in which he is prepared to act as if there were no smell.

The difference between suggestion and attention lies thus only in this: the motor response in attention aims towards a fuller clearness of the idea, for instance, by fixating, listening, observing, searching; while the motor response in suggestion aims towards the practical action in which the object of the idea is accepted as real. In attention, we change the object in making it clearer; in suggestion, we change ourselves in adapting ourselves to the new situation in which we believe. If you consider attention as a psychophysical process open to physiological explanation, you have surely no reason to seek anything mysterious in the process of suggestion; and no new principle is involved, if we come from the effect of the smallest suggestive hint to the complex and powerful suggestions which overwhelm the whole personality.

The two great types of suggestion, the suggestion of actions and the suggestion of ideas, have now come nearer together since we have seen that the suggestion of ideas is really a suggestion of the practical acceptance of ideas, and that means, of a preparation towards a certain line of action. In the one case I suggest the idea of a certain action and this motor idea leads to the action itself, and in the other case I suggest a certain preparatory setting for action and that will lead to the appropriate action whenever the time for action comes. Every suggestion is thus ultimately a suggestion of activity. The most effective suggestion for an action results, of course, if both methods are combined, that is, if we suggest not only the will to perform the action, but at the same time the belief that the end of the action will be real. Suggestion reaches us usually from without. Yet there is again no new principle involved, when the new motor setting results from one's own associations and emotions. Then we speak of auto-suggestion. It is the same difference which exists between the attention called forth through an outer impression and the attention directed by our own will. Loud noise demands our attention, and even a whispered word may awaken associations which stir up the attention. In both cases the channels for adjustment become opened without our intention. But if we are expecting something of importance, if we start to watch a certain development and to find something which we seek, we open the channels by our own effort beforehand and produce our own settings thus through a voluntary attention. In this way suggestion too may start from without,—by a spoken word, by a movement, by a hint; or may start within us and may give us our caprices and our prejudices.

We must not neglect one other feature of the suggestion. Not every proposition to action or to belief can be called a suggestion. Essential too remains the other side of it, the overcoming of the resistance. A mere request, " Please hand me the book on the table," or a mere communication, " It rains," may produce and will produce the fit motor response, the movement towards handing over the book or opening of the umbrella, and yet there may be no suggestive element involved. We have a right to speak of suggestion only if a resistance is to be broken down, that is, if the antagonistic impulse, or the motor setting for the antagonistic action is relatively strong. If I say to the boy, " Hand me the book," when he was anxious to hide the book from my eyes and thus had the wish not to hand it to me and the tone of my request overwhelmed his own intention, then to be sure suggestion is at work. The stronger the resistance, the greater the degree of suggestive power which is needed to overcome the motor setting. If I say to the normal man, " It rains," while he sees the blue sky and the dry street, his impression will be stronger than my suggestion; but if he is suggestible and I tell him that it will rain, he may accept it and take an umbrella on his walk, even if no indication makes a change of weather probable. The present impression of the dry street was strong enough to resist the suggestion, the imaginative idea of that which is to be expected in the next hour was too weak, and was overwhelmed by the suggestion of the weather prophecy.

It is clear that the whole suggestive effect, being one of a new motor setting, depends thus entirely on the equilibrium of the personality which receives the suggestion. Every element which reaches the mind through sense organs or through associations must have influence in helping the one or the other side, that is, in opening the channels of action in the sug-

gested direction or in the antagonistic one. The
results appear surprising only if we forget how endlessly complex this psychomotor apparatus really is.
If we disregard this complexity we may easily have
the feeling that one person has an unexplainable influence over another, as if the will of the one could
control in a mysterious way the will of the other.
But as soon as we see that every action is the result of
the coöperation of hundreds of thousands of psychomotor impulses which are in definite relation to
antagonistic energies, and that the result depends upon the struggling and balancing of this most complex
apparatus, then we understand more easily how outer
influences may help the one or the other side to preponderance: as soon as the balance turns to the one
side, a completely new adjustment must set in. And
we understand especially that there is nowhere a sharp
demarcation line between receiving communications
and receiving suggestions. By small steps suggestion
shades over into the ordinary exchange of ideas,
propositions, and impressions, just as attention shades
over into a neutral perception.

To be suggestible means thus to be provided with
a psychophysical apparatus in which new propositions
for actions close easily the channels for antagonistic
activity. Such an apparatus carries with it the dis-
advantage that the personality may too easily be
guided contrary to his own knowledge and experience.
He will be carried away by every new proposition and
will accept beliefs which his own thoughts ought to
reject. On the other hand, it has the advantage that

he will be open to new ideas, be ready to follow good examples, never stubbornly close his mind to the unaccustomed and the uncomfortable. It is easy to determine the degree of suggestibility. Take this case. I draw on the blackboard of a classroom two circles of an equal size, and write in the one the number fourteen and in the other the number eighty-nine, and ask the children which is the larger circle. The suggestible ones will believe that the circle with the higher number in it is really larger than the other, the unsuggestible children will follow the advice of their senses and call both equal, and there may be a few children with negative suggestibility who would call the circle with the higher number the smaller circle. What happened to the suggestible ones was that the higher number brought about a motor attitude which faced that whole complex as being more imposing and this new motor setting was with them strong enough to overcome the motor adjustment which the circles alone produced. Such experiments of the psychological laboratory can be varied a thousandfold, and it might not be unwise to introduce them into many practical fields. Everybody knows for instance how much may depend upon the suggestibility of the witness in court. The suggestible witness believes himself to have seen and heard what the lawyer suggests. The memory picture which such a witness has in mind offers, of course, much less resistance to the opposite action and attitude and belief than the immediate impression. If I show the witness a colored picture of a room and close the

book and ask him whether there were three or four
chairs in the picture and whether the curtain was
green or red, the suggestible man will decide for one
or the other proposition, even if there were only two
chairs and a blue curtain. The perception would
have resisted the suggestion, the fading memory
image cannot resist it. Thus suggestibility is really
a practical factor in every walk of life. And it is in
the highest interests of psychotherapy that this intimate connection between suggestion and ordinary talk
and intercourse, between suggestion and ordinary
choice of motives, between suggestion and attention be steadily kept in view and that suggestion
is not transformed into a kind of mysterious
agency.

To be sure, the importance of suggestion for psychotherapy is not confined to these suggestive processes of daily life. They play a rôle there, as we
shall see, and we shall claim that even the mere presence of the physician may have its suggestive power
and so may every remedy which he applies. But no
doubt many of his suggestive effects depend on a
power which far transcends the suggestions of our
daily life. Yet the psychologist must insist again
that no new principle is involved, that even in the
strongest forms of suggestion, in hypnotism, nothing
depends upon any special influence emanating from
the mind of the hypnotizer or upon any special power
flowing over from brain to brain; but that everything
results from the change of equilibrium in the psychomotor processes of the hypnotized, and thus upon the

interplay of his own mental functions. All that is needed is a higher degree of suggestibility than is found in the normal life. In a more suggestible mind even the direct sense impressions may be overwhelmed by the proposition for an untrue belief and the strongest desires may yield to the new propositions of action. This library may then become a garden where the hypnotized person picks flowers from the floor, and the wise man stands on one leg and repeats the alphabet, if the hypnotizer asks him to do so. Let us consider at first this extreme case. By a few manipulations I have brought a man into a deep hypnotic state. He is now unable to resist any suggestion, either suggestion of impulse or suggestion of belief, and as every one of the hypnotic phenomena can be explained in this way, we may claim that the hypnotic state is in its very nature a state of reënforced suggestibility. Whether I say, "You will not move your arm," or whether I say, "You cannot move your arm," awakening in the one case the impulse to the suppression of the movement, in the other case the belief in the impossibility of the movement, in either case the result is the same; the arm remains stiff and any effort of his to move it is inhibited. I may go to the extreme and tell him that our friend by my side has left the room; he will not see him, he will not even hear a word which the friend speaks. If I take a hat in my hand and put it on the friend's head, the hat appears to hang in the air. Every impression of sound or sight or touch which comes from the friend is entirely inhibited. The direct sense im-

pression of eye and ear is thus completely overwhelmed by the suggestion.

What has happened?   Are the manipulations
which I applied sufficient to produce the changes by
their physical influence?   Certainly not; they are of
the most different kinds and yet all may have the same
effect.   Perhaps I may have used the easy method
of making the subject stare at a shining button held
in front of his forehead.   Or I may have used slight
tactual impressions, while he was lying with closed
eyes, or I may have produced the abnormal state by
monotonous noises of falling waterdrops, or I may
have simply spoken to him and asked him to think of
sleep and to relax and to feel tired, while I held my
hand on his forehead or while I held his hand in mine.
Or I may have relied upon mild talking without
touching him at all; and yet every time the result was
reached in the same degree.   There is thus certainly
no special physical energy which like a magnetic force
flows over.   It cannot even be said that my will is engaged.   I have often hypnotized without even thinking of the subject before me, going through adjusted
manipulations while my thoughts were engaged in
something else.   I have even hypnotized over the
telephone; and a written note may be substituted with
the same result.   I write to the patient that two minutes after receiving this letter by mail, he will fall
into hypnotic sleep.   The effect sets in; and yet at
that time, I may not remember sending the note at all.

It is thus entirely evident that the hypnotic effect
results only from the mental conditions of the subject.

Whatever may stimulate his mind to the right kind of reaction will produce the desired result. The increased suggestibility thus sets in by his own imagination which may be stirred up by slight visual or tactual or acoustic stimuli or by monotonous words or by feelings of relaxation and especially by words which encourage sleep. But just because it is the play of his own imagination, the most essential factor certainly is the will and expectation of the subject. No one can really be hypnotized against his own will. And to expect strong hypnotic effect from a certain hypnotist is often in itself sufficient to produce hypnotic sleep. Thus there is no special personal power necessary to produce hypnotism. Everybody can hypnotize. And almost with the same sweeping statement it may be said everybody can be hypnotized, provided that he is willing to enter into this play of imagination. The young child or the insane person is therefore unfit.

Of course, not everybody can be hypnotized to the same degree. Just as the normal suggestibility showed itself very different with different persons, the degree of artificial reënforcement varies still more. Practically everybody can be brought to that breakdown of the resistance in which he can no longer open the eyes against the order of the hypnotist, but rather few can be brought to the point of seeing extended hallucinations, or accepting the disappearance of persons who are speaking, or of yielding to the impulse to a dangerous action. The highest reported degree, in which even criminal actions are performed by honest men, exists in my opinion only in the imagination of amateurs; it is certainly not difficult to produce sham crimes for performance' sake, with paper daggers and toy pistols, but that is no proof at all that the hypnotized person would commit a crime under conditions under which he has the conviction that he faces a real criminal situation. But if we abstract from real crime, we certainly have to acknowledge that actions can be performed which appear in striking contrast with the habits and character of the normal personality, upset his knowledge, and are based on beliefs which would be immediately rejected under ordinary conditions. These higher degrees of hypnotic state are easily followed by complete loss of memory for all that happened during the abnormal state.

How have we to interpret such a surprising alteration of mind? It lies near to compare it with sleep. The brain seems powerless to produce its normal ideas, the associations do not arise, the normal impulses have disappeared and a general ineffectiveness has set in; in short, the brain cells seem unable to function. Of course, the explanation of sleep itself may offer difficulties. Is it a chemical substance which poisons the brain during the sleep, or are the brain cells contracted so that the excitement cannot run over from the branches of one nerve cell into those of another? Or are the blood-vessels contracted so that an anæmic state makes their normal function impossible? But whatever the physical condition of sleep may be, have we really a right to em-

phasize the similarity between sleep and hypnosis?
After all that we have discussed, we ought rather to
recognize that the hypnotic state too comes much
nearer to the process of attention than to the process
of sleep. We saw that in every act of attention the
process of inhibition is essential. All that is not in
harmony with the attended idea is suppressed. Yet
we should hesitate to say that in attention parts of
our brain are asleep.

We should feel reluctance to group such inhibition
together with sleep because it would be a sleep which
at any moment can pass from one part of the brain
to others and which certainly leaves at every moment
most of the cell groups unaffected. We saw that attention does not at all focus on one narrow point, but
that an abundance of impressions, of ideas and associations, of thoughts and emotions can enter the
field of attention, if they all lead to one and the same
motor attitude, and that only the one part is inhibited
which involves the opposite action. Such a jumping
sleep which at every moment selects a special part
would be, of course, just the contrary of that which
characterizes the sleep state of the fatigued brain.
But exactly these characteristics of attention belong
to hypnotism too. It is not true that the mind of the
hypnotized is asleep and that perhaps only one or the
other idea can be pushed into his mind. On the contrary, his mind is open to an abundance of ideas, just
as in the normal state. If I tell him that this is a
landscape in Switzerland, he sees at once the mountains and the lakes, and his mind provides all the de-

tails of his reminiscences, and his imagination furnishes plenty of additions. His whole mind is awake;
the feelings and emotions and volitions, the memories
and judgments and thoughts are rushing on, and only
that is excluded which demands a contrary attitude.
This selective process stands decidedly in the center
of the hypnotic experience and makes it very doubtful
whether we are psychophysically on the right track,
if we make much of the slight similarity between
hypnosis and sleep.

This has nothing to do with the fact that hypnosis
is best brought about by suggesting the idea of sleep,
that is, the belief that sleep will set in.   This belief
is indeed effective in removing all the ideas which are
awake in the mind which would interfere with the
willingness to submit to the suggestions of the hypnotizer.   But the fact that belief in sleep and expectation of sleep bring with them the hypnotic state is
not a proof that the hypnotic state itself is sleep.
Even the mental experiences which can remain in sleep,
the dreams, are characteristically different from the
hypnotic experience.   Thus the dreams show that un-
selective awakening of ideas which is to be expected
from a general decrease of functioning. The hypnotic
variation is characterized just by its selective nar-
rowing of consciousness.   For the same reason,
hypnotism is strikingly different from such diseases of
the mind as dementia.   Certainly in dementia too,
many associations are cut off, but it is not a selective
inhibition, it is a haphazard destruction resulting
from the degeneration in the brain.

The fundamental principle of the hypnotic state lies in its selective character. Inhibited and cut off are those states which are antagonistic to the beliefs in the suggested ideas, and as their antagonism consists in their connection with opposite actions, the whole is again a question of motor setting. No doubt, such new motor setting can precede the normal sleep too; thus the sleeper may be insensitive to any surrounding noises, but perhaps awake at the slightest call from a patient who is intrusted to his care. In that case, one special feature of hypnotism is superadded to sleep but the sleep itself is not hypnotic. Again sleep may go over into a state which shares many characteristic features with hypnotism, that is, somnambulism, and it may be said with a certain truth that hypnotism is artificial somnambulism. But somnambulism, while arising in sleep, is not at all a feature of sleep.

While sleep is characterized by a decrease of sensitiveness and of selective powers, the selective process of hypnotism rather reënforces sensitiveness and memory in every field which is covered by the suggestive influence. Stimuli may become noticeable which the normal man is unable to perceive, and long-forgotten experiences which seem inaccessible to the search of the waking mind may reproduce themselves and may vividly enter consciousness. Again we have there symptoms which rather characterize the state of over-attention than the state of sleep. We might add further that we know states with all the characteristics of hypnotism in which even the subjective idea of sleep is entirely absent, for instance, all those which are usually called states of fascination. A certain shining light or a glimpse of an uncanny eye may startle and upset the imagination of the subject and throw him into a state of abnormally increased suggestibility. It is well known that whole epidemics of such captivation have occurred and have resulted in hysterias of the masses in which the subjects become the slaves of their impulse, perhaps to imitate what they see or hear, or to realize ideas in which they believe without logical warrant. They surely are not asleep, are not even partially asleep. Every center of their brains would be ready to work, if the captivated attention were not forcing the mind in one direction and selectively suppressing every impulse to opposite actions. The developed hypnotism finally shades off into innumerable states of hypnoid character in which the sleeplike symptoms are entirely in the background.

Thus the increased suggestibility of the hypnotic state will result not from a partial sleeplike decrease of functioning but the decrease of function is a motor inhibition which results from over-attention. In the ordinary attention, our motor setting secures only an increase in clearness and vividness of the attended ideas, but in an abnormal over-attention the new motor setting produces a complete acceptance with all its consequences. Abnormal or heightened attention thus goes directly over into the belief and into the impulse without resistance. There is no hypnotism which does not contain from the first stage this definite relation to certain objects of attention, usually to a particular person. All the manipulations, passes, fixation, monotonous speaking, and so on narrow the contents of consciousness but hold the idea of the hypnotizing person steadily in the center of attention. The awakened expectation of sleep, the associated feeling of tiredness all help to cut off attention from the remainder of the world, but as no real sleep sets in, this cutting off from the remainder reënforces the focusing of attention on the one central idea of the hypnotizing personality. Every word and every movement of this personality become therefore absorbed with that over-attention which leads at once from a mere perceiving and grasping to a complete sinking into the suggested idea with the suppression of all opposites, and thus to a blind acceptance and belief. We saw before that such belief is indeed nothing else but a motor setting in which certain ways of action are prepared. We are to think in accordance with the belief in the suggested idea and the channels for discharge in the opposite direction are closed. Even the ordinary life shows us everywhere that the step from attention to belief is a short one. The effort to grasp the object clearly works as a suggestion to accept that which we are seeking as really existing, and that from which we are to abstract and which we are to rule out through our attention, we believe to be non-existent. The prestidigitator does his tricks in order to sidetrack our attention, but he succeeds in making us believe that we see or do not see whatever he wishes.

That the motor setting alone determines those changes and that a real sleeplike inability of the centers does not set in, can also be demonstrated by the results of later hypnotizations. I ask my hypnotized subject not to perceive the friend in the room; he is indeed unable to see him or to hear him. Yet his visual and acoustic centers are not impaired, the defect is only selective, inasmuch as he sees me, the hypnotizer, and not the friend. But even this selection inhibits only the attitude and not the sensorial excitement. If I hypnotize him again to-morrow and suggest to him now to remember all that the friend did and said during yesterday's meeting, he is able to report correctly the sense impressions which he got, which were inhibited only as long as they contradicted the suggestion, but now rush to consciousness as soon as the suggestion is reversed. As a matter of course, he must therefore have received impressions through eye and ear in his hypnotic sleep of yesterday from all that happened, only he was not aware of it because the channels of the accepting attitude were blocked.

As soon as the over-attention has produced the acceptance of the belief, all further effects are automatic and necessary. If I tell the hypnotized person that he cannot speak and he absorbs this proposition, with that completeness in which he accepts it as a fact, not speaking itself unavoidably results. The motor ideas with which the speech movement has to start are cut off and the subject yields passively to the fate that he cannot intonate his voice. Thus a special influence on the will is in no way involved. If the idea is accepted, and that means, if the preparatory setting for the action has been completed, the ideas of opposite activity must remain ineffective; the suggested idea must discharge itself in action without resistance. As a matter of course the new line of action will then surround itself with its own associations and will thus give to the subject the impression that he is acting from his own motives. As soon as the psychophysical principles are understood, there is indeed no difficulty in going from the simplest experience to those spectacular ones where we may suggest to the profoundly hypnotized person that he is a little child or that he is George Washington. In the one case, he will speak and cry and play and write as in his present imagination a child would behave; in the other case, he will pose in an attitude which he may have seen in a picture of Washington. There is nothing mysterious and his utterances are completely dependent upon his own ideas, which may be very different from the real wisdom of a Washington and the real unwisdom of a child. I may suggest to him to be the Czar, by that he will not become able to speak Russian. In the same way I may suggest changes of the surroundings; he may take my room for the river upon which he paddles his canoe, or for the orchard in which he picks apples from my bookshelves.

Finally there is no new principle involved, if the action which is prepared by any belief has to set in after the awaking from hypnotic sleep, the so-called post-hypnotic suggestion. As a matter of course, just these have an eminent value for psychotherapy. I may suggest to-day that the subject will overcome to-morrow his desire for the morphine injection, or that he will feel to-night the restfulness which will over-come his insomnia. But if the suggestion of an idea means belief, and if belief means a preparation for action, we have indeed no new factor before us if the action for which we prepare the subject is from the start related to a definite time. If we do not link it with the consciousness of a special time or of a special occasion which will occur later, the suggestion soon fades away. That my library is an orchard is for-gotten perhaps within ten minutes, if I have not come back to it in the conversation. But if I say that after awaking as soon as I shall knock on my desk three times, you will be in the orchard again, the psycho-physical apparatus is prepared, a new setting has set in, the three knocks will bring about the complete transformation. In short the difficulties disappear as soon as we are consistent in interpreting all sug-gestive influences as changes in the motor setting and as the result of the antagonistic character of all of our motor paths.

We say the difficulties disappear. Of course, that is meant in a relative sense only. It means essentially. that we are able to bring the complex state of hypno-tism down to the similar state of attention and motor adjustment, but of course we must not forget that we are far from a satisfactory explanation of the proc-ess in attention itself. We know that the opening of motor channels in one direction somewhat closes the channels for discharge in the opposite direction, but what mechanism does that work is still very obscure. Whichever principle of hypothetical explanation we might prefer, it certainly leads to difficulties in view of the extreme complexity of attention in states of suggestion and hypnotism. We might think of a mechanism which through the medium of the finest blood-vessels should produce a localized anæmia in those centers which lead to the antagonistic action. Or we might fancy that by extremely subtle machinery the resistance is increased in those tissues which lie between the various neurons, or we might even think of toxic and antitoxic processes in the cerebral regions; and any day may open entirely new ways of explanation. We may add that even if the mechanism of attention were completely explained, we are also still far from understanding the physiological changes which go on in the sphere of the blood-vessels or of the glands and the internal organs. We understand easily that the idea of the subject that he cannot move his arm keeps the arm stiff; but that his idea to blush really dilates the blood-vessels of his cheek is much less open to our causal understanding; still less that in very exceptional cases perhaps a part of the skin becomes inflamed, if we make believe that we touch it with a glowing iron. And yet here too we see that we move in the same direction and that we have to explain these exceptional and bewildering results by comparing them with the simpler and simpler forms, that the process of attention contains all the germs for the whole development.

In claiming that hypnotism depends upon the over-attention to the hypnotizing person, we admit that the increased suggestibility belongs entirely to suggestions which come from without. Only that which at least takes its starting point from the words or the movements of the hypnotizer finds over-sensitive suggestibility. Ideas which arise merely from the associations of the subject himself have no especially favorable chance for acceptance. But surely we also know states in which the suggestibility for certain of one's own ideas is abnormally increased. Great individual differences exist in that respect in normal life. There are normal hypochondriacs who believe that they feel the symptoms of widely different diseases under the influence of their own ideas, and others who are torturing themselves with fears on account of unjustified beliefs. But the abnormal increase of suggestibility parallel to that of hypnotism for suggestions from without exists for suggestions from within, mainly in nervous diseases, especially in neurasthenic, hysteric, and psychasthenic states. Within certain limits, we might almost say that this increase of suggestibility for autosuggestion is the fundamental characteristic of these diseases, just as increase of suggestibility for heterosuggestions characterizes hypnotism.

Especially in earlier times, the theory was often proposed that hypnosis is an artificial hysteria. Such a view is untenable to-day; but that hysteria too shows abundant effects of increased suggestibility is correctly indicated by such a theory. The hysteric patient may by any chance pick up the idea that her right arm is paralyzed or is anæsthetic and the idea at once transforms itself into a belief and the belief clings to her like an obsession and produces the effect that she is unable to move the arm or that she does not feel a pinprick on the skin. These autosuggestions may take a firmer hold of the mind than any suggestions from without, but surely such openness to selfimplanted beliefs must be acknowledged as symptomatic of disease, while hypnosis with its impositions can be broken off at any moment and thus should no more be classed among the diseases than are sleep and dreams. The hysteric or psychasthenic autosuggestion resists the mere will of breaking it off. Here, therefore, is the classical ground for strong mental counterinfluences, that is, for psychotherapeutic treatment. Experience shows that the strongest chance for the development of such autosuggestive beliefs exists wherever an emotional disposition is favorable to the arriving belief. But emotion too is after all fundamentally a motor reaction. The whole meaning of emotion in the biological sense is that it focuses the actions of man into one channel, cutting off completely all the other impulses and incipient actions. Emotion is therefore for the expressions of man what attention is for the impressions. An emotional disposition means thus in every case a certain motor setting by which transition to certain actions is facilitated. It is thus only natural that a belief can settle the more easily, the more it is favored by an emotional disposition, as the motor setting for the one must prepare the other. Hypnosis and hysteria thus represent the highest degrees of suggestibility, the one artificial, the other pathological; the one for suggestions from without, the other for suggestions from within. But between these two and the normal state there lie numberless steps of transition. The normal variations themselves may go to a limit where they overlap the abnormal artificial product, that is, the suggestibility of many normal persons may reach a degree in which they accept beliefs hardly acceptable to other persons in mild hypnotic condition. Thus there is no sharp demarcation between suggestions in a waking state and suggestions in a hypnoid state. And the expectation of coming under powerful influence may produce a sufficient change in the motor setting to realize any wonders. Moreover probably every physician who has a long experience in hypnotizing has found that his confidence in the effectiveness of the deep hypnotic states has been slowly diminished, while his belief in the surprising results of slight hypnotization and of hypnoid states has steadily grown and has encouraged him in his psychotherapeutic efforts.

VI

THE SUBCONSCIOUS

THE story of the subconscious mind can be told in three words: there is none. But it may need many more words to make clear what that means, and to show where the misunderstanding of those who give to the subconscious almost the chief rôle in the mental performance sets in. The psychology of suggestion, for instance, which we have now fully discussed without even mentioning the word subconscious, figures in most popular books in the treatises of both physicians and ministers as a wonderful dominance of the subconscious mind. The subconscious mind alone receives the suggestions and makes them effective, the subconscious mind controls the suggestive processes in consciousness, and the subconscious mind comes into the foreground and takes entire hold of the situation when the hypnotic state sets in.

But we are always assured that there is no need of turning to the mystery of suggestion and hypnotism to find that uncanny subpersonality in us. We try to remember a name, or we think of the solution of a problem; what we are seeking does not come to consciousness and now we turn to other things; and suddenly the name flashes up in our mind or the solution of the problem becomes clear to us. Who can doubt that the subconscious mind has performed the act? While our attention was given over to other questions, the subconscious mind took up the, search and troubled itself with the problem and neatly performed what our conscious mind was unable to produce. Moreover in every situation we are performing a thousand useful and welladapted acts with our body without thinking of the end and aim. What else but the subconscious mind directs our steps, controls our movements, and adjusts our life to its surroundings? And is not every memory picture, every reminiscence of earlier experiences a sufficient proof that the subconscious mind holds its own? The poem which we learned years ago did not remain somewhere lingering in our consciousness, and if we can repeat it today, it must be because our subconscious mind has kept it carefully in its store and is ready to supply us when consciousness has need for it.

Surely if we think how this, our subconscious mind, is able to hold all our memories and all our learning, and how it transacts all the work of controlling our useful actions and of bringing up the right ideas, we may well acknowledge that compared with it our conscious life is rather a small part. It is as with the iceberg in the ocean; we know that only a small part is visible above the surface of the water and a ten times larger mountain swims below the sea. It seems, therefore, only logical to attach this whole subconscious mental life to a special subconscious personality. Then we come to the popular theory of the two minds in us, the upper and the lower, of which we can hardly doubt that the lower one has on the whole the larger part of the business to perform. And we certainly have no right to give to the word lower mind the side-meaning that the activity is of a lower order. The most brilliant thoughts of the genius are not manufactured in his upper consciousness, they spring suddenly into his mind, their whole creation belongs thus to the assiduous work of the subconscious neighbor. There the inventor and discoverer gets his guidance, there the poet gets his inspiration, there the religious mind gets its beliefs. In short, the constitution of the mental state allows on the whole to the upper consciousness a rather decorative part while the real work is left for the lower house.

Yet it must be acknowledged that the scholars somewhat disagree as to the dignity of the lower mind. Considering the usually accepted fact that in hypnotism the lower mind comes entirely over the surface, just these hypnotic events can indeed suggest two different views of the subconscious and this doubleness is reënforced if we still add the entertaining material which comes to light by the automatic writing of mediums in their trance. The hypnotized person is ready to perform any foolishness, is not influenced by any considerations of tact and taste and wisdom and respect, and thus some of the chief believers in the subconscious personality stick to the diagnosis that the lower mind in us which shows up in hypnotism is a rather brutal, stupid, lazy, cowardly, immoral creature which ordinarily rather deserves to be subdued by our noble and wise upper personality. And the automatic writings of the mediums indorse this disrespectful view, for it is difficult to gather more idiotic slang than the emanations of these letters of the planchette. On the other hand, the hypnotized person shows an increase of sensitiveness and hyperæsthesia in which perhaps optical impressions or smells may be noticed which the ordinary man cannot perceive. Moreover the memory of the hypnotized is, as we saw, abnormally sharpened. Entirely forgotten experiences may awake again. The same holds true for the hysteric in whom also, of course, the subconscious takes hold of the inner life. Thus it seems entirely safe to say that the powers of the subconscious personality far surpass those of the upper conscious fellow, and that agrees with all those facts as to the subconscious origin of the work of the genius. Further, has it not been found again and again that the hypnotized and the hysteric cannot only remember long-forgotten parts of the past but have telepathic knowledge for distant events and even mysterious premonitions of the field of occurrences of the future?

Hypnotism is essentially the same as the old mesmerism, and mesmerism was widely acknowledged as clairvoyance, and all that harmonizes again with the experiences of the mediums whose subconscious mind in trance enters into contact with the spirits of the dead. The subconscious personality is thus really

a metaphysical power which transcends the limitations of the earthly person altogether and has steady
connection with the endless world of spirit and the
inner soul of the universe. Most popular books, it
is true, do not demand from their readers the choice
between the one or the other type of the lower personality, between that brutal, vicious, ignorant creature and that far-seeing, inspired, powerful soul.
They simply mix the two and adapt the special faculties of this underground man to the special requirements of the particular chapter, the subconscious being
unusually wise or unusually stupid in accordance with
the special facts which are just then to be explained.
Even that does not always settle all difficulties. They
may discover, for instance, that the subconscious
mind with which we deal in the hypnotized person
has again itself a subconsciousness. If we tell the
hypnotized person not to see a certain picture on the
wall, this subconscious personality perceives the whole
room with the exception of the picture. Yet after all
someone sees this picture, because if we hypnotize him
the next time and ask him what the picture contained,
he now knows its contents. Thus they must have been
recognized in a sub-subconsciousness, and we therefore come to a personality which lives on a floor still
below the basement. But experiment can demonstrate that even this most hidden personality has
still its secrets which are handed downwards. In
short, we finally have not merely two but a number
of personalities in us.

But now let us leave these fantasies of psychological fiction. Let us turn to the concrete facts, let us see them in the spirit of modern scientific psychology, let us try to explain them in harmony with the principles of psychological explanation, and let us discriminate the various groups of facts which have led to that easy-going hypothesis of the subconscious. Discrimination indeed is needed, as it would be impossible to bring the whole manifold of facts under one formula, but there is certainly no unification reached by simply putting the same label on all the varieties and behaving as if they are all at once explained when they are called the functions of the subconscious. Two large groups may be separated. Facts are referred to the subconscious mind which do not belong to the mind at all, neither to a conscious nor to a subconscious one, but which are simply processes in the physical organism; and secondly, facts are referred to the subconscious mind which go on in the conscious mind but which are abnormally connected. Thus the subconscious mental facts are either not mental but physiological, or mental but not subconscious.

What does the scientific psychologist really mean by consciousness? We must now think back to our discussion of the principles which control the fundamental conceptions of modern psychology. We saw clearly that the psychology which is a descriptive and explanatory science of mental phenomena can by no means have the ambition to be a full interpretation of the inner reality. Our inner life, we saw, is not a series of phenomena, is not a chain of objects which we are aware of and which we therefore can describe, and which finally we can explain. But in its living reality, we saw that it is purposive, has a meaning and aim, is will and intention, and can thus be understood in its true character, not by describing and explaining it but by interpreting it and appreciating it. This is the life attitude towards personalities when we deal man to man. We do not at first consider ourselves or our fellows as mental objects to be explained but always as subjects to be understood in their meaning. If we pass from this primary attitude to the attitude of the scientific psychologist we gain, as we saw, an artificial perspective. We must consider then our inner experience of ourselves with all our states as a series of objects made up of elements connected by law. Instead of the real things which in our real life are objects of will and purpose, tools and means for us, the psychologist knows only objects of awareness, objects which have no meaning, but which simply exist and which are no longer related to a will but are connected with other objects as causes and effects. Now we deal no longer with the chairs and tables before us but from a psychological point of view they become perceptive ideas of chairs and tables, ideas which are not in the room but in our own minds. While these objects of our will and of our personality become mere ideas, our will and personality themselves become, too, a series of phenomena. Our self is now no longer the purposive will but is that group of sensations and ideas which clusters about the perception of our organ-

ism and its actions; in short, our self itself becomes
an object of awareness.

Our whole inner experience thus becomes a manifold of objects. Our self and the actions of our self
are thus alike for the psychologist mere phenomena,
mere objects which are perceived. Will and emotion,
memory idea and thought—they all are now passing
appearances like the sunshine and rain, the flowers
and waves. By this transformation the immediate
will character of real life is given up, but instead of
it a system of objects is gained, that allows description and explanation. If we are to deal at all with
inner life not from a purposive but from a causal
point of view, we are obliged to admit this reconstruction. Without it we cannot have any science
of the mind, without it we can understand the intentions of our neighbor and appreciate the truth and
morality of his meanings but we cannot causally explain his experiences or determine which effects are
to be expected. It is thus not an arbitrary substitu-
tion but a procedure just as necessary and logically
obligatory as the work of the chemist who substitutes
trillions of invisible atoms for the glass of water
which he drinks. The possibility of causal explanation of the successive facts demands this remolding
of the outer and of the inner world. We have discussed that before and now only have to draw the
consequences.

Thus for the psychologist the mental world is a
system of mental objects. To be an object means of
course to be object of some subject which is aware of

it. What else could it mean to exist at all as object
if not that it is given to some possible subject? But
the world of objects is twofold; we have not only the
mental objects of the psychologist but also the physical objects of the naturalist. Science must characterize the difference between those two and we pointed
once before to the only fundamental difference.
Physical objects are those which are possible objects
of awareness for every subject; psychical objects are
those which are possible objects of awareness for one
subject only. The tree which I see is as physical tree
object for every man, it is the same tree which you
and I see; my psychical perception of the tree is object for one subject only. My perception can never
be your perception. Our perceptions may agree but
each has his own. As to the physical objects, we can
entirely abstract from such reference to the subjects.
We say simply: the tree exists or is part of nature;
and only the philosopher is aware that we silently
mean by it that it exists for every subject and that it
is therefore not necessary to refer to any particular
subject. But the perception of the tree which is either
your idea or my idea evidently gets its existence only
if it is referred and attached to a particular subject
which is aware of it. Such subject of awareness is
that which the psychologist calls consciousness and all
the ideas and volitions and emotions and sensations
and images which make up the mental life are then
contents of the consciousness or objects of the consciousness. To have psychical existence at all means
thus to be object of awareness for a consciousness.

Something psychical which simply exists but is not object of consciousness is therefore an inner contradiction. Consciousness is the presupposition for the existence of the psychical objects. Psychical objects which enjoy their existence below consciousness are thus as impossible as a wooden piece of iron.

If consciousness is nothing but the subject of awareness for the individual objects, we see at once certain consequences which are too often forgotten in the popular, haphazard psychology. In the scientific system of psychology, consciousness has for instance nothing whatever to perform, that is, consciousness itself is in no way active. The active personality of real life has been left behind and has itself been transformed into that self which is merely content of consciousness. The person who acts and performs the deeds of our life is then only a central content of our consciousness which is crystallized about the idea of our organism. It has thus become one of the contents of which consciousness itself is passively aware. Consciousness is an inactive spectator for the procession of the contents. Thus consciousness itself cannot change anything in the content nor can it connect the contents. No other function is left to consciousness but merely that of awareness. Every change and every fusion and every process must be explained through the relations of the various contents to one another. Consciousness has, therefore, not the power to prefer the one idea or to reject the other, to reenforce the one sensation and to inhibit the other. From a psychological point of view, we have seen before that even attention does not mean an activity of consciousness but a change in the content of consciousness. Certain sensations become more impressive, more clear, and more vivid, and others fade away, become indistinct and disappear, but all that goes on in the content of consciousness and the spectator, consciousness itself, simply becomes aware of those changes. Consciousness has also in itself no special span, ideas appear or disappear not because consciousness expands or narrows itself but because the causal conditions awaken or suppress the various contents.

Consciousness has in itself no limit; all organization belongs to the content. Whatever psychical states are attributed to one organism belong thus to its consciousness but all the connections are entirely connections of the content. We, therefore, have not even the right to say that consciousness, as such, has unity. Unity too belongs to the organization of the content. One part of the content hangs together with the other parts but consciousness is only the constant condition for their existence. Where there is no unity, there it cannot have any meaning to speak of the double or triple existence. There may be a disconnection in the various parts of the content and a dissociation by which the normal ties between the various contents may be broken but consciousness itself cannot fall asunder. Thus consciousness cannot have any different degrees. The same consciousness experiences the distinct clear content and the vague fading confused content. Thus also consciousness can never be aware of itself and the word self-consciousness is easily misleading. In psychology, it can never mean that the consciousness which is a subject of all experience is at the same time object of any experience. Its whole meaning lies in its being the passive spectator. That of which consciousness becomes aware in self-consciousness is the idea of the personality, which is certainly a content. The personality, the actor of our actions, is thus never anything but an object in psychology, and consciousness never anything but a subject. Consciousness itself is thus in no way altered when the idea of the personality is changing. Only if all this is carelessly confused, if consciousness is sometimes treated as meaning subject of consciousness, and at another time as meaning the content of consciousness, and again at another time the unified organization of the content, and at still another time the connection of the content with the personality, and if finally all that is confused with the purposive reality of the immediate personal life—only then, do we find the way open to those tempting theories of the subconscious personality.

If, instead, we stick to the scientific view, we find the following facts. First, we have everywhere with us the fact that the earlier experiences may again enter into consciousness as memory images or as imaginative ideas, that is, in the order in which they are experienced a long time before or in a new order, either with a feeling of acquaintance or without it. Certainly at no time is the millionth part of what we may be able to reproduce present in our consciousness. Where are those words of the language, those faces of our friends, those landscapes, and those thoughts; where have they lingered in the time of their seclusion? Scientific psychology has no right to propose any other theory as explanation but that no mental states at all remain and that all which remained was the disposition of physiological centers. When I coupled the impression of a man with the sound of his name, a certain excitement of my visual centers occurred together with the excitement of my acoustical centers; the connecting paths became paths of least resistance, and any subsequent excitement of the one cell group now flows over into the other. It is the duty of physiology to elaborate such a clumsy scheme and to make us understand in detail how those processes in the neurons can occur and it is not the duty of psychology to develop detailed physiological hypotheses. Psychology has to be satisfied with the fact that all the requirements of the case can be furnished by principle through physiological explanation. Least of all ought we to be discouraged by the mere complexity of the process. If a simple sound and a simple color sensation, or a simple taste and simple smell sensation, can associate themselves through mere nervous conditions of the brain, then there is nothing changed by going over to more and more complex contents of consciousness. We may substitute a whole landscape for a color patch or the memory of a book for a word, but we do not reach by that a point where the physiological principle of explanation, once admitted, begins to lose its value. Complexity is certainly in good harmony with the bewildering manifoldness of those thousands of millions of possible connections between the brain cells.

Every experience leaves the brain altered. The nerve fibers and the cells have gone into new stages of disposition for certain excitements. This disposition may be slowly lost. In that case the earlier experience cannot be reproduced; we have forgotten it. But as long as the disposition lasts—it is quite indifferent whether we conceive it more in terms of chemical changes or physical variations, as processes in the nerve cells or between the nerve cells—the physiological change alone is responsible for the awakening of the memory idea under favoring associative conditions. Of course, someone might reply: can we not fancy that there remains on the psychical side also a disposition? Each idea which we have experienced may have left a psychical trace which alone may make it possible that the idea may come back to us again. But what is really meant and what is gained by such a hypothesis?

First, do not let us forget that such a proposition could only have one possible end in view, namely, the explanation of the reappearance of memories. But when we discussed the basis of physiological psychology, we convinced ourselves that mental facts as such are not causally connected anyhow. Our real inner life has its internal connections, connections of will and purpose, but as soon as we have taken that great psychological step and look on inner life as merely psychological objects, then the material is connected only through the underlying physiological processes and we can never explain causally the appearance of an idea through the preceding existence of another idea. We may expect one after the other, but we have no insight into the mechanism which makes the second follow after the first. Such insight into necessary connection we find only on the physical side, and we saw that just here lies the starting point for the modern view of physiological psychology. If that holds true for the connections between idea and idea, of course it holds true in the same way for the connection between mental disposition and the corresponding memory. We can understand causally that a chemical disposition in the nerve fibers brings about a chemical excitement in those neurons, but how a mental disposition is to create mental experience we could not understand; and to explain it casually, we should need again a reference to the underlying physiological processes. The hypothesis of mental dispositions would thus be an entirely superfluous addition by which we transcend the real experience without gaining anything for the explanation.

Secondly, if we really needed a mental disposition for each memory picture, in addition to the physiological disposition of the brain cells, can we overlook that exactly the same thing would then be necessary for every perception also? The outer impression produces, perhaps through eye or ear or skin, an excitement of the brain cell and this excitement is accompanied by a sensation; and no one fancies that the appearance of this sensation is dependent upon a special disposition for it on the mental side. No one fancies it, because it is evident that such a hypothesis again would be entirely useless. If every new perception needed such a special mental disposition, we should have to presuppose dispositions for everything which possibly can come into our surroundings. Every smell, every word, every face which comes anew to us would need its special ready-made disposition. In other words, our mind would contain the disposition for every possible idea and that would mean that these dispositions would be in no way helps for explanation. If the disposition exists for everything, no one particular thing can be explained by the existence of that disposition. Again we should have to rely entirely upon the physiological brain excitement for explaining that this word or that word is perceived by our mind. But if the brain excitement alone is sufficient to explain the new perception in the mind, then no reason can be found why the renewed brain excitement would not be sufficient to renew the mental experience. Thus there is nowhere room for mental dispositions below the level of consciousness.

Thirdly, what could we really mean by such mental dispositions? A physiological disposition for a physiological action is certainly not the action itself. The finger movement in piano playing finds only a disposition in my brain centers, in case I am trained; the movement itself does not last. But the disposition is at least itself a change in the physical world. The molecules are somehow differently placed, the disposition has thus as much objective existence as the resulting movement. Nothing at all similar can be imagined in the sphere of psychical contents. Such mental dispositions would have to exist entirely outside the world of concrete mental experiences and, if we scrutinize carefully, we soon discover that such theories are only lingering reminiscences of the purposive view of life, and do not fit at all into the causal one. If we take the purposive attitude, then every idea and every will contains indeed all that its meaning involves and everything which we can logically develop out of it is by intention contained in it. All mathematical calculations are then contained in the thought of figures and forms, but they are contained there only by intention, they are logically inclosed; psychologically the consciousness of the figures and forms does not contain any disposition for the development of mathematical systems. We indeed have no right to throw into a psychological subconsciousness all that which is not present but involved by intention in the ideas and volitions of our purposive life.

If thus the memory idea is linked with the past experience entirely by the lasting physiological change in the brain, we have no reason to alter the principle, when we meet the memory processes of the hypnotized person or the hysteric. It is true their memory may bring to light earlier experiences which are entirely forgotten by the conscious personality, but that ought to mean, of course, only that nerve paths have become accessible in which the propagation of the excitement was blocked up before. That does not bring us nearer to the demand for a subconscious mental memory. The threshold of excitability changes under most various conditions. Cells which respond easily in certain states may need the strongest stimulation in others. The brain cells which are too easily excited perhaps in maniacal exultation would respond too slowly in a melancholic depression. Hypnotism, too, by closing the opposite channels and opening wide the channels for the suggested discharge, may stir up excitements for which the disposition may have lingered since the days of childhood and yet which would not have been excited by the normal play of the neurons. Quite secondary remains the question of how these reproduced images finally appear in consciousness, that is, whether they appear with reference to earlier happenings and are thus felt as remembrances, or whether they enter as independent imaginations, or whether they finally, under special conditions, take the character of real, new perceptions. The latter case is well-known in crystal-gazing, where long-forgotten memory ideas project themselves into the visual field like hallucinations. But for the theory of the subconscious, even these uncanny crystal visions do not mean more than the simplest awakening of the experience of a landscape image of yesterday.

We turn to a second group of facts and again we have no fault to find with the observation of the facts, even of the most surprising and exceptional ones. Our objection refers to the interpretation of them. This second group contains the active results of such physiological nervous dispositions. In the first group, the dispositions come in question only as conditions for a new excitement which was accompanied by mental experience. In this second group, the dispositions are causes for other physiological processes which either lead to actions or to influences on other mental processes. The dispositions are here working like the setting of switches which turn the nervous process into special tracks. In the simple cases, of course no one doubts that a purely physiological basis is involved. The decapitated frog rubs its skin where it is touched with a drop of muriatic acid in a way which is ordinarily referred to the trained apparatus of his spinal cord, as no brain is left, and the usefulness of the action and its adjustment is very well understood as the result of the connecting paths in the nervous system.

From such simple adjustment of reactions of the spinal cord, we come step by step to the more complex activities of the subcortical brain centers, and finally to those which are evidently only short-cuts of the higher brain processes. That we react at every change of position with the right movements to keep our bodily balance, that we walk without thinking of our steps, that we speak without giving conscious impulse for the various speech movements, that we write without being aware of the motor activity which we had to learn slowly, that we play the piano without thinking of the special impulses of the hands, that we select the words of a hasty speech, if we have its aim in mind, without consciously selecting the appropriate words—all that is by continuous transitions connected with those simplest automatic reactions. And from here again, we are led over gradually perhaps to the automatic writings of the hysteric who writes complex messages without having any idea of their content in consciousness. It is in such cases certainly a symptom of disease that the activity of these lower brain centers can go over into the motor impulse of writing without producing secondary effects in the highest conscious brain centers; it is hysterical. But that the message of the pencil can be brought about by such operation of lower brain centers, or at least with imperfect coöperation of the higher brain centers, is certainly entirely within the limits of the same physiological explanation.

On the other hand, nothing is changed in the theoretic principles of the case if the effect of these automatic processes in the nervous system is not an external muscle action at first, but an influence on other brain centers which may furnish the consciousness with new contents. We try to remember a name, that is, a large number of neuron processes are setting in which normally lead to the excitement of that particular process which furnishes us the memory image of the name. But those brain cells may not respond, the channels may be blocked somehow or the excitability of those cells may be lowered. Now new excitements engage our psychophysical system. We are thinking of other problems. In the meantime, by

the new equilibrium in the brain the blockade in
these first paths may slowly disappear or the threshold
of excitability may be changed. The physiological
excitement may now be carried effectively into those
tracts. The cell response sets in and suddenly the
name comes to our mind. This purely physiological
operation in our brain paths must thus have exactly
the same result which it would have had, if more
parts of the process had been accompanied by conscious experience. And again from mere remembering a forgotten name, we come by slow steps to the
solution of a problem, to the invention, and finally to
the creation of the genius.

Superficiality of thought is easily inclined to object to such a physiological interpretation and perhaps
to denounce it pathetically as a crude materialism
which lowers the dignity of mental work. Nothing
shows more clearly the confusion between a purposive
and causal view of the mind. In the purposive view
of our real life, only our will and our personality have
a meaning and can be related to the ideas and higher
aims. Nature is there nothing but the dead material
which is the tool of our will and which has to be
mastered by the personality. In that world alone lie
our duty and our morality. But as soon as we have
gone over to the causal aspect of our life and have
taken the point of view of the psychologist, making
our inner life a series of contents of consciousness, of
psychical phenomena, we have transformed our inner
experience in such a way that it has become itself
nothing but nature.

It is mental nature, nature of psychical stuff, but each part of it is nothing but a mental element, a mental atom without any meaning and without any value; nothing but a link in the chain, nothing but a factor in the explanation of the whole, nothing to which any ethical or æsthetic or logical or religious significance can any longer be attached. The psychical sensations and the physical atoms are equally material for naturalistic explanation. To understand causally a certain effect, for instance the creation of a work of art, of a discovery or a thought or a deed as the product of psychical processes, is thus in no way more dignified or more valuable than to understand it as the product of physiological brain processes. The one is not more dignified than the other because both alike have nothing whatever to do with dignity. Both alike are the necessary results of the foregoing processes, and to attach a kind of sentimental preference to the explanation through conscious factors is nothing but a confused reminiscence again of the entirely different purposive view of life. And surely nothing is gained for the higher values of life if this confusion sets in, because if the popular mind becomes unable to discriminate between the secondary, causal, artificial aspect of science and the primary, purposive aspect of life, the opposite effect lies still nearer: the values of the real life suffer and are crowded out by the knowledge of the scientific facts. Man's moral freedom is then wrongly brought in question, as soon as it is learned that every action is the product of brain processes. Life and science alike will gain the more, the more clearly the purposive and the causal point of view are separated and the more it is understood that this causal aspect itself is demanded by certain purposes of life. The oratory of those who denounce the physiological theories as lacking idealism in reality undermines true moral philosophy. There is no idealism which can really flourish merely by ignoring the progress of science and confusing the issues. The true values of the higher life cannot be safely protected by that thought-less idealism which draws its life from vagueness and which therefore has to be afraid of every new discovery in scientific psychology. Our real ideals do not lie at all in the sphere in which the problem of causally explaining the psychological phenomena arises.

Our conscious experiences are thus indeed not only here and there, but usually the products of chains of processes which go on entirely on the physiological side. We have no reason at all to seek for those preceding actions any mental accompaniment outside of consciousness, that means, any subconscious mental states. Then, of course, this physiological explanation also covers entirely those after-effects of earlier experiences, especially emotional experiences, which the physician nowadays likes to call subconscious "complexes." We shall see what an important rôle belongs to these facts, especially in the treatment of hysteria and psychasthenia, but the interpretation again ought to avoid all playing with the conception of the subconscious. Emotional experiences may produce there some strong stable dispositions in the brain system which become mischievous in reënforcing or inhibiting certain thoughts and actions without awakening directly conscious experiences. The whole psychological switch system may have been brought into disorder by such abnormal setting of certain parts, but the connection of each resulting accident with the primary emotional disturbances does not contradict the fact that all the causes lie entirely in disturbances of the central paths. It is a change in the neurons and their connections. To discover it we may have to go back to early conscious experiences, but in the process itself there is no mental factor, and therefore no subconscious emotion is responsible for the mischief carried out.

Both groups of facts which we have studied so far, have dealt with processes which were indeed not conscious but which we had no right to call subconscious inasmuch as they contained no mental process at all but only physiological dispositions and actions. We turn finally to the other smaller and more abnormal group of so-called subconscious facts in which the facts are mental indeed and not only physiological, but not at all outside of consciousness and thus again not subconscious. A conscious fact may easily suggest the appeal to subconscious theories to those who have accepted such theories for other reasons. There are, for instance, plenty of mental experiences which we do not notice or which we do not recognize. Yet if we find later that they must have influenced our mind, we are easily inclined to refer them to subconscious activity. But it is evident that to be content of consciousness means not at all necessarily to be object of attention or object of recognition. Awareness does not involve interest. If I hear a musical sound, I may not recognize at all the overtones which are contained in it. As soon as I take resonators and by them reënforce the loudness of those overtones, they become vivid for me and I can now notice them well even when the resonators are removed. I surely was aware of them, that is, had them in consciousness all the time but there were no contrast feelings and no associations in consciousness which gave them sufficient clearness to attract attention.

In this way I may be again led by gradual stages to more and more complex experiences. I may overlook and yet include within my content of consciousness most various parts of my surroundings; and yet the neglected is not less in consciousness itself than the attended. Much that figures in literature as subconscious means indeed nothing else but the unattended. But it belongs to the elements of psychological analysis to recognize that the full content of consciousness is always larger than the narrow field of attention. This narrow field on the other hand has certainly no sharp demarcation line. There is a steady shading off from the most vivid to the least vivid. We cannot grasp those least vivid contents of consciousness, we cannot fixate them as such, because as soon as we try to hold them, they move from the periphery of the content into its center and become themselves vivid and clear. But as we are surely aware of different degrees of clearness and vividness in our central mass of contents, we have no difficulty in acknowledging the existence of still lower degrees of vividness in those elements which are blending and fusing into a general background of conscious experiences. Nothing stands out there, nothing can be discriminated in its detail. That background is not even made up of whole ideas and whole memories and whole emotions and feelings and judgments and volitions, but of loose fragments; half ideas and quarter ideas, atoms of feelings and incipient impulses and bits of memory images are always mixed in that half-dark background. And yet it is by principle not less in consciousness, and consciousness itself is not different for these contents. It is not half-clear consciousness, not a lower degree of awareness, only the objects of awareness are crumbled and fading.

Whether these background objects really exist can only be made out by studying carefully the changes which result under different conditions, the influences which those loose parts have on the structure of the whole, and the effect of their complete disappearance. I may never really notice a little thing in my room and yet may be aware that it has been taken away. The visual image of it was an element of my mental background, when I was sitting at my desk, but it never before moved to the center of my conscious content. But this center itself is also constantly changing. Sometimes the one, sometimes the other idea may enter into it, but in this alternation that which is not

in the focus either remains in consciousness unattended or when it disappears from it it loses its mental
character altogether. If I attend a tiresome lecture
while my mind is engaged with a practical problem
of my own life, there may be a steady rivalry between
the words which come with the force of outer stimulus
to my brain and make me listen and my inner difficulties which claim my attention. I listen for a while,
and then suddenly, without noticing it, my own
thoughts may have taken the center of the stage and
again without sudden interruption a word may catch
my attention. While I was thinking of my own
problem the sounds of the lecturer were really outside of my field of attention, yet some remark now
pushes itself again into the center. That does not
mean that a subconscious mind is listening while my
lucid mind was thinking, but it does mean that those
words were unattended and remained in the periphery
of the field of consciousness. But when some of the
sentences stirred up in that peripheral field some important associations, they were strong enough to produce a new motor reaction by which the mental
equilibrium became changed again and by which the
lecturer overwhelmed my private thoughts. Yet even
this state of mind, without any break, can go over
into an absolutely physiological process. I may for
a while really inhibit the lecturer's voice completely
and remain in the thoughts of my own imagination.
After a minute or two, the resistance against the
acoustical stimulus will certainly be broken and the
sound will again enter into my consciousness, but in

that interval there was no subconscious and not even
any unattended mental function; there was no mental
process at all. The sound reached my brain but as
the motor setting was adverse, the sounds did not
bring about that highest act of physiological transmission which is accompanied by mental contents.
Thus it became entirely physiological. Yet of course
every word reached my brain and left traces there.
If I were hypnotized after the lecture and thus the
threshold for the real awakening of brain excitements
lowered, it might not be impossible that some of the
thoughts of the lecturer which did not enter my consciousness at all, are now afterwards in the hypnotic
state stirred up in me. Yet even that would not indicate that they had become mental and thus subconscious at the time of the lecture.

The so-called subconscious, which in reality is fully
in consciousness but only unnoticed, easily shades
over into that unconscious which is also in consciousness but dissociated from the idea of the own personality and thus somewhat split off from the interconnected mass of conscious contents. Wherever we
meet such phenomena, we are in the field of the abnormal. The normal mental life is characterized by
the connectedness of the contents. Yet even that
holds true, of course, only if we think of those mental
states which exist at one and the same instant in consciousness. As soon as we consider the succession of
mental events, we cannot doubt that even normal experience shows breaks, lapses, and complete annihilation of that which a moment before was a real content

in our consciousness. We may have looked at our watch and certainly had in glancing at the dial a conscious impression, but in the next moment we no longer know how late it is. The impression did not connect itself with our continuous personal experience, that is, with that chief group of our conscious contents which we associate with the perception of our personality. Under abnormal conditions of the brain, larger and larger parts of the completely conscious experience may thus be cut off from the continuity of conscious life. But to be in consciousness, and therefore to be not-subconscious, does not mean to be through memory ties connected with the idea of our own personality.

The somnanbulist, for instance, may get up at night time and write a letter, then go to bed again and not know anything of the event when he awakes in the morning. We have no reason to claim that he had no knowledge of the letter in his consciousness when he wrote it. It is exactly the same consciousness from a psychological standpoint as the one with which he wakes up. Only that special content has in an abnormal way entirely disappeared, has not left a possibility of awakening a memory image, and the action of the personality in writing has thus become separated and cut off from the connected experiences of the man. But while the nocturnal episode may be entirely forgotten, it was not less in consciousness for the time being, than if a normal man should leave his bed hastily to write a letter. Moreover under abnormal conditions, as for instance in severe hysteric cases, those dissociated contents may form large clusters of mental experiences in the midst of which a new idea of the own personality may develop. Considering that through such disconnection many channels of discharge are blocked, while others are abnormally opened, it seems only natural that the idea of the own acting personality becomes greatly changed. Thus we have in such an episode a new second personality which may be strikingly different in its behavior and in its power, in its memories and in its desires, from the continuous normal one, and this secondary personality may now develop its own continuity and may arise under special conditions in attacks which are connected among one another by their own memory bonds.

The two personalities may even alternate from day to day and the normal one may itself become pathologically altered. In that case the two alternating personalities would both be different from the original one. But again we have even in such most complex and exceptional cases only an alternation in the contents, not an alternation in the consciousness itself. Different ideas of the own personality with different associations and impulses follow each other in consciousness and the abnormality of the situation lies in the lack of memory connections and of mutual influences, but consciousness remains the same throughout. It remains the same, just as we do not change consciousness if we feel ourselves in one hour as members of our family, in the next hour as professional workers in our office, again later as social personalities at

a party or as citizens at a political meeting or as
æsthetic subjects at the theater. Each time we are to
a high degree a different personality, the idea of our
self is each time determined by different groups of
associations, memories, emotions, and impulses. The
differentiation is to be considered as normal only because broad memory bridges lead over from one to the
other. The connection of the various contents with
the various ideas of the own personality constitutes
thus in no way a break of consciousness itself and
relegates no one content into a subconscious sphere.

Finally the same holds true, if the idea of the personality as content of consciousness in the patient is
split into two simultaneous groups, of which each one
is furnished with its own associations. Yet the interpretation here becomes extremely difficult and arbitrary. Take the case that a patient in severe
hysteria at our request writes down the history of her
life. We should not hesitate to say that she is doing
it consciously but now we begin to talk with her and
slowly the conversation takes her attention while her
pencil is continuing to write down the connected story
of her youth. Again the conversation by itself gives
the impression of completely conscious behavior. As
both functions go on at the same time, the person
who converses does not know what the person who
writes is writing, and the writer is uninfluenced by the
conversation. Various interpretations are possible.
Indeed we might think that by such double setting in
the pathological brain two independent groups in
the content of consciousness are formed, each one

fully in consciousness and yet both without any mutual influence and thus without mutual knowledge. In the light of such interpretation, it has been correctly proposed to speak of coconscious processes, rather than subconscious. Or we may interpret it more in harmony with the ordinary automatic writing or with other merely physiological reactions. Then we should suppose that as soon as the conversation sets in, the brain centers which control the writing movement work through channels in which no mental factors are involved. One of the two characteristic reaction systems would then be merely physiological. We saw before that the complexity of the process is no argument against the strictly physiological character of the event. That various activities can coexist in such a way that one of them may at any time slide down from the conscious centers to the merely physical ones, we all know by daily experience. We may go home through the streets of the busy town engaged with our thoughts. For a while the idea of our way and of the sidewalk is in our consciousness, when suddenly we reach our house and notice that for a long while we have no longer had any thought at all of the way. We were absorbed by our problems, and the motor activity of walking towards our goal was going on entirely in the physiological sphere. But whether we prefer the physiological account or insist on the coconscious phenomena, in either case is there any chance for the subconscious to slip in? That a content of consciousness is to a high degree dissociated or that the idea of the personality is split

off is certainly a symptom of pathological disturbance, but it has nothing to do with the constituting of
two different kinds of consciousness or with breaking
the continuous sameness of consciousness itself. The
most exceptional and most uncanny occurrences of the
hospital teach after all the same which our daily experience ought to teach us: there is no subconsciousness.

PART II

THE PRACTICAL WORK OF PSYCHO-THERAPY

VII

THE FIELD OF PSYCHOTHERAPY

WE have discussed the psychological tools with which the psychotherapist has to work but we have not spoken as yet of psychotherapy itself. All that we have studied has been by way of preparation; and yet the right preparation is almost the most important factor for the right kind of work. To rush into psychotherapy with hastily gathered conceptions of mental life may be sometimes successful for the moment, but must always be ultimately dangerous. It is often most surprising what a haphazard kind of psychology is accepted as a basis for psychotherapy even by scientifically schooled physicians who would never believe that common sense would be sufficient to settle the problems of anatomy and physiology; as soon as the mind is in question, no serious study seems needed. Can we be surprised then that in the amateur medicine of the country within and without the church any fanciful idea of mental life may flourish? If we are to recognize the rights and wrongs of psychotherapy in a scientific spirit, a sober analysis of the mental facts involved was indeed at the very first most essential. Now we can easily draw the conclusions from our findings.

We recognized from the start the fundamental difference between two different attitudes which we can take towards the inner life of any personality, the purposive view and the causal. We recognized the sphere to which each belongs and we saw that all medical treatment demands the causal view, thus dealing with inner life as part of the causal chain of events. Each inner experience became therefore a series of so-called contents of consciousness. These contents can be described and must be analyzed into their elements. The basis of psychotherapy is therefore an analytic psychology which conceives the inner experience as a combination of psychical elements.

But the final aim was the causal connection. The appearance and disappearance of those millions of elements and their connection had to be explained. We recognized that such an explanation of the contents of consciousness was possible only through the connections between the accompanying brain processes. Every psychical change had to be conceived as parallel to a physiological change. The psychology which is to be the basis of psychotherapy had to be therefore a physiological psychology.

We recognized that these psychophysiological processes were processes of transmission between impressions and expressions, that is, between incoming nervous currents and outgoing nervous currents, between stimuli and reactions. Thus we have no central process which is not influenced by the surroundings and which is not at the same time the starting point of an action. We have normal health of the personality as long as there is a complete equilibrium in the functions of the organism which adjusts the activities to the surroundings. Every abnormality is a disturbance of this equilibrium. A psychology which is the basis of psychotherapy thus conceives every mental process in relation to both the ideas and the actions; it avoids all one-sidedness by which the mind is cut off either from its resources or from its effects. The relations to the impressions are usually the less neglected: and we must the more emphasize the fact that the psychology needed for psychotherapy knows no mental fact which does not start an action and that every change in the system of actions involves a change in the central experience. Wherever this equilibrium of adjusted functions is disturbed, some therapy of the physician has to set in: whether psychotherapy is in order depends upon the special conditions.

We have recognized that there are no mental facts outside of those which are in consciousness and that from a psychological point of view consciousness itself does not have different degrees and different levels, that all varieties of experience refer thus only to the special content and its organization. There is thus no subconscious. On the other hand, we saw

that there is no conscious experience which is not
based on a bodily brain process. By these two fundamental facts of scientific psychology, every possible
psychotherapy gets from the start its clear middle
way between two extreme views which are popular
today. The one school nowadays lives from the
contrast between consciousness and subconsciousness
and makes all psychotherapy work with and through
and in the subconscious. The other school creates a
complete antithesis between mind and body and
makes psychotherapy a kind of triumph of the mind
over the body. Practically every popular treatise on
psychotherapeutic subjects in recent years belongs to
the one or the other group; and yet both are fundamentally wrong. And while, of course, this mistake
is one of theoretical interpretation, it evidently has
its practical consequences. The fantastic position allowed to a subconscious mind easily gives to the doctrine a religious or even a mystical turn and the artificial separation between the energies of the mind and
those of the body leads easily to a moral sermon.
Whether this amalgamation of medicine with religion
or with morality may not be finally dangerous to true
morality and true religion is a question which will interest us much later. Here we only have to ask
whether it is not harmful to the interests of the patient and thus to the rights of medicine, and indeed
that must be evident here at the very threshold.
Both schools must have the tendency to extend psychotherapy at the expense of bodily therapy and to
narrow down psychotherapy itself to a therapy by

appeals which in the one case are suggestions to the
subconscious and in the other case persuasions and
encouragements to the conscious will. As soon as
we have overcome the prejudices of those two rival
schools and have recognized that both are wrong,
that there is no subconscious and that there is no psychological fact which is not at the same time a physiological one, we see at once that this common procedure of both schools is unjustified and dangerous.
Mental therapy and physical therapy ought to be
most intimately connected parts of the same therapeutic effort and mental therapy includes by far more
than mere suggestions and appeals. All that involves of course that its systematic application belongs in the hands of the well-trained physician and
of nobody else, but on the other hand, it involves that
every physician ought to be well schooled in psychology.

As soon as a disturbance to be cured is considered
as a lack of equilibrium in psychophysical functions,
every mental influence, every suggestion and appeal
becomes itself an excitement or an inhibition of nerve
cells. The sharp demarcation line between a psychical
agency and a physical one disappears altogether;
the spoken word is then considered as physical air-
waves which stimulate certain brain centers and in
the given paths this stimulation is carried to hundreds
of thousands of neurons. The protracted warm bath
or the cold douche influences, too, large brain parts
by changing the blood circulation which controls the
activity of those neurons; or the bromides absorbed in

the digestive apparatus, or the morphine injected, also reach the neurons and again have a different kind of influence on them, and the electric current may stimulate the nervous system in still a different way. It may be, and under many conditions certainly is, essential to influence the brain cells just in that particular way which results from the spoken word, but there too the causal influence remains a function of the physical effect and thus by principle there is no sharp separation from other physical means. Thus to believe in psychotherapy ought never to mean that we have a right to make light of the other means which, as experience shows, may help towards the treatment of disturbances in the central equilibrium. Suggestions and bromides together may secure an effect which neither of them alone will bring about. It is most unfortunate that not without some guilt on the part of the physicians themselves, the large public has begun to believe that orthodox psychotherapy has to mean a rejection of drugs and a contempt for the doctors who prescribe them.

Of course a discussion of psychotherapy cannot enter into the study of these physical agencies of treatment, but at the threshold, we have to insist that there exists no opposition between psychophysiological and physiological means of influencing the brain. It may be true that drugs and baths and electricity have no influence on the subconscious, but the trouble is not that the drugs are inefficient but that they cannot influence what does not exist. In the same way

disappears now that new boundary line for psychotherapy which wants to limit it to mere suggestion
and appeal. If psychotherapy employs all the means
by which we can influence mental states in the interest
of the health of the personality, we have no reason to
confine it either to a persuasion of the subconscious
through suggestion and hypnotism or a persuasion of
the conscious, in which it works as a moral appeal.
Suggestion and hypnotism certainly must play a large
part in psychotherapy and that part does not become
smaller by the fact that we reject the subconscious interpretation of them and consider them entirely as
psychophysical processes. And in the same way un-
doubtedly we have to acknowledge the psychophysiological effect of persuasion and of the appeals to the
conscious intellect and will. But for us as psychotherapists all those factors have no moral value but
only a therapeutic one, and thus stand in line with
any other influence that may help, even though from
a purposive point of view it stands on a much lower
level. A mere mental distraction by enjoyment and
play and sport, an æsthetic influence through art, a
mere stimulus to automatic imitation, an enforced
mental rest, an involuntary discharge of suppressed ideas, and many similar schemes and even
tricks of the mental physician belong with the same
right to psychotherapy.

It is really doubtful whether the moral and religious appeals are always helpful and not sometimes
or often even dangerous for the health of the individual; and it is not doubtful that morally and reli-

giously indifferent mental influences are often of the
highest curative value. The more we abstract from
everything which suggests either the mysticism of the
subconscious or the moral issues of a mind which is
independent of the body, the more we shall be able
to answer the question as to the means by which
health can be restored. This question is neither a
moral nor a philosophical one but strictly one of experience. In this connection, we must remember
that we also have had to give up the artificial demarcation line between organic and functional diseases. We recognized that every so-called functional disease has its organic basis too, and that it is
entirely secondary whether we are able to find visible
traces of the organic disturbance. We had to acknowledge, to be sure, the difference between reparable and irreparable disturbances, but such grouping expresses only in another form the fact that experience alone can show whether the methods of
treatment which we know so far will be successful or
not. Not a few disturbances of the equilibrium
which appeared irreparable to an earlier time yield to
the treatment of to-day, and no one can determine
whether much which appears irreparable today may
not be accessible either to psychotherapeutic or to
physical therapeutic means tomorrow. If we were
carelessly to identify the reparable troubles with
those which we cannot recognize visibly, we should
be at a loss to understand why, for instance, many
forms of insanity are entirely beyond our psychotherapeutic influences. On the other hand, every

physician who uses psychotherapeutic means is surprised to see the effective bodily readjustment where serious disturbances perhaps of the circulatory system or the digestive system existed. What the methods can do and what they cannot do must simply be left to experience, but of course to an experience which is eager to expand itself by ever new experimental curative efforts.

From this point of view we can see clearly the general division of the whole field of possible psychotherapy. Psychotherapy influences psychophysical states in the interest of health. There are only two possibilities open: either the disturbance is in the psychophysical system itself or it is outside of it, that is in the other parts of the body which are somehow under the influence of the mind. In the first case when the disturbance occurs in the mind-brain system itself, we ought to separate two large groups, first those cases in which the system itself is normal and the disturbance comes from without, and second those in which the constitution of the system itself was abnormal and led to disturbances under conditions in which a normal system would not have suffered. We have to consider both groups somewhat more in detail, as each again allows a large variety of cases.

Thus we have before us, first the normal mind-brain system into which a disturbance breaks, injuring more or less severely and for a longer or shorter time the equilibrium of the psychophysical functions. Here belong any bodily processes which produce pain or any bodily defects which produce blanks in the content of consciousness; the pain of sciatica or of rheumatism, or the defect of the blind or of the deaf, certainly interferes in a disturbing way with the perfect harmony of psychophysical activities. But here also belongs the suffering which results from conditions in the surroundings, the loss of a friend, a disappointment in life, any source of worry and grief. Social and bodily conditions alike may thus work to break up the equilibrium. The pain sensation interferes with the normal flow of mental life and the grief may undermine the mental interests. The psychotherapeutic effort may be directed toward removing the source of the disturbance, bringing the patient under other conditions, curing the diseased organ, and where that is not possible, may work directly on the psychophysical state, inhibiting the pain, suppressing the emotion, substituting pleasant ideas, distracting the whole mind, filling it with agreeable feelings, until the normal equilibrium is restored.

The psychophysical system itself was not really harmed by such influences. In the following groups, such is no longer the case. We here think at first of those severe injuries which have their sources in abnormal processes outside of the brain. The anæmia of the patient or the low state of his nutrition or the fever heat of his blood impairs the harmony of the mental functions. Another and for the psychotherapist much more important group is that in which the impairment results from toxic influences. Alcohol, morphine, cocaine, tobacco, and many other drugs may have been misused and may have produced a most marked alteration in the mind-brain system. Desires may have developed which completely destroy the balance of the normal functions and yet the satisfaction of which increases the poisoning effect. But here belongs further the effect of poisons which the body itself produces: the toxic disturbance of uræmia or the coma in diabetes, or especially the grave disturbances resulting from the abnormal action of the thyroid gland, the source of cretinism. Many indications suggest that a near future will consider this group much larger than we are really justified in doing today, probably soon connecting a number of other mental diseases like dementia præcox with toxic effects of bodily origin. Experience shows that in this group not a few chances exist for successful psychotherapeutic influence. Yet the means may be various in character and their effect may be a direct or an indirect one. A psychical shock may remove directly the mental disturbance of the alcoholic state, but it is more important that mental suggestion can remove the alcoholic disturbance indirectly by suppressing the desire for alcoholic excesses. Even where cure by psychotherapeutic means is out of the question, as is the case with feverish delirium or uræmic excitements, no skilled physician ignores the aid which a well-adjusted mental influence can offer to the patient.

We come to a third group. Some outside cause has harmed the central nervous system directly, and has left it in a disabled state after the cause itself has disappeared. Such causes may have been at first purely functional: for instance, a neglect of training, or a wrong training, or an over-activity, but the ill-adjusted function which involved, of course, every time an ill-adjusted organic activity or lack of activity, has led to a lasting or at least relatively lasting disturbance in the system of paths. The neglect of training, for instance, in periods of development may have resulted in the retardation which yields the symptoms of a feeble-minded brain, or the wrong training may have created vicious habits, firmly established in the mind-brain system and gravely disturbing the equilibrium. Above all, the overstrain of function, especially of emotional functions, may lead to that exhaustion which produces the state of neurasthenia. It is true that not a few would doubt whether we have the right to class neurasthenia here where we speak of the harm done to the normal brain. Many neurologists are inclined to hold that neurasthenia demands a special predisposition and is therefore dependent upon a neurotic constitution of the brain itself. But if defenders of such a view, as for instance, Dubois, acknowledge that " we might say that everybody is more or less neurasthenic," we can no longer speak of any special predisposition. Certainly there exists a constitutional neurasthenia sometimes but we have hardly a right to deny that overstrain in the brain activity may produce a series of neurasthenic symptoms in any brain, and the special predisposition is responsible rather for the particular selection among the innumerable symptoms.

Neurasthenia certainly is the classical ground for

the psychotherapist. The patient's insomnia and his
headache, his feeling of tiredness and his disgust with
himself, his capricious manias and his absurd phobias,
his obsessions and his fixed ideas all may yield to the
"appeal to the subconscious," and as a neurasthenic
easily believes in the existence of various organic diseases in his body, Christian Science can perform here
even "miracles." In the case of retardation, the
psychical influence will have to be in the first place
one of training. Yet it would be narrow to overlook that in neurasthenia, too, suggestion has to be
only a part of the psychical treatment. Training
and rest, distraction and sympathy and many other
factors have to enter into the plan. Incomparably
small, on the other hand, is the aid which psychotherapy can offer in cases of real destructions in the
brain, as in the case of tumors, hemorrhage, paresis
or the degeneration by senility. More effective may
be its work in concussion of the brain and especially
with traumatic neuroses, as in the case when a railroad accident has put the mind-brain system out of
gear.

So far we presupposed that the central system itself
was normal. No sharp separation line, however,
lies between all these disturbances and the equally
large group of psychophysical disabilities resulting
from a defective constitution of the brain. The
normal brain shades over by smallest differences into
the abnormal one; yes, even the varieties of temperament and character and intellectual capacity and industry and energy represent, in the midst of our

social surroundings, large deviations from the standard. That which might still pass as normal under
certain conditions of life would be unadjusted and
thus abnormal under other conditions. In the same
way, we certainly cannot point out where the natural
constitution of a brain ceases to be fit for its organic
purposes and where the structural variations are ill-
prepared for the struggle for existence. Just as we
claimed that an entirely normal brain might be
brought by an emotional overstrain to a state of exhaustion and disability, we may claim on the other
side that a brain which nature has poorly provided
may yet be protected against damage and injury.
The inborn factor does not alone decide the fate.
Psychophysical prophylaxis may secure steadiness of
equilibrium to a system which inherited little resistance. Yet this large borderland region, where an ill-
adjusted brain may be saved or lost in accordance
with favorable or unfavorable circumstances, shades
off again to the darker regions where the inner evolu-
tion leads by necessity to disaster even under favorable conditions.

We might begin this large group of the constitutional disturbances with that neurasthenia which develops on the basis of inherited disability. Lack of
energy resulting from a feeling of tiredness, a quick
exhaustion, a mood of depression, an easy irritation,
even despair and self-accusation, sullenness and fits of
anger, cranky inclinations and useless brooding over
problems, headache and insomnia characterize the
picture which everyone finds more or less developed

in some of his acquaintances. If we classify symptoms, we may separate from it that which we nowadays are inclined to call psychasthenia. An abnormal suggestibility for autosuggestions stands in the foreground. Fixed ideas and fixed emotions, especially fears, trouble the patient. He may pick up his obsession by any chance experience and no goodwill liberates him from the intrusion perhaps for years. The patient is perfectly well aware that his ideas and his emotions are unjustified, he himself does not believe in them, and yet they come with the strength of an outer perception and with the vividness of a real attitude, and his whole mental equilibrium may be upset by the continuous fight against these involuntary interferences. In the light cases, sometimes the one and sometimes the other autosuggestion may hold the stage; in the severe cases, mental life turns more and more around certain definite fears and yet it may all still be in the limits where the daily work can go on and the world may not know of the hidden tortures. Here belongs the fear of open places or the fear of touching certain objects, the fear of doing harm to others or the fear of deciding actions wrongly, the fear of destroying valuable things or the fear of being the center of public attention, the fear of crowds or of closed doors, of altitudes or of bridges. And in all cases emotional reaction may set in with anxieties, and bodily symptoms such as palpitation of the heart may result, whenever an effort is made to disregard the nervous fear. There is perhaps no group of patients which so much deserves the most careful efforts of the psychotherapist. Still more than the hysterics they suffer from the fate of seeing their ills counted as not real. For them everybody has the good advice that they ought to overcome their fancies; and yet they feel their life ruined with their endless fight against the overpowering enemy. And if anywhere, it is here that the psychotherapist is successful. Psychasthenic fear can be removed, while the developed melancholic depression, for instance, is entirely beyond the reach of psychical influence.

We have after all the same psychasthenic state before us when the obsession has impulsive character, from the mere abnormal impulse of lying, or making noise in a quiet place or crying in the dark, or touching certain places, to that of stealing, indecent speech, arson, and perhaps even murder. The symptoms might easily be mistaken for those of graver diseases. Yet the fact that the patient himself really does not will the effect at which he is aiming separates, mostly without difficulty, the diagnosis of psychasthenia from that of insanity. Quite nearly related to it are the manifold variations of abnormal and perverse sexual tendencies. The psychiatrists are perhaps too much inclined to bring all these pathological impulses and desires, fears and anxieties, into the nearest neighborhood to real insanity. The indisputable success of psychotherapy in these spheres ought to add a warning against these expansions of the strictly psychiatric domain. The psychologist will be more inclined to emphasize their relation to simple neurasthenia which itself imperceptibly shades over into our normal life.

All neurasthenic and psychasthenic disabilities show a certain emotional continuity and uniformity. It is the emotional instability and the quick alternation of symptoms which characterize hysteria or rather the hysterias. It seems as if science were near to the point of explaining the hysterical disease by one common principle, but certainly the symptoms are an inexhaustible manifold. The rapid changes of the intense moods of the patient usually stand in the center. Torturing obsessions, abnormal impulses, over-suggestibility, hypochondriac depressions, paralysis of arms or legs, anæsthesia and paræsthesia, a mental stupor and confusion, illusions and perceptions of physiological symptoms may work together in spite of his, or rather her clear intelligence. It is probably on a hysteric basis also that somnambulic states arise during the night, and from them a straight way leads to those mental attacks after which the memory is entirely lost, or for which fundamental associative connections are cut off. And from here we come to the exceptional cases of alternating personality. The more we recognize the myriad symptoms in the hysteric patient as products of the emotional instability, of autosuggestibility and of inhibition, the more we understand the almost miraculous result of psychotherapeutic treatment. Autosuggestions can be fought by countersuggestions, anæsthesia and paræsthesia can be removed often in an instant, dissociated personalities may be built up again through hypnotism, the most severe bodily symptoms may disappear by influences in a waking state. Hysteria alone would justify the demand that every physician in his student days pass with open eyes through the field of psychology. Quite near stand chorea and the epidemic impulses to imitative movements. And we might bring into this neighborhood also the disturbance in the equilibrium of the speech movements through all degrees of stammering and severe impairment. Up to a certain degree, though not often completely, they too yield easily to psychotherapeutic influence.

We enter now that region of constitutional disturbances in which psychotherapy is of small help. It leads from epilepsy to the periodic diseases, especially the maniacal depressive insanity, the paranoia which develops late, and finally to states of idiocy which cover the whole life. We are far from claiming that psychical influences are entirely powerless, the more as we insisted that psychotherapy goes much beyond mere suggestions and appeals. No psychiatrist will work without psychological tools when he deals with the exultations of the maniac and the depressions of the melancholic, with the hallucinations of persecution or the erotic insanities of the paranoiac. Still more the whole register of psychology has to be used, when we are to educate the idiot and the imbecile. But the disappearance of the disease or of the chief symptoms through the mental agencies is in all these cases out of the question. Only in incipient cases, especially of melancholia and mania, the psychotherapeutic work seems not entirely hopeless; and for epilepsy some distinct successes cannot be denied.

We have reviewed the whole field of psychophysical disturbances, those produced through external conditions in the normal brain and those resulting from abnormal brain constitution. We have seen that the work of the psychotherapist is of very unequal value in different parts of the field; in some, as in neurasthenia, in psychasthenia, in hysteria and similar regions most effective, in others like paresis or paranoia reduced to an almost insignificant factor. Where it can help and where not we recognize as a mere question of experience. Certainly the severity of the symptoms alone does not decide it. As the treatment is entirely empirical, no one can foresee whether or not the situation may change tomorrow. We may find psychotherapeutic schemes by which epilepsy or maniacal depressive insanity or traumatic neuroses may become accessible. We simply do not know why we may remove stammering or synthesize a dissociated personality or overcome an inborn sexual perversity, while we are unable to remove the depression of the melancholic. Certainly the symptoms of the circulatory insanity disappear completely in the free intervals; there is no reason to give up hope that psychotherapy might find the way to hasten the appearance of such a normal period.

But we have emphasized from the start that the psychotherapeutic work has not only to set in when the disturbance itself lies in the psychophysical system. We may utilize the influence which the mind-brain system has for the whole body and thus may apply the psychical tool to work on the disturbances in the bodily apparatus. We may discriminate a direct and an indirect influence in the psychical treatment of bodily diseases. Transition from the foregoing group of psychical disturbances offers itself perhaps most easily through the state of insomnia.

The causes of sleeplessness may still lie in the psychophysical sphere; restless thoughts may inhibit the idea of sleep. The effect of sleep is again in the sphere of the mind, the annihilation of conscious contents. But the center which regulates and creates the sleep, probably by contracting the blood-vessels, lies outside of the psychophysical system in the lower centers of the brain. The real disturbance thus lies in the inactivity of this purely bodily apparatus and mental influence which is to create sleep has therefore to work downwards from the mind to a bodily organ. In the same way many other non-psychical centers of the brain may be brought to efficiency through psychophysical regulation.

But the therapeutic effect is certainly not confined to the central nervous system. Whithersoever the centrifugal nerves lead there the mind-brain system may have its curative influence. In the most startling way that is true for the digestive apparatus. The secretions of the stomach, the activity of the intestines can be influenced to a degree which it is difficult to explain. Important also is the relation to the circulatory system, especially the disturbances of the heart: innervation may be corrected, abnormal dilations and contractions of blood-vessels may be regulated. The bladder, uterus, even the pancreas and the liver seem to be influenced by the peripheral effects of the central excitement. And while no warning can be serious enough against the absurd belief that diseases like cancer or tuberculosis can be cured by faith, it must be admitted that psychical influences under special conditions may have a retarding influence on any pathological process in the organism. Much of that certainly is indirect influence but the physician would be reckless if he should ignore the aid which may result from such indirect assistance. Even if psychotherapy could not do more in the treatment of bodily diseases than to secure a joyful obedience to the strict demands of the physician, it would yet have to be accredited with an extremely important service.

In a parallel line comes the effective aid by the stimulation of hope and the suppression of fear, by suggestion of a feeling of encouragement and the inhibition of the emotions of worry. This is a field where even the average physician is most easily inclined to play the amateur psychotherapist. He knows how convalescence is disturbed by psychical depression and how much more quickly health returns, if it is confidently expected; he knows how many dangerous operations are disturbed by despondency and helped by bravery; he knows what a blessed change has come into the treatment of tuberculosis since a psychical factor of social interest has set in; he knows how many ills disappear when regular occupation and interesting work are established or the strain of distasteful work removed. Even the mere suppression of the pain works backwards on the bodily disease which produces it. The pain was a starting point for disturbing reactions; with its disappearance through psychotherapeutic influence, the reactions of the irritated brain come to rest, the diseased body can carry on its struggle without interference and may win the day. Often the psychical influence may not even change the symptoms at all but may remove other troublesome effects. The sufferer from locomotor ataxia may learn to walk again through mental education without any restitution of his spinal cord. In short, there are endless ways in which psychical influence may work towards the general health and towards the victory over bodily disease; and all that may be acknowledged without the slightest concession to the metaphysical creeds of mental healers and Christian Scientists. But to make use of those means and to harness such influences, it cannot be enough to rely on the common-sense of the physician any more than we should trust the common-sense of the surgeon to use his knife without condescending to the study of anatomy. The psychological study of the anatomy of the soul shows a not less complicated system of mental tissues and mental elements.

To enter into the full richness of this whole, large field of course lies entirely beyond the scope of our short discussion, which seeks as its only aim a clear recognition of the principles. Yet it seems essential to illustrate at least this sketch of the field by a more detailed account of actual developments. Various ways of procedure might appear in order and the most natural one would be, of course, to pass down from disease to disease and sketch special cases from diagnosis to cure. We might go through the various stages of neurasthenia and then through psychasthenia and then through hysteria and so on. And if we had to write a handbook for physicians, it would certainly be the desirable way, in spite of the too frequent repetitions which would become necessary. But as our aim is only a discussion of principles of psychotherapy, we have no right to use this method. Moreover, such a method would suggest the misleading view that the psychotherapist is called and is able to treat diseases. All that he treats are symptoms and he ought not to pretend that he can do more, as long as he abstracts from all other therapeutic agencies. Psychotherapeutic influence may remove the phobia of a psychasthenic or the obsession of a neurasthenic or the emotion of a hysteric, and thus may bring not only momentary relief but a change which may be favorable for general improvement, but certainly the neurasthenia and psychasthenia and hysteria are not really removed by it. Of course, even the treatment of symptoms demands a constant reference to the whole background of the disease. The depression of the neurasthenic must not be treated like the depression of the melancholic, the obsession of the psychasthenic must not be mixed with the fixed ideas of a paranoiac, the hysteric inability to walk must not be confused with an injury of the motor nerves; in short, each symptom has to be treated as part of a complete situation. The efforts of the psychotherapist will move over as large a part of the disease as possible and cover, perhaps, the causes of the disturbance as far as they are of psychical origin. Yet it would remain dilettanteism if we were to accept the popular view that the mere psychotherapeutic aid is a sufficient treatment of the whole disease. The physician has to be much more than a psychotherapist. Our discussion only seeks to point out that whatever else he may be, he must be also a psychotherapist.

The more conservative method which befits us may be, therefore, the method of dealing with symptoms only and abstracting from the more ambitious plan of discussing the diseases entire. We simply separate the mental symptoms and the bodily symptoms which the psychotherapist is to remove. And just in order to classify somehow the manifold mental symptoms, we might separate those in the sphere of ideas, those in the sphere of emotions, and those in the sphere of volitions. Of course, nothing is further from such a plan than the old-fashioned belief that intellect, feeling, and will represent three independent faculties of the soul. Modern psychology has not only substituted the millionfold phenomena for the schematic faculties, but emphasizes above all the interconnectedness of the mental facts. There is no experience into which ideas, and feelings, and impulses do not enter together. And correspondingly we emphasized that on the physiological side too, every sensory excitement is at the same time the middle point of central irradiation and the starting point of motor activity. Thus there can be no disturbance of ideas which does not influence feeling and will, and vice versa. Yet it would be artificial to deny that any one of those various sides of the psychical process may come to prominence, sometimes the impulse, sometimes the emotion, and sometimes the interplay of ideas. The separation means only an abstraction, but it is an abstraction which is justified and suggested by the actual experiences. Thus we shall deal with the psychical treatment of ideational, emotional, volitional, and bodily symptoms.

Common to our discussions will be only the effort to avoid everything which is exceptional and by its unusual complications apparently unexplainable and mysterious. The greater complexity of the case certainly adds much fascination. Yet since we do not want to stimulate mere curiosity but clear understanding of the elements, we avoid every startling record. We confine ourselves carefully to those perhaps trivial experiences which daily enter into the view of those who come in contact with suffering mankind. There will be no startling stories of dissociated personalities, such as appear perhaps every few years on the horizon of the medical world, but we shall speak of those who every day in every town carry their trouble to the waiting room of the doctor and who might return more happily if he had more well-trained interest in the psychotherapeutic factors. Yet before we analyze some typical symptoms, it might be wise to review the whole series of means and tools which the psychotherapist finds at his disposal.

VIII

THE GENERAL METHODS OF
PSYCHOTHERAPY

THE psychological work of the physician does not begin with his curative efforts. Therapy is always only the last step. Diagnosis and observation have to precede, and an inquiry into the causes of the disease is essential, and in every one of these steps psychology may play its rôle. The means of psychodiagnostic are not less manifold than those of psychotherapy. Moreover there the technique may be more complex and subtle. The whole equipment of the modern laboratory ought to be put at its disposal. Perceptions and associations, reactions and expressions ought to be examined with the same carefulness with which the conscientious physician examines the blood and the urine.

A particular difficulty of the task more or less foreign to every other medical inquiry is the intentional or unintentional effort of the patient to hide the sources of the trouble and to mislead as to their true character. Too often he is entirely unconscious of the sources of trouble or else he has social reasons to deceive the world and himself, and ultimately the physician. And yet no psychical treatment can start successfully so long as the patient is brooding on secret thoughts at the bottom of his mind. The desire to hide them may often be itself a part of the disease. It is surprising how often unsuspected vistas of thoughts and impulses and emotions are opened by an inquiring analysis where the direct report of the patient does not awaken the least suspicion. In the field of insanity, naturally the physician at once goes to an examination on his own account, but in the borderland regions of the psychasthenics and hysterics and neurasthenics, the intellectual clearness of the patient too easily tempts one into trusting the sincerity of his story; and yet the most important ideas clustering perhaps about love or ambition, about vice or crime, about business failure or family secrets, about inherited or acquired diseases may be cunningly withheld and may frustrate every psychotherapeutic influence. Where suspicion is awake and mere confidential talk and persuasion seem insufficient, the physician may feel justified in the interest of his patient in drawing the thoughts out of their hiding-place by artificial means. Skill, tact, and experience are needed there.

As a matter of course, in the overwhelming mass of cases the frankness and the good will of the patient himself will support the physician and accordingly his examination is not obliged to trap the patient but simply to guide him to important points. But then begins the most essential study of diagnostical differentiation. With all the means not only of psychology but of neurology and internal medicine, he has to separate the particular case from similar ones and to examine whether he deals with, for instance, a hysteric or with a paranoiac, with a neurasthenic or with a case of dementia præcox; and he will not forget that there exist almost no symptoms of serious diseases which the nervous system of the hysteric may not imitate for a time. Not ours is the task of analyzing special methods of neurological and mental differential diagnosis such as are used in the psychiatric clinic and in the office of the nerve specialist. There the family history with reference to nervous and other diseases, the history of the patient himself, the infectious diseases which he has passed through, his habits and anomalies, his use of alcohol and of drugs, his experiences in social life, the demands of his profession, his recent troubles and their first origin are to be recorded carefully. Then begins the physical examination, the study of his sense organs and his nerves, of the motor inabilities, the pains, the local anæsthesias and paræsthesias, the disturbances of the reflexes, of the spasms, tremors, convulsions, and incoordinations, of the vasomotor and trophic disorders, and so on. In a similar way the psychical examination tests the hallucinations and illusions, the variations and defects of memory and attention, of judgment and reasoning, of orientation and self-consciousness, of emotions and volitions, of intellectual capacities and organized actions. But we do not have to enter here into a discussion of such diagnostic means; our chief interest belongs to the therapy.

The variety of the psychotherapeutic methods is great and only some types are to be characterized here. But one rule is common to all of them: never use psychotherapeutic methods in a schematic way like a rigid pattern. Schematic treatment is a poor treatment in every department of medicine, but in psychotherapeutics it is disastrous. There are no two cases alike and not only the easily recognizable differences of sex and age, and occupation and education, and financial means, and temperament and capacity are decisive, but all the subtle variations of prejudices and beliefs, preferences and dislikes, family life and social surroundings, ambitions and prospects, memories and fancies, diet and habits must carefully be considered. Every element of a man's life history, impressions of early childhood, his love and his successes, his diseases and his distresses, his acquaintances and his reading, his talent, his character, his sincerity, his energy, his intelligence—everything—ought to determine the choice of the psychotherapeutic steps. As it is entirely impossible to determine all those factors by any sufficient inquiry, most of the adjustment of method must be left to the instinct of the physician, in which wide experience, solid knowledge, tact, and sympathy ought to be blended. Even the way in which the patient reacts on the method will often guide the instinct of the well-trained psychotherapist.

It is therefore certainly not enough that the knowledge of the physician simply decide beforehand on a definite course of psychical treatment and leave the carrying out to a well-meaning minister or any other medical amateur who schematically follows the indicated path. The finest adjustment has to come in during the treatment itself and the response of the patient often has to suggest entirely new lines of procedure. More than in any other field of medicine, the physician himself has to extend his influence far beyond the office hours and the strictly medical relations. And yet, on the other hand, there is no department of medicine in which the treatment might not profit by the psychotherapeutic influence. With a few vague words of encouragement mechanically uttered, or with a routine of tricks of suggestion by bread pills and colored water and tuning forks, not much will be gained even in the ordinary physician's practice. Subtle adjustment to the personal needs and to the individual conditions is necessary in every case where the psychical factor is to play an important rôle. It cannot be denied that the one great obstacle in the work of the routine physician is the lack of time and patience which is needed for successful treatment. To prescribe drugs is always quicker than to influence the mind; to cure a morphinist by hyoscine needs less effort than to cure him by suggestion.

The first method to bring back the psychophysical equilibrium is of course the one which is also demanded by common-sense, namely, to remove the external sources of the disturbance. External indicates there not only the outer world but also the own body outside the conscious parts of the brain. If we take it in the widest meaning, this would evidently include every possible medical task from filling a painful tooth to operating on a painful appendix, as in every case where pain results, the mental equilibrium is disturbed by it and the normal mental life of the patient reduced in its efficiency. But in the narrower sense of the word, we shall rather think of those sources of trouble in the organism itself which interfere directly with the mental functions. The examination of any public school quickly leads to the discovery that much which is taken for impaired mental activity, for lack of attention, for stupidity, or laziness may be the result of defective hearing or sight or abnormal growth of the adenoids. Growths in the nose may be operated upon, the astigmatic or the shortsighted eye may be corrected by glasses, the child who is hard of hearing may at least be seated near the teacher; and the backward children quickly reach the average level. No doubt in the life of the adult as well, often almost insignificant and from a strictly physical point of view unimportant abnormities in the bodily system, especially in the digestive and sexual spheres, are sources of irritation which slowly influence the whole personality. To be sure, the brain disturbance may have reached a point where the mere removal of the original affliction is not sufficient to reinstate the normal balance of mental energies, but wherever such a bodily irritation goes on, it is never too late to abolish it in the interests of psychotherapy.

The less evident and yet even more important source of the painful intrusions may lie outside of the organism in the social surroundings and conditions of life. Most of that has to be accepted. The physician cannot bring back the friend who died or the fortune which was lost in speculation or the man who married another girl. He will even avoid suggesting far-reaching social changes in the private life of the patient, changes like divorce in an unhappy marriage or the breaking of the home ties, however often he may get the impression that such a liberation would stop the source of the mental trouble. He will be the more careful not to overstep his medical rights as he seldom has the possibility to judge fairly on the basis of the one-sided complaint, and the probability is great that the character and temperament of the complainant may be a more essential factor of the ailment than the personalities which surround him. Yet even the conservative physician will find abundant opportunities for advice which will remove disturbing energies from the social surroundings of the sufferer. Even a short release from the burdening duties, a short vacation from the incessant needs of the nursery, a break in the monotony of the office, may often do wonders with a neurasthenic. Often within a surprisingly short time the brain gathers the energies to overcome the frictions with unavoidable surroundings.

Yet here the physician has to adjust the prescribed dose of outing very carefully to the special case. We may be guided by the psychological experiments which have been made in the interest of testing the fatigue induced by mental work. If perhaps four hours of concentrated work are done without pauses, experiment shows that the quality of the work deteriorates, measured for instance by the number of mistakes in quick calculation. If certain relatively long pauses

are introduced, the standard of work can be kept
high all through. But if frequent pauses are made,
and each short, the result is with many individuals the
opposite. The experiment indicates that these frequent pauses are working as interruptions which
hinder the perfect adjustment to the work in hand.
That is suggestive. Our neurasthenic may complain
about the life which he has to live and yet after all
he is frequently so completely adjusted to it that it
may not be in his interest to remove him far away
from the conditions which cannot ultimately be
changed but to which he has to return. The instinct
of the physician has to find the middle way between a
temporary removal of irritation which really allows
a development of new energies and a mere interruption which simply damages the acquired relative adjustment. Every cause of friction which can be per-
manently annihilated for the patient certainly should
be removed.

This negative remedy demands its positive supplement. The patient must be brought under conditions
and influences which give fair chances for the recu-
peration of his energies. Too often from the standpoint of the psychologist, the prescription is simply
rest. As far as rest involves sleep, it is certainly the
ideal prescription. There is no other influence which
builds up the injured central nervous system as safely
as sound natural sleep, and loss of sleep is certainly
one of the most pernicious conditions for the brain.
'Again rest is a great factor in those systematic rest
cures which for a long while were almost the fashion

with the neurologist. Experience has shown that their stereotyped use is often unsuccessful, and moreover that the advantage gained by those months spent in bed completely isolated and overfed is perhaps due to the separation and changed nutrition more than to the overlong absolute rest. Yet used with discrimination, the physiological and the psychical effect of lying in bed for a few weeks has certainly often been a marked improvement, especially with young women. But more often the idea of rest in bed during daytime is not meant at all when the nerve specialist recommends rest to his over-strained patient. It is simply meant that he give up his fatiguing daily work, even if that work is made up of a round of entertainments and calls and social engagements. The neurasthenic and all similar varieties are sent away from the noise of the city, away from the rush of their busy life, away from telephones and street cars, away from the hustling business and politics.

Indeed it is the dogma of most official and unofficial doctors that the restlessness and hurry and noise which all are characteristic of the technical conditions of our time are the chief sources of the prevailing nervousness. There was no time in the history of civilization in which the average man was overwhelmed by so many demands on his nerve energy, no time which asked such an abundance of interests even from the school child. The wild chase for luxury in the higher classes, reënforced by the commercialism of our time, the hard and monotonous labor in our modern mills and mines for the lower classes, the over-excitement brought to everybody by the sensationalism of our newspapers and of our public life all injure the brain cells and damage the equilibrium. That is a story which we hear a thousand times nowadays. Yet it is doubtful whether there is really much truth in such a claim and whether much wise psychotherapy can be deduced from it.

We may begin even with the very justifiable doubt whether nervousness really has increased in our time. Earlier periods had not so many names for those symptoms and were not able to discriminate them with the same clearness. Above all, the milder forms of abnormities were not looked on as pathological disturbances. If a man has a pessimistic temperament, or has fits of temper, or cannot get rid of a sad memory idea, or imagines that he feels an illness which he does not have, or has no energy to work, even today most people are still without suspicion that a neurasthenic or a psychasthenic or a hysteric disturbance of the nervous system may be in its beginning. Earlier times surely may have treated even the stronger varieties of this kind as troublesome variations in the sphere of the normal. On the other hand, there can be no doubt that, for instance, the Middle Ages developed severe diseases of the nervous system in an almost epidemic way which is nearly unknown to our time.

As to the conditions of life itself, there are certainly many factors at work which secure favorable influences for our cerebral activity. The progress of scientific hygiene has brought everyone much nearer to a harmonious functioning of the organism, and the progress of technique has removed innumerable difficulties from the play of life. Of course, we stand today before a much more complex surrounding than our ancestors but still more quickly than the complexity have grown the means to master it. We have to know more: yet the effort has not become greater since it has become easier to acquire knowledge. We have to endure much disturbing noise, and yet we forget how the sense organs of our forefathers must have been maltreated, for instance, by flickering light. We are in a rush of work and stand in thousandfold connections; and yet the neural energy which is demanded is not large because a thousand devices of our technical life have become our obedient servants. There is no nation on earth which is more proud of its rush and its hurry than the American people; and yet what an abundance of time is leisurely wasted that would have to be used for work if the country could not live from its richness. Moreover our life has probably become cooler, there is less emotionalism, less sentimentality, more business-like attitude, and that all means less inner friction and excitement; in public life too, less fear of war and less religious struggle. All has become a question of administration and efficiency. Our time is certainly not worse off on the score of neurasthenia than its predecessors.

Above all the intensity of mental stimuli is always relative. The psychologist knows the experiments which determine that we perceive the difference of impressions as alike when the stimuli are propor-

tional. If I have a ten-pound weight in one hand, I
may find that I must have one pound more in the
other hand to discriminate the difference. Now if I
take twenty pounds in the one hand, then it is
not sufficient to have one pound more in the other,
but I must have twenty-two pounds in the other to
feel a difference, and if I take thirty pounds, the
other weight must be thirty-three. We feel equal
differences when the weights stand in the same relation. The man who owns a hundred dollars will
enjoy the gain of five and regret the loss of five just
as much as the owner of a hundred thousand dollars
would feel the gain or loss of five thousand. This
fundamental law of the relativity of psychical impressions controls our whole life. The rush of stimuli
which might mean a source of nervous disturbance
for the villager whose quiet country life has brought
about an adjustment to faint impressions may cause
very slight stimulation for the metropolitan accustomed for a lifetime to the rhythm of the surroundings. Yet that quiet countryman may react in his
narrow system not less when the modest changes in his
surroundings provoke him. The gossip of his neighbor may undermine his nervous system just as much
as a political fight or the struggles of the exchange
that of the city man.

The same holds true for the purely intellectual
engagements. The work which the scholar undertakes
should not be measured by the effect which the same
appeal to concentrated attention would make on the
average man of practical life. There, too, an adjust-

ment to the demand has resulted during the whole period of training and professional work. Every effort should be estimated with reference to the standard of the particular case. This relativity of the mental reaction on the demands of life must always be in the foreground of the psychotherapeutic régime. Even the best physicians too often sin against this principle and accuse the life which a man or woman leads as too exhausting and overstraining simply because it would be overstraining and exhausting to others who are not adjusted to that special standard. Simply to withdraw a patient from the one kind of life and to force on him a new kind with new standards may not be a gain at all. A new adjustment begins and smaller differences from the standard may bring about the same strong intensities of reaction as the large differences brought before. Complete rest, for instance, for a hard brain-worker hardly ought to be recommended unless a high degree of exhaustion has come on. If routine prescriptions are to be admitted at all, they should not be complete rest or complete change of life for any length of time but a continuation of the life for which adjustment has been learned with a reasonable reduction of the demands and stimulations. The intellectual worker ought to decrease his work, the overbusy society woman ought to stay in bed one day in the week, the man in the midst of the rush of life ought to cut down his obligations, but probably each of them does better to go on than simply to swear off altogether.

Their rest ought to have the character of vacation;

that means interruptions without the usual activity ought to be short periods spent with the distinct feeling that they are interruptions of that which must last and that they are not themselves to become lasting states. Thus the inner adjustment to the work ought to be kept up and ought not to be substituted by a new adjustment to a less exacting life. In this way the episode of the vacation rest ought to be in a way included in the strenuous life almost as a part of its programme. Strenuosity must not mean an external rush with the gestures of overbusy excitement, but certainly the doctrine of the lazy life is wretched psychotherapy, as long as no serious illness is in question. By far the best alteration is, therefore, even in the periods of interruption, not simply rest but new engagements which awaken new interests and stimulate neglected mental factors, disburdening the overstrained elements of mental life. The most effective agency for this task is contact with beauty, beauty in nature and life, beauty in art and literature and music. To enjoy a landscape ought to be not merely a negative rest for the man of the office building, and good literature or music absorbs the mental energies and harmonizes them. In the second place come games and sport, which may enter into their right if fatigue can be avoided. Harmonious joyful company, as different as possible from the depressing company of the sanitariums, will add its pleasantness.

While the advice of the physician ought thus to emphasize the positive elements which work, not towards rest, but toward a harmonious mental activity, we must not forget some essential negative prescriptions. Everything is to be avoided which interferes with the night's sleep. Furthermore, in the first place, alcohol must be avoided. There cannot be any doubt that alcoholic intemperance is one of the chief sources of brain disturbances and that the fight against intemperance, which in this country is essentially the fight against the disgusting saloon, is a duty of everyone who wants to prevent nervous disaster. There may and must be divergence of opinion as to the safest way to overcome intemperance. The conservative physician will feel grave doubt whether the hasty recommendation of complete prohibition is such a safe way, whether it does not contain many conditions of evil, and whether the fight against the misuse of alcohol will not be more successful if a true education for temperance is accepted as the next goal. But for the man of neurasthenic constitution and for any brain of weak resistance, the limit for permissible alcoholic beverages ought to be drawn very narrow and in such cases temporary abstinence is usually the safest advice. Individual cases must indicate where a glass of light beer with the meal or a glass of a mild wine may be permissible. Strong drinks like cocktails are absolutely to be excluded. In the same way a strong reduction is advisable in tobacco, tea, and especially coffee. A complete withdrawal of all stimulations to which a nervous system has been accustomed for years is not wise, or at least mild substitutes ought to be suggested, but if coffee can be ruled out at once, often much is gained. In the same way all passionate excitements are to be eliminated and sexual life to be wisely regulated. An especial warning signal is to be posted before all strong emotions, and if the patient cannot be asked to leave his worry at home, he can at least be asked to avoid situations which will necessarily lead to excitement and quarrel and possible disappointment.

It is one of the surest tests of psychotherapeutic skill to discriminate wisely whether one or the other of these features of general treatment ought to be emphasized. They usually demand more insight than specific forms of psychotherapy like hypnotic suggestions. These general efforts are also much more directed against the disease itself where the specific methods are merely directed against the symptoms. The separation from disturbing surroundings, the reduction of engagements and work, the complete rest, the suppression of artificial stimulants, the enjoyment of art, of nature, of sport, the distractions of social life, each might be in one case a decisive help and indifferent, perhaps even harmful in another. All is a matter of choice and adjustment to the particular needs in which all the personal factors of inherited constitution, acquired adjustments, social surroundings, temperament, and education, and the probable later development have to be most tactfully weighed. Yet this general treatment may take and very often ought to take the opposite direction, not towards rest but towards work, not towards light distraction but towards serious effort, not towards reduction of engagements but towards energetic regulation. We said that it was an exaggeration to blame the external conditions of our life, the technical manifoldness of our surroundings as the source of the widespread nervousness. The mere complexity of the life, the rapidity of the demands, the amount of intellectual effort is in itself not dangerous and our time is not more pernicious than the past has been; but it is perhaps no exaggeration to say that our time is by many of its features more than the past tending towards an unsound inner attitude of man.

Much of the present civilization leads the average man and woman to a superficiality and inner hastiness which undermines sound mental life much more than the external factors. We look with a condescending smile at the old-fashioned periods in which the demands of authority and discipline controlled the education of the child and after all the education of the adult to his last days. We have substituted for it the demand of freedom with all its blessings, but instead of the blessings we too often get all its vices. A go-as-you-please method characterizes our whole society from the kindergarten to the height of life. We eulogize the principle of following the paths of own true interest and mean by that too often paths of least resistance. Study becomes play, the child learns a hundred things but does not learn the most important one, to do his duty and to do it accurately and with submission to a general purpose. The power of attention thus never becomes trained, the energy to concentrate on that which is not inter-

esting by its own appeal is slowly lost, a flabby superficiality must set in which is moved by nothing but the
personal advantage and the zigzag impulses of the
chance surroundings.   He who has never learned
obedience can never become his own master, and whoever is not his own master through all his life lacks
the mental soundness and mental balance which a
harmonious life demands.   Flippancy and carelessness, haphazard interests and recklessness must result,
mediocrity wins the day, cheap aims pervade the
social life, hasty judgments, superficial emotions,
trivial problems, sensational excitements, and vulgar
pleasures appeal to the masses.   Yellow papers and
vaudeville shows—vaudeville shows on the stage, in
the courtroom, on the political platform, in the pulpit
of the church—are welcome, and of all the results,
one is the most immediate, the disorganization of the
brain energies.

   A sound mind is a well-organized mind in which a
controlling idea is able to inhibit the opposites and
is in no danger of being overrun by any chance intrusion into the mind.   This power is the act of attention.   An attention which is trained and disciplined
can hold its ideas against chance impulses.   An untrained attention is attracted by everything which is
loud and shining, big and amusing.   The trouble is
not with the rush and hurry of the impressions which
demand our attention; the trouble is with our attention which seeks a quick change of new and ever new
impressions because it is not disciplined to hold firmly
to one important interest.   We want the hundred

short-cut superficial magazines because we lack the energy to study one large volume; we want the thousand engagements because we are not concentrated enough to devote ourselves fully to one ideal task. The strong mind may find its sound adjustment even without such training for concentrated attention through obedience and discipline but the weak mind has to pay the penalty. For not a few it will mean social disaster. Yet our society is sufficiently adapted to this state so that it gives some good social chances to the superficial too, and this not only to the rich, but to those on every level. Only the nervous system cannot so easily be adjusted to the new régime. The loose interplay of the brain cells without the serious training of discipline must involve disorganization of the mind-brain system which may count often most powerfully in those spheres in which the mere needs of life are felt the least. There is only one great remedy: discipline, training for concentrated attention, for a work in submission of will to a steady purpose. And psychotherapeutic effort will often demand such a training for work rather than a reduction of work and rest.

The most alarming product of the neglect in training is found in many of those retarded children who at fifteen show the intelligence of a boy of eight. They are not imbeciles and do not belong in the psychiatric domain; their development has simply been suspended by a mistaken education. Of course no neglect would have led to it without a constitutional, inherited weakness of the central nervous system, but the weakness would never have led to the retardation if perhaps a mistaken parental indulgence had not allowed a life without forced effort and, therefore, without progress. Even such extreme cases may not show on the surface. The boy may pass as all right if we meet him at a ball; only his tutor knows the whole misery. Still less does the surface view of many a grown-up neurasthenic alarm us who seems to live a well-ordered, perhaps an enviable life, and yet who suffers the penalty of a life without concentrated effort, really without anything to do in spite of a thousand engagements. Moreover this lack of important activity may often be forced on our patients. Married women without children, without household responsibilities, and without interests of their own and without strong nervous constitution will soon lose the power of effort and their brain will succumb. A dreary monotony is dangerous even for the worker; for the non-worker it may be ruinous.

Yet mere flippant excitement and superficial entertainment is nothing but a cheap counterfeit of what is needed. Voluntary effort is needed, and this is the field where the psychotherapist must put in his most intelligent effort. There is no one for whom there is not a chance for work in our social fabric. The prescription of work has not only to be adjusted to the abilities, the knowledge, and social condition, but has to be chosen in such a way that it is full of associations and ultimately of joyful emotions. Useless work can never confer the greatest benefits; mere physical exercises are therefore psychophysically not as valuable as real sport while physically, of course, the regulated exercises may be far superior to the haphazard work in sport. To solve picture puzzles, even if they absorb the attention for a week, can never have the same effect as a real interest in a human puzzle. There is a chance for social work for every woman and every man, work which can well be chosen in full adjustment to the personal preference and likings. Not everybody is fit for charity work, and those who are may be entirely unfitted for work in the interest of the beautification of the town. Only it has to be work; mere automobiling to charity places or talking in meetings on problems which have not been studied will, of course, be merely another form of the disorganizing superficiality. The hysterical lady on Fifth Avenue and the psychasthenic old maid in the New England country town both simply have to learn to do useful work with a concentrated effort and a high purpose. From a long experience I have to confess that I have seen that this unsentimental remedy is the safest and most important prescription in the prescription book of the psychotherapist.

There is one more feature of general treatment which seems almost a matter of course, and yet which is perhaps the most difficult to apply because it cannot simply be prescribed: the sympathy of the psychotherapist. The feelings with which an operation is performed or drugs given do not determine success, but when we build up a mental life, the feelings are a decisive factor. To be sure, we must not forget that we have to deal here with a causal and not with a pur-

posive point of view. Our sympathy is therefore not
in question in its moral value but only as a cause of
a desired effect. It is therefore not really our sympathy which counts but the appearance of sympathy,
the impression which secures the belief of the patient
that sympathy for him exists. The physician who,
although full of real sympathy, does not understand
how to express it and make it felt will thus be less
successful than his colleague who may at heart remain
entirely indifferent but has a skillful routine of going
through the symptoms of sympathy. The sympathetic vibration of the voice and skillful words and
suggestive movements may be all that is needed, but
without some power of awakening this feeling of
personal relation, almost of intimacy, the wisest
psychotherapeutic treatment may remain ineffective.
That reaches its extreme in those frequent cases in
which social conditions have brought about an emotional isolation of the patient and have filled him with
an instinctive longing to break his mental loneliness,
or in the still more frequent cases where the patient's
psychical sufferings are misunderstood or ridiculed as
mere fancies or misjudged as merely imaginary evils.
Again everything depends upon the experience and
tact of the physician. His sympathy may easily
overdo the intention and further reënforce the patient's feeling of misery or make him an hypochondriac. It ought to be sympathy with authority and
sympathy which always at the same time shows the
way to discipline. Under special conditions it is even
advisable to group patients with similar diseases to-

gether and to give them strength through the natural mutual sympathy; yet this too can be in question only where this community becomes a starting point for common action and common effort, not for mere common depression. In this way a certain psychical value must be acknowledged for the social classes of tuberculosis as they have recently been instituted.

From sympathy it is only one step to encouragement, which indeed is effective only where sympathy or at least belief in sympathy exists. He who builds up a new confidence in a happy future most easily brings to the patient also that self-control and energy which is the greatest of helping agencies. The physical and mental efforts of the physician are alike deprived of their best efficiency if they are checked by worry and fear that the developments of the disease will be disastrous. As soon as new faith in life is given, and given even where a sincere prognosis must be a sad one, a great and not seldom unexpected improvement is secured. There is no doubt that the routine physician is doing by far too little in these respects. His instinctive feeling that disease is a causal process, and that he should therefore keep away from the purposive attitude, leads him too easily to a dangerous narrowness. He treats disease as if it were an isolated process and overlooks the thousandfold connections in which the nervous system stands with the patient's whole life experience in past and future. The physician is thus too easily inclined to underestimate the good which may come in the fight against disease from the ideas and emotions which form the background of the mind of the patient. Even if the disease cannot be vanquished, the mental disturbances which result from it, the pains and discomforts, may be inhibited, as soon as hopes and joyful purposes gain a dominating control of the mind. The nervous patient often needs a larger hold upon life, while the routine prescriptions may too easily reduce that hold by fixing the attention on the symptoms.

Here then is the right place for the moral appeal and the religious stimulation. How psychotherapy is related to the church will interest us later. At this moment morality and religion are for us not inspirations but medicines. But from such a causal point of view, we should not underestimate the manifold good which can come from the causal effect of religious and ethical ideas. Those faith curists who bring mutual help by impressing each other with the beauty and goodness of the world really bring new strength to the wavering mind; and the most natural channel for religious help remains, of course, the word of the minister and the own prayer. Religion may work there causally in a double way. The own personality is submerging into a larger all-embracing hold and thus inhibits the small cares and troubles of merely personal origin. The consciousness sinks into God, a mental process which reaches its maximum in mysticism. The haphazard pains of the personality disappear and are suppressed by the joy and glory of the whole. This submission of will under a higher will and its inhibitory effect for suppression of dis-

turbing symptoms must be wonderfully reënforced by
the attitude of prayer.   Even the physiological conditions of it, the clasping of the hands, the kneeling,
and monotonous sounds reënforce this inhibition of
the insignificant dissatisfactions.   On the other hand,
contact with the greater will must open the whole
reservoir of suppressed energies, and this outbreak
of hidden forces may work towards the regeneration
of the whole psychophysical system.   Neglected functions of the brain become released and give to the
mind an energy and discipline and self-control and
mastery of difficulties which restitutes the whole
equilibrium, and with the equilibrium comes a new
calmness and serenity which may react almost miracu-
lously on the entire nervous system and through it on
the whole organism and its metabolism.

Seen from a causal point of view, however, there is
no miracle in it at all.   On the contrary, it is a natural
psychophysical process which demands careful supervision not to become dangerous.   It is not the value
of the religion which determines the improvement,
and it is not God who makes the cure; or to speak
less irreligiously, the physician ought to say that if it
is God who cures through the prayer, it is not less
God who cures in other cases through bromide and
morphine, and on the other side just as God often refuses to cure through the prescribed drugs of the drug
store, God not less often refuses to cure through
prayer and church influence.   But the real standpoint
of the physician will be to consider both the drugs
and the religious ideas merely as causal agencies and

to try to understand the conditions of their efficiency and the limits which are set for them. From such a point of view, he will certainly acknowledge that submission to a greater power is a splendid effect of inhibition and at the same time a powerful effect for the stimulation of unused energies; but he will recognize also that the use of those silent energies is not without dangers.

Certainly nature has supplied us with a reservoir of normally unused psychophysical strength, to which we may resort just as the tissues of our body may nourish us for a few days when we are deprived of food, but such supply, which in exceptional cases may become the last refuge, cannot be used without a serious intrusion and interference with the normal household of mind and body. To extract these lowest layers of energies may mean for the psychophysical system a most exhausting effort which may soon bring a reaction of physical and nervous weakness. The chances are great that such a religious excitement, if it is really to have a deep effect, may go over into a mystic fascination which leads to hysteria or into an exhausting eruption of energies which ends in neurasthenic after-effects. The immediate successes of the strong religious influence on the weakened nervous system, especially on the nervous system of a weak inherited constitution, are too often stage effects which do not last. From a mere purposive point of view, they may be complete successes. They may have turned the immoral man into a moral man, the skeptic into a believer, but the physician cannot overlook that the result may be a moral man with a crippled nervous system, a believer with psychasthenic symptoms. From the point of view of the church, there cannot be too much religion; from a therapeutic point of view, religion works there like any other nervous remedy of which five grains may help and fifty grains may be ruinous.

Moreover this power of inhibiting the little troubles of the body and of bringing to work and effectiveness the deepest powers of the mind belongs not less to any other important idea and overpowering purpose. The soldier in battle does not feel the pain of his wound, and in an emergency everybody develops powers of which he was not aware. The same effect which religion produces may thus be secured by any other deep interest: service for a great human cause, enthusiasm for a gigantic plan, even the prospect of a great personal success. Thus in a psychotherapeutic system, religion has only to take its place in line with many other efforts to inhibit the feeling of misery and to reënforce will and self-control by submission under a greater will. That in the case of religion this submission, from an entirely different purposive point of view, also has a moral and religious value, has in itself no relation to the question of its therapeutic character. It ought not to lead to any one-sided preference, inasmuch as religiously indifferent agencies may be in the particular case a more reliable means of improvement. Moreover the psychological symptoms are, after all, only a fraction of the disease and very different bodily factors, digestion and nutrition, heart and lungs and sexual organs may be most intimately connected with the disturbance of the equilibrium. Medicine today no longer believes that hysteria originates in the diseases of the uterus or that neurasthenia necessarily results from insufficiencies of the stomach, but it would be a graver mistake to believe that mental factors alone decide the progress of the disease, however prominent the mental symptoms may be in it.

From the physician's encouragement and the minister's influence towards new faith in life, a short way leads to the influence of suggestion. It is on the whole the way which leads from the general psychotherapeutic treatment to the specific one directed against particular symptoms.

THE SPECIAL METHODS OF
PSYCHOTHERAPY

O F course there is no abrupt division between special and general methods. Yet the different tendency is easily recognized, if we turn only, for instance, from the mere sympathy and encouragement to the method of reasoning with the patient about the origin of his special complaint. Just now the medical profession moves along this line a great deal. Of course no well-trained psychotherapist will make the blunder of arguing with the insane. To dispute by argument with the paranoiac and to try to convince him would not be only without success, but easily irritating. This does not mean that the not less amateurish way ought to be taken of accepting his delusions and appearing to be in full agreement with him. A tactful middle way, preferably a disciplinary ignoring atttitude, ought to be taken. But it is entirely different with the mental states of the psychasthenic. The mere statement and objective proof that his obsession is based on an illusion would be ineffective. He knows that himself, but he may take the disturbance as the beginning of a brain disease, as a form of insanity, as a lasting damage which lies entirely beyond his control. Now the physician explains to him how it all came about. He shows to him that the symptoms resulted merely from autosuggestion or are the aftereffects of a suggestion from without or of a forgotten emotional experience of the past. That is a new idea to the patient and one which changes the aspect and may have an inhibitory influence.

Of course, the patient does not accept the explanation at once. He feels sure that he is not accessible to suggestion and that he has least of all a tendency to autosuggestions, but the skillful psychotherapist will find somewhere an opening for the entering wedge. He may develop to the patient the modern theories of the origin of neurotic disturbances, all with entire sincerity and yet all shaped in a way which gives to the special case an especially harmless appearance. He may even enter into experimental proof that the patient is really accessible to autosuggestions. A very simple scheme for instance is to put some interesting looking apparatus with a few metal rings on the fingers of the subject and connect it with a battery and electric keys. The key is then pushed down in view of the patient and he is to indicate the time when and the place where he begins to feel the galvanic current. The feeling will come up probably very soon in the one or the other finger, and as soon as he feels sure that the sensation is present, the physician can show him that there was no connection in the wires, that the whole galvanic sensation was the result of suggestion.

Such a method demands patience and good will.

The prejudices and deeply-rooted hypochondriac ideas, foolish theories of the patient and pessimistic emotions which have become habitual, must be removed piece by piece until the central symptoms themselves can be undermined and explored. It often takes hours of careful and fatiguing reasoning, in which at any time the patient may suddenly slip back to his old ideas. Yet if the explanatory arguments have once succeeded in making the patient himself believe firmly that his whole trouble resulted from suggestion only, the inhibitory effect of this idea may be an excellent one. The only serious defect of the method is that it often does not work. The credit which neurologists of today give to its effectiveness seems to me much too high. Even slight neurasthenic and psychasthenic disturbances remain too often in complete power when the patient is fully convinced that they originated with an emotional excitement which has long since lost its feeling value or that it resulted from a chance suggestion picked out from indifferent surroundings. The patient knows it and yet goes on suffering from the fruitless fight of his will against the intruder. Where mere reasoning is entirely successful, I am inclined to suspect that an element of suggestion has always been superadded. The authority of the physician has created a state of reënforced suggestibility in which the argument convinces, not by its logic but by its impressiveness.

This element of suggestion is quite obvious when the argument takes the form of persuasion, a psychotherapeutic method which has found its independent development. Whoever seeks to persuade relies on the mental fringe of his propositions. The idea is not to work by its own meaning but by the manner of its presentation, by its impressiveness, by the authority, by the warmth of the voice, by the sympathy which stands behind it, by the attractiveness with which it is offered, by the advantages which are in sight. Thus persuasion relies on personal powers to secure conviction where the logic of the argument is insufficient to overcome contradictions. But just for that reason persuasion is after all only a special kind of suggestion.

Other methods work on the same basis. Prominent among them is the psychotherapeutic effect of a formal assurance. The psychotherapist assures the patient that he will sleep the next night or that the pain will disappear or that he will be able to walk with such firmness that the counter-idea is undermined. It depends on the type of patient whether such suggestions of belief work better when it is assured with an air of condescension, spoken with an authority which simply ignores every possible contradiction, or with an air of sympathy and hope. Experience shows that it is favorable to connect such assurance with the entrance of a definite signal. " You will sleep to-night when the clock strikes ten," " The pain will disappear when you enter the door of your house," or perhaps, " Read this letter three times quietly in a low voice, and at the end of the third reading your fear will suddenly stop." Psy-

chological insight will further decide whether it is
wiser in the particular case to assure the patient of
the resulting effect or rather of the power to bring
about the effect.   With some people, it works better
to insist that the result will happen, with others to
promise that they themselves can secure it; in the one
case they feel themselves as passive instruments, in
the other as real actors.   To some hysterics, it is
better to say: " You will walk," to others, " You can
walk."

This belief in the future entrance of a change frequently demands an artificial reënforcement.   There
belongs first the application of external factors which
awaken in the background of the mind the support-
ing idea that something has been changed in the
whole situation or that some helpful influence has
made the improvement possible.   Medicines of colored and flavored water, applications of electric instruments without currents, in extreme cases even the
claptrap of a sham operation with a slight cut in the
skin, may touch those brain cells which words alone
cannot reach with sufficient energy and may thus secure the desired psychophysical effect.   The patient
who by merely mental inhibition has lost his voice for
weeks may get it back as soon as the physician has
looked into his larynx with a mirror and has held an
electrode without battery connection on the throat.
Another way of helping by make-believe methods is
to give the impression that a decided improvement is
noticeable.   The uneducated patient believes it easily
when the physician at his very entrance into the office

expresses his surprise about the external symptoms of
a change for the better, perhaps seen in the color of
the skin or the shading of the iris in the eye and re-
affirmed by some pseudotests of the muscle reflexes.
All that is not very edifying and the decent physician,
who justly feels somewhat dragged down to the level
of the quack in applying such means frequently, will
abstain from them wherever possible. He knows
that in the long run, even the psychasthenics are best
treated with frankness and sincerity and he will therefore only in exceptional cases resort to such short-cut
treatment by making believe. Yet that it is sometimes almost the only way to help the patient cannot
be denied.

A neater way to secure the sufferer's belief in the
possibility of a cure is by securing the desired effect
at least once through little devices. As soon as it is
once reached, the patient knows that it can be reached
and this knowledge works as a suggestion. The
hysteric who cannot speak when he thinks of his
words, or who cannot walk when he thinks of his
legs, may by the skillful physician be brought to a
few words or steps before he himself is aware of it
by completely turning his attention to something else
and producing the stimulus toward the movement in
a reflex-like way. Still more successful is the effort
to resolve the inhibited action into its component
parts and to show to the patient who cannot perform
the action as a whole that he can go through the parts
of it after all. As soon as he has passed through a
few times, a new tactual-visual image of the whole

complex is secured for his consciousness and this image works then as a new cue for the entire voluntary action, overcoming the associated counter-idea.

Another excellent way to overpower a troublesome idea or impulse or emotion is to reënforce the opposite idea by breaking open the paths for its motor expression. The effort to hold the counter-idea before consciousness may be unsuccessful so long as it is only an idea which tries in vain to produce any motor effect; but if the action itself has been repeatedly gone through, the idea will find it easier to settle and it becomes vivid in proportion to the openness of the channels of motor discharge. This holds true even for emotional states. A certain word perhaps picked up by the psychasthenic in a particular experience may produce whenever it is seen a shock and a depressing emotion. If we ask the patient to go artificially through the movements which express joy and hilarity, make him intentionally grin and open wide the eyes and expand the arms and inhale deeply, and after training this movement complex of joyful expression, speak the dreaded word at the height of the movement a new feeling combination clusters about the sound and may overcome the antagonism. Sometimes you will give to the desirable idea sufficient strength by mere repetition, sometimes you force the attention better by unusual accentuation, connecting the suggestion with a kind of shock. From here it is only one step to the suggestion in the form of a sharp order which breaks down the resistance just by its suddenness and loudness, supported perhaps by a quick arm movement which gives a cue for imitative reflexes. In the case of a youngster even a slap may add to the nervous shock; also a sudden clapping of the hands may favor effectiveness of the suggestive order.

Often it is wise to give the suggestion, not from without but to prescribe it in the form of autosuggestions. For instance, advise the patient not only to have the good will and intention of suppressing a certain fixed idea or by producing a certain inhibited impulse but to speak to himself in an audible voice, every morning and every evening, saying that he will overcome it now. Here, too, the autosuggestion may become effective by the frequency of the repetition or by the urgency of the expression or by the accompanying motor reactions. As a matter of course any associations which reënforce the idea may be used for assistance. Especially near-lying is the appeal to the man's conscience, but just such associations which touch the idea of the own personality and its deepest layers of feelings are always risky. They may touch and stir up old memories which interfere with success or they may awaken a feeling of contrast between duty and fulfillment which may disturb the whole equilibrium. If the physician knows that the good-will of the patient is insufficient to overcome the pathological disturbance, he ought not to make him feel ashamed or guilty, and that not only for moral reasons but also for strictly psychotherapeutic reasons.

In certain easily recognizable cases, it is essential to give the suggestion with avoidance of any emphasis, only as a hint, passing as if the suggestion almost slipped from the tongue of the doctor without his real intention. The hysteric who is resisting the suggestion which is intentionally given to her is sometimes surprisingly trapped by a half-hidden suggestion, perhaps not spoken to the patient herself at all but spoken in a low voice to a colleague in the room. Sometimes we have to trick those who suffer by "negativism," that is by an obstinacy which exaggerates that of the ordinary stubborn man. In such cases the suggestion not to perform an action works best if we want the action performed. There is hardly an end to the list of such methods for bringing beliefs and attitudes with suggestive power to the mind of the sufferer. Definitely to describe the conditions under which the one or the other form ought to be applied would be no wiser than to tell a statesman what steps are to be taken in every possible diplomatic situation. The instinctive selection of the right means among the many possible ones characterizes both the true statesman and the true doctor.

So far we have spoken only about the character of the suggestion, presupposing that the receiver remains in his natural state. This presupposition is certainly often entirely correct, but as far as it is correct, the results of the suggestion vary greatly with the different individuals. On the whole, we might say that such suggestions given to the subject in his normal state are effective only when the subject is by nature a suggestible being.   In considering the psychology of suggestion, we recognized at once that the degree of natural suggestibility varies excessively. The non-suggestible mind is only to a slight degree influenced by any of these proposed forms of suggestion as long as the suggestibility itself is not heightened.   To be sure, the question whether the person is suggestible by nature or not cannot be settled simply by his own impression.   Many of the most suggestible persons believe firmly that they are superior to any suggestive influence.

To bring suggestions to greater effectiveness and to exert their influence practically upon every possible subject, we have thus not only to give suggestions or to advise autosuggestion but in both cases we have to secure, especially for the naturally less suggestible patients, a somewhat heightened suggestibility.   Yet no one can overlook that some of the methods which we described have in themselves the tendency to reenforce the mental suggestibility.   Those methods of emphasis and order, of assurance and make-believe, of practical training and of awakening counter-ideas, of persuasion and even of reasoning, wherever they are in a high degree successful probably always gain a certain part of their success by the increased suggestibility which the whole situation brings with it.

This reënforcement of the psychophysical readiness for suggestions results indeed quite directly both from expectation of the unknown and of the half-way mysterious, and from the confidence in the doctor. Of course it can work very differently.   The expectation can upset the nervous system and produce unrest instead of suggestibility and, instead of confidence, the patient may feel that discouraging diffidence which settles easily upon those who have tried one fashionable physician after another. But where there is real confidence, based perhaps on the fame of the doctor and on the reports of his powerful achievements, there the conditions for effective suggestions are greatly strengthened. Still better is it if this confidence in the man is combined with a sincere hope for recovery. To lie down on a lounge on which hundreds have been cured fascinates the imagination sufficiently to give to every suggestion a much better chance to overcome the counter-idea. The expectation that something wonderful will happen can even produce an almost hypnoid state. The effect will be the greater, the less the barriers of systematic knowledge hinder the entrance of suggested ideas. The uneducated will on the whole offer less resistance to suggestions, just as superstitions find the freest play in the minds of the untrained. It is not by chance that the earlier epidemics of pathological suggestibility have on the whole disappeared with the better popular education. In a similar way work fatigue and exhaustion. The resistance has grown weaker, the suggested idea goes automatically into activity.

Skillful artificial means can still surpass the effect of these natural conditions. Here belongs everything which accentuates the authority and dignity of the originator of the suggestion. The psychologically trained physician has no difficulty in heightening the effect by simple surprises, if he cares for such tricks. If the patient for whom a mental treatment is recognized as necessary shows himself too skeptical to submit to the powers of the psychotherapist, such captivation of his belief can easily be secured. Let the man perhaps fixate a penny on the table with his right eye, while the left is closed and you show him that you can make another penny suddenly disappear when you move it a certain distance to the right and appear again when you move it still further. As the man has never heard of the blind spot in the retina, he accredits you with a special power. Many similar psychological illusions can well be used to prepare the mind for unsuspected healing powers.

Still stronger is the effect of personal contact. The psychophysiology of love indicates the most complex influence which contact sensations have on the whole nervous system and especially on the vasomotor apparatus of the body. Probably such vasomotor effect enters in, changing the blood circulation in the brain, when a personal contact between the transmitter and receiver of the suggestion is brought about. If the physician's hand rests quietly on the forehead of the patient who lies with closed eyes, or if he holds for a long while the hand of the patient, he may secure a nervous repose and submission which gives to the suggestions the most fertile soil. Needless to say that here again everything depends upon the accessories. An unsympathetic doctor may be entirely powerless where his neighbor has complete success. Neither a lifeless hand nor an agitating one will bring the desired repose, neither a cold nor a rough one. There must be strength and energy and even discipline, and yet sympathy in the pressure of the fingers. Again a psychologically different effect and yet one often to be preferred results from mild stroking movements, the stroke always to be repeated in the same direction, never up and down. The slow change in the position of the tactual sensations evidently produces a rather strong influence on the equilibrium of nervous impulses, and here again vasomotor reflexes seem to arise easily. Another variety of such bodily influences is given by artificial changes of the positions, for instance by bending the head of the subject backward while the eyes are closed. It may be that a certain lack of balance sets in in which the self-equilibrium is disturbed and an external influence can thus more easily get control of the psychophysical system. Again a certain monotony of speaking may easily add to the increase of the suggestibility.

Everyone knows that another most fruitful cause of this change is any mystic inspiration, any emotion in which the individual feels himself in contact with something higher or larger or stronger. Of course, the church can secure this effect easily, and here again the maximum will be reached if a bodily contact with the symbol of religious exaltation can be established. The patient who can touch the relics of the saints or bathe in the waters of Lourdes or at least feel on his forehead the hand of the minister, is wrought up to a state of suggestibility which makes suggestions easily effective. The objective value of religion again has nothing to do with it, as exactly the same effect can result from the most barbarous superstition. The amulets of a gypsy might secure the same re-setting of the psychophysical system which the most sacred symbols awaken, and even many an educated person is unable to cross the threshold of a palmist or an astrologist, or to attend the performance of a spiritist, or to sit down with a purchasable trance medium without feeling an uncanny mental state which is objectively characterized by an increased suggestibility. But finally, the same effect sets in when the symbols of other emotional spheres are ap-plied, perhaps for the patriotic soldier the flag of his country.

All the states of increased suggestibility which we have characterized so far still remain within the limit of normal wakefulness. We may turn now to the methods of the psychotherapist which produce in the interest of the suggestions an artificial state. How-ever we have no right superficially to claim that the effectiveness of the suggestions is always greater in such unnatural states. On the contrary, we know that sometimes well applied suggestions work on wideawake persons with increased suggestibility more strongly than on hypnotized subjects. Here even the instinct of the experienced physician may easily go astray, and it may need practical tests to find out which way will be the most accessible to the par-ticular case. Often a certain rôle belongs even to natural sleep. It cannot be denied that some people can be influenced to some degree by words spoken to them during sleep. Most adults either wake up or show no signs of influence beyond effects on their dreams. But some absorb especially whispered words in such a way that their power becomes evident after the waking of the sleeper. Much more is this true of children. A suggestion to give up vicious habits, perhaps in the sexual sphere, or to speak fluently and no longer stammer may thus be beneficial. Yet the danger of this method is not small and extensive use of it is certainly not advisable. The more easily it can be carried into every bedchamber and can thus give to every mother and nurse the tools of a rather powerful therapy, the more a danger signal ought to be displayed. Interference with the natural sleep by outer influences creates abnormal conditions which cannot be removed at will. The chances are great that many unintended bad effects slip in and that not a few hysterias may be created by a method at the first glance so startling. Much less objectionable is it to make use of the effect of that period of half-sleep which precedes the natural sleep, and which is for many a period of increased suggestibility for autosuggestions. A resolution or the formulation of a belief which would be ineffective in a wide-awake state seems to get an accentuated effect on the mind, if it is repeatedly expressed in this transitional state. The psychasthenic who in such a half-dozing stage assures himself that he will no longer be afraid of going over a bridge or hearing a thunderstorm or will feel a disgust for whiskey or will have the energy for work, has a certain chance that such autosuggestions become reality the next morning. With many others there seems no effect to be obtained and not a few seem unable to catch the right moment. As soon as they begin to speak they become wide awake or fall asleep before they talk.

Incomparably more value belongs to the artificial sleep, the mesmeric state of earlier days, the hypnotism of our time. We have discussed its theory and recognized that an abnormally increased suggestibility is indeed its chief feature. We know hypnotism in most various degrees; the lowest can be reached practically by everyone, the highest by rather few. It is almost arbitrary to decide where those waking states with high tension of suggestibility end and the hypnotic states begin, and not less arbitrary to call the higher degrees only hypnotism and to designate the lower degrees as hypnoid states. If we do it, we certainly should acknowledge from the start that the hypnoid states are for therapeutic purposes not a bit less important than the full hypnotic states. Certainly the hypnoid states do not allow complex hallucinations and absurd posthypnotic actions, but they offer excellent starting points for the removal of light obsessions and phobias and for the reënforcement of desirable impulses, volitions, and emotions. Many persons cannot under any circumstances be brought beyond such a hypnoid degree. The physician who has not theoretical experiments but practical success in view ought therefore never to trouble himself with the inquiry exactly which degree has been reached.   This advice is given because nothing interferes with the progress of hypnotic influence so badly as the constant testing.   It must naturally often lead to a point where the subject finds that he can very well still do what the hypnotizer told him not to do.   If the doctor assures him that he can no longer move his arm and the patient is yet able to move it, the doctor secures the very superfluous knowledge that this special degree of suggestibility has not been reached, but the patient is sliding backward and the lower degree which actually had been reached will be less accessible later.   The physician might rather resort to the opposite course and assure the patient, even after the first treatment which might have been a slight success, that he saw from definite symptoms that hypnosis had set in.   That will greatly smooth the way for real hypnotic effects the next time.

The best method of hypnotizing is the one which relies essentially on the spoken word, awakening through speech the idea of the approach of sleep. If the hypnotizer assures the subject in monotonous words that a feeling of fatigue is setting in, that he is feeling a tiredness creeping over his shoulders and arms and legs, that his memories are fading away and that he is now hypnotized, for not a few all is done that is needed.   The hypnotic state will come and will hold until the verbal suggestion takes it off again.   Perhaps the hypnotizer says that he will count three and at three the subject is to open his eyes and feel perfectly comfortable. It is wise to tell the patient beforehand that he will not lose consciousness and that he will remember afterward whatever happens as many people believe that loss of memory belongs to the hypnotic state, and that they were not hypnotized if they can remember what happened. Such a skeptical after-attitude can seriously interfere with the success of the treatment.

Yet in most cases, it will be safer not to rely on words only but to supplement them by manipulations which all converge towards the effect of increasing the suggestibility and thus of overcoming the resistance to the suggestions introduced. It is well known that for this purpose it is advisable to begin the influence with some slight fatiguing stimulations. The effect is most easily reached when the patient fixates perhaps a shining button held over his eyes or listens to monotonous sounds. A particularly strong effect belongs again to very slight touch stimuli. If the subject with his eyes closed is touched perhaps by two pencils at various and unexpected points of the face and hands, a skillful playing on his tactual senses soon produces a half-dozing state of hypnoid character. In the same group belong those so-called passes which evidently have a reflex influence in the blood-vessel system. It is advisable to combine the various elements in such a way that at first physical stimuli upon eye or skin produce an over-suggestible state and that only as soon as this state is reached the verbal suggestion sets in, perhaps with the words,

" I shall hypnotize you now." Under such conditions every subject may soon be brought to that degree of hypnotization which is accessible to him. Yet more than one treatment is usually necessary for the higher degrees. Much less importance for therapeutic purposes belongs to that hypnoid state which is reached without the idea of sleep where the subject comes with open eyes into a kind of fascination, produced perhaps by a sudden flash of light or by the firm eye of the hypnotizer. It is a state which can lead to a strong submission of will and which has its legal importance. Therapeutically it can hardly secure an effect which cannot better be secured through the real sleeplike hypnotism. Under certain conditions, chemical substances may well prepare for the hypnotic treatment, for instance bromides or alcohol. Others rely on the suggestive effect of flavored water. But all that is unwise. The confidence of the patient is the best preparation for the securing of the helpful degree of hypnotism.

Of course only a small part of the therapeutic usefulness is secured during the hypnotic state itself. A pain may be removed, sleep be secured, an idea be inhibited, a movement be reënforced in cases where non-hypnotic suggestions would have found insurmountable obstacles. During the hypnosis we may also open the storehouse of memory and bring to light the ideas which disturbed the equilibrium of the suffering mind. Further in those most complex hysteric cases of dissociated personality, new memory connections may be formed during the hypnosis by which a synthesis of the double or triple personalities into the old one may be secured. Yet the general effect which the physician has to hope for from hypnotic treatment is the posthypnotic one. Not what happens during the hypnosis but what the suggestion will produce after hypnosis is essential to him. The fixed idea is to disappear forever, the paralyzed limb is under control, the desire for morphine and cocaine is gone for all future time, the perverse longing is annihilated, the old energy is to remain again for all time. It is the posthypnotic after-effectiveness which gives to the hypnoid and to the hypnotic states their importance for the treatment of the most exasperating symptoms. To be sure, the treatment often must be a prolonged one. A man who for years has used thirty grains of morphine a day cannot be rid of the desire after two or three hypnotic sittings. In such a case the treatment may cover three or four months, if it is to be of lasting value and without any damage during the treatment.

Still we are not at the end of the psychotherapeutic methods and we may turn to a fascinating group of curative efforts which has especially come to the foreground in recent years. We mentioned before that mischief cannot seldom be traced back to earlier experiences with a strong unpleasurable feeling. In certain cases, the subject remembers such particular experiences as the beginning of his discomfort; in others, especially those of hysteric character, the starting point may have long been forgotten, and yet that early impression evidently left traces in the brain which produce disturbances in conscious life. The psychotherapist nowadays calls these groups of traces "complexes." We recognized clearly that there is no reason to refer such forgotten remainders of the past to any subconscious mind; they are physical after-effects which keep their influence over the equilibrium of the psychophysical system. Now modern psychotherapy finds that the entire disturbances which arise from such emotional disagreeable experiences, forgotten or not forgotten, can often be removed by psychical means. Two ways in particular seem open. As soon as the idea is fully brought back to consciousness again, the patient must be made to express the primary emotion with full intensity. Subtle analysis has repeatedly shown that many of the gravest hysteric symptoms result from such a suppression of emotions at the beginning and disappear as soon as the primary experience comes to its right motor discharge and gains its normal outlet in action. The whole irritation becomes eliminated, the emotion is relieved from suppression and the source of the cortical uproar is removed forever.

Practically still more important seems the other case which refers alike to hysterics and psychasthenics and which is applicable for the forgotten experience not less than for the well-remembered ones. This second way demands that the psychotherapist bring this primary experience strongly to consciousness and then by a new training link it with new and more desirable associations and reactions. The disturbing idea is thus not to be discharged but to be sidetracked so that in future it leads to harmless results. The new setting works towards an entirely new equilibrium. What was a starting point for abnormal fears now becomes an indifferent object of interest and all its evil consequences are cut off. It may be acknowledged that the full elaboration of these methods still belongs to the future. Both methods, the discharging, or the so-called cathartic one, and the side-tracking method evidently demand the discovery of the starting point in the service of the therapy and here again several methods are at the disposal of the psychologist.

A promising way to this end is the inexhaustible association test which we mentioned when we discussed the contributions of the psychological laboratory to the medical diagnosis. A series of short words are spoken to the patient and, as soon as he hears one, he is to pronounce as quickly as possible the first word which comes to his mind. If we use fifty words, we should be able to learn something as to the inner states of the man and as to the working of his mind, if we analyze carefully his particular choices. But two further conditions ought to be fulfilled. The time of the association ought to be measured. Of course there will be wide differences. A word which is often in a certain connection will quickly bring the habitual association. Abstract words will call forth their associations more slowly than concrete words, familiar words more rapidly than unfamiliar words. To measure such association time with fullest accuracy, as it is necessary for the purpose of scientific investigations, delicate electrical instruments are needed that indicate thousandths parts of a second. For the purpose of the practical physician such accuracy would be superfluous. His examination will be perfectly successful if it is carefully done with a stop-watch which shows the fifth part of a second, like those which are used at races. He speaks a word, presses at the same time the button of the watch, and presses the stopper when he sees the lips of the patient moving. He is thus able to examine not only the involuntary choice of association but also the time of every associative process. But a second condition ought also to be fulfilled. After some indifferent words, others ought to be mixed into the series which touch in a tentative way on various spheres corresponding to the possible suspicions. The groups to which the hidden thoughts of psychasthenics, for instance, belong are not many. As soon as our series of words strikes such a group, the reaction of the mind may be discriminated. The effect may be a general perturbation resulting either in an unusual delay of the fitting association or in an effort to cover the sore spot by an unfitting association. Sometimes the dangerous association may rush forward even with unusual rapidity but, as soon as it is uttered, it gives a shock to the mental system, brings the whole associative process into disorder, and the result is that the next following associations are abnormally delayed. The skilled psychologist will quickly take such a change as a cue for the selection of the later words in his series. Of course, he will at first return to neutral words, but as soon as he has found a danger spot, he will approach it from various sides, perhaps in every fourth or fifth word, and may then find out which particular experiences are disquieting the patient. Words like women or money or career or family or disease are often sufficient to get the first inkling of a mental story.

With less diagnostic elegance we sometimes reach the same end by taking careful records of pulse and breathing and involuntary movements during an apparently harmless conversation. The instruments at the disposal of the psychologist are those familiar to every psychological laboratory: the pneumograph, which registers the movements of respiration; the sphygmograph, which writes the pulsation of the artery in the wrist; the automatograph, or other instruments, which register the slight unintentional movements of the arm. If the examiner is skillful, he will not fail to discover the changes in breathing and pulse and reaction as soon as the painful groups of ideas are approached. More of theoretic interest and too cumbersome for practical diagnosis is the unfailing galvanic reaction from the skin in which the glands change their activity and their resistance to the galvanic current under the influence of hidden emotions. Yet all these methods, with exception of the last, are essentially useful only if the starting experience is still accessible to the memory of the patient. He may be unaware that it had anything to do with his nervous symptoms but he recognizes the experience

still as soon as his attention is directed towards it.
The psychologically more interesting but probably
more exceptional situation is the one in which it is
not only forgotten but cannot be recognized when it
is brought to consciousness. The shortest way to get
hold of such past impressions is the hypnotic one.
The hypnotic state sharpens the memory and experiences of early childhood or apparently insignificant experiences of later life may be brought back
when they would have been inaccessible to any intentional effort of the attention. Even still more
surprising is the success if the association is left to a
dreamy play of ideas suggested perhaps by gazing
into a crystal ball or by a meaningless talking. Perhaps the patient lies with closed eyes on the couch
while the physician holds his hand. A few words
are given to him as a starting point and then he is
thoughtlessly to pronounce whatever comes to his
mind, not only unfinished sentences but loose phrases,
single words, apparently without meaning and slowly
ideas arise which betray the original intrusion. At
last memories and lost emotions come again to the
surface, and the watchful psychotherapist may discover the complex, which is then to be removed by
discharge or by sidetracking. This is the so-called
psychoanalytic method.

Finally the psychotherapist may go still one step
further. After all it often seems inexplainable that
just this or that emotional experience made such a
deep and lasting impression while a thousand other
experiences passed by without leaving any mischie-

vous after-effect. It seems that indeed the conditions are still more complicated. That emotional disturbance operated dangerously perhaps only because it itself appealed to a suppressed desire and this seems to hold true especially for suppressed emotions of the sexual sphere. The desire for gratification in normal or abnormal channels was perhaps attached by the mind to some group of objects. It was completely suppressed but it left an abnormal tension in the central system. If now a chance experience touches on this group of ideas, there results an explosive reaction; and movements, convulsions, spasms, obsessions, and fears set in which get their particular character not through the secondary intrusion but from the primary desire. To discharge that intrusion leads therefore only to the elimination of those symptoms which resulted from it, but the primary disturbance goes on and any new chance intrusion will produce new explosions. The psychotherapist should therefore go deeper and relieve the mind from those primary desires which may belong to early youth and which are entirely forgotten. Even the method of automatic writing may here sometimes lead to an unveiling of those deepest layers of suppressed desires. In the same way a careful, subtle analysis of dreams may support the search for the hidden source of interference.

We have spoken of the technical methods of the psychotherapist. It would be short-sighted to ignore the great manifoldness of secondary methods which he shares with the ordinary intercourse between man and man, the methods which the teacher uses in the schoolroom, which the parents use in the nursery, which the neighbor uses with his neighbor, methods which build up the mind, methods which train the mind, methods which reënforce good habits and suppress unwholesome ones, methods which stimulate sound emotions and inhibit a quarrelsome temper, methods which indeed are not less important in the psychiatric clinic and in the hospital than in our daily life, and which certainly have central importance in that borderland region which is the particular working field of the psychotherapist.

X

THE MENTAL SYMPTOMS

W E have discussed both the psychological theory and the practical work of psychotherapy in a systematic order without any reference to personal chance experience. After studying the fundamental principles, we have sketched the whole field of disturbances in which psychotherapeutic influence might be possible and all the methods available. It seems natural that our next step should be an illustrating of such work by a number of typical cases. Here it seems advisable to leave the track of an objective system and to turn to the record of personal observation. As this is not a handbook for the physician, dealing with the special forms of disease, we emphasized before that we avoid even any attempt in such a direction because it would have to introduce not only the questions of diagnosis, but above all the highly important questions of treatment by physical agencies. We saw that for us nothing else can be desirable, but to show the way in which the various symptoms which suggest mental treatment occur, and how they yield to the psychical methods. We had also agreed beforehand that for a first survey we might separate the mental from the bodily symptoms and group the mental ones with reference to the predominance of ideational, emotional, and volitional factors. And finally it may be said that we abstain from everything which is exceptional or even unusual, and confine ourselves to the routine observations with which the psychotherapist comes in contact every day and the simplest country physician surely every week.

Thus I turn from systematic objectivity to my unsystematic reminiscences of many years. Of course, they abound with eccentric abnormities and startling phenomena. As I have devoted myself to psychotherapeutics, always and only from scientific interest, as a part of my laboratory studies and therefore have refused to spend any time on cases which offered no special psychological interest to me, the striking and sensational cases have prevailed in my practice even to an unusual degree. Yet they are unessential for our purposes here, the more as their interest lies mostly in the complex structure of the mental state while the curative features are in the background. Our purpose of demonstrating practical cases as they occur in every village, and as they ought to be understood and treated by every doctor, thus rules out just those experiences which would be prominent in a theoretical study of abnormal psychology. We want to select only simple commonplace cases. Only those who have not learned to see are unaware that such cases are everywhere about them.

As a matter of course, I also leave out everything which refers to insanity, that is, every mental dis-

turbance which lies essentially outside of the domain
of psychotherapy. The helpful influence which
psychical factors can exert in the asylums for the insane is, as we emphasized, entirely secondary. The
psychotherapeutic methods in the narrower sense of
the word are in the present state of our knowledge
ineffective in the insane asylum. I should also be
unable to speak of laboratory experience with insanity, as I insist on sanitarium treatment in every such
case. The question of how to differentiate the diagnosis of insanity from that of the other mental abnormities is not our question at this moment. I select
the few illustrations which seem to me desirable for
the purpose of making more concrete our abstract
discussion of methods, essentially from the class of
neurasthenics, psychasthenics, hysterics, and so on.

In all these reports, I shall confine the account to
the few points which are to illustrate the psychical
factors, thus abstaining entirely from the further details which any medical history of the cases would
demand and from all results of further examination
and other particulars. As a matter of course, I exclude the possibility of identifying the patient. I
may start with a typical case of obsessing ideas of
simplest character and with simple routine treatment
illustrating the emphasis on antagonistic ideas.

A man of mature age, well educated, well built and in
every respect in good health, without nervous history and
without other nervous symptoms, suffered vehemently by
the persistent recurrence of a visual image which entirely

absorbed his attention. He knew exactly the development
of his trouble. A woman acquaintance of his had committed
suicide by poisoning herself. He knew her slightly and
the emotion of personal loss played hardly any rôle in the
case. But he had met her at a gay dinner a short time
before her death. The news of the suicide came to him
when he was overtired from work. The idea of the contrast between seeing his friend partaking of the dinner and
imagining her drinking the poison gave him a strong shock.
There was hardly any grief mixed in. He remembers that
he shivered at the thought of the contrast, and in that moment the visual image of the woman raising a glass of
poison to her mouth flashed into his mind and thus became almost a part of the shock. From that time on, the
memory image of this scene returned more and more frequently. At first it associated itself with any chance mentioning of death or suicide and to a very slight degree with
the idea of a meal. More and more any element of a
meal and of social life, the word soup or meat, the word
gown or dance, brought up at once the picture of the
woman, which had in the meantime lost every element of
personal relation. Any sad thought of her ending had
faded away. It remained merely a troublesome impression.
The man fought against it by trying to suppress the idea
but the more he fought against it, the more insistently it
rushed forward through new and ever new association paths.
Any advertisement in the newspaper referring to food, anything in a shop window referring to ladies' dresses, any
household utensils related to a meal, and especially the meals
themselves, forced the visual image into the centre and captured the attention to such a degree that a confusing distraction from the real surroundings resulted. The struggle
against the idea became more and more exasperating, made

life a torture, almost suggested despair, even faint thoughts
of suicide, and especially a growing fear that it was a symptom of the beginning of insanity.

When he came to me, a number of physical cures, especially bromides and electricity, had been tried in vain by
the physician. Some weeks in the country had not changed
the distress. He came to me with the direct request as a
last resort to try hypnotic treatment. I found in spite
of the fact that he and his physician had constantly spoken
of visual hallucinations that the visual image had no hallucinatory character at all, that is, he never believed that
he saw the image of that woman as if it were actually present, he never took the product of his imagination for reality,
nor had it the vividness and character of reality. It was
hardly more vivid than any landscape which he tried to
remember, only that it controlled the interplay of ideas in
such a persistent way. I found that he was a strong visual-
izer and easily suggestible. I told him beforehand that I
should hypnotize him only to a slight degree, that he would
not lose consciousness, that he would remember everything
which I told him. Then I asked him to lie down and had
him gaze on a crystal only for half a minute, then close
the eyes. I asked him to relax and to think of sleep. With
the two blunt points of a compass, I touched his two cheeks
at corresponding places, then his forehead. And now I
told him that I would begin with the hypnotic influence. I
put my hand on his forehead and spoke to him in a monotonous way, saying that he felt a fatigue in his shoulders,
and in his arms, creeping over his whole body and assured
him that he was now fully hypnotized. To what degree
he really was hypnotized cannot be said as no effort was
made to test it by any experiments, thus avoiding any possible reaction against the feeling of submission. Expression

and breathing indicated a slight hypnoid state. Then I removed my hand and spoke to him in a warm and assuring way.

I told him that in future he would give his full attention to his meal, and not give the slightest attention to any image of his friend. If he should think of the friend the memory would appear indifferent, he would not even notice the image and would give his whole mind to the objects with which he was engaged. In the same way, when he should be reading newspapers or looking in shopwindows, his whole attention would belong to that which he really perceived. Any passing inner image would be ignored. Then I awoke him from his sleep. He was unwilling to believe that he had been in hypnosis at all. I told him that the effect would prove it and in his fully wakeful state I explained to him why there was not the slightest fear of insanity justified, that it was a psychasthenic state resulting from fatigue and shock and from a wrong attitude of his attention during the past months, and then I asked him to return the next day. Intentionally I had not given the suggestion that the image would disappear. I could not expect it would disappear entirely after a first treatment and even a faint appearance of it would have at once fascinated the attention and brought about the whole disturbance of the equilibrium which might become habitual. Instead of it I gave the impulse to the counteridea, that is, I reënforced the attention towards that which he really saw around him and thus withdrew the attention from the rival image in the mind. The success was complete. He came the next day in a much happier frame of mind, reporting that he still had seen the image of the woman every few minutes, especially strongly at the breakfast table, but it had no longer troubled him. It was more in the background of consciousness, sometimes it appeared transparent, it no longer held his attention, and he felt free to give his full attention to the actual surroundings.

On that basis I hypnotized him the second day and he had hardly heard me saying that he ought to try to sleep when he was evidently in a much deeper hypnotic state than the first time. Again I suggested only the opposite attitude, the positive turning to the surroundings and the complete neglect and indifference for the possible memory image. This time the effect was still stronger. On the third day he reported that he still saw the image but he no longer minded it, as it was like a veil through which he looked at real objects and that left him entirely indifferent. His mind was hardly engaged with it any more. The real spell of the attention was broken. On the basis of this situation, I took the last step and suggested that the image of the woman would disappear altogether and would not trouble him any more. In the next twenty-four hours, it still returned two or three times, but colorless and faint. The following day I was able to eliminate it altogether. Even when the last trace of the inner struggle between the memory and the perceived surroundings had disappeared, I went on with two hypnotic sittings to give stability to the new equilibrium, to insist that the image would not come back and to settle completely that inner repose with which every fear of possible disease evaporated. I feel sure that the cure would not have been reached so quickly, possibly not at all, if the second suggestion, the disappearance of the image, had been given at the first step. The improvement was secured because the antagonistic process itself was used for the suggestion. On the other hand, there was no doubt that in this case the strong will of the patient or suggestion in a normal state would not alone have been sufficient. The hypnotic treatment was indicated by the symptoms and justified by the results.

I may take another typical case in which also the obsession was brought about by an idea without emotional value or at least by an idea which had lost its emotional character; the idea came somewhat nearer to hallucination, but had its chief elements on tactual ground where the transition from image to hallucinatory perception is easier. I add this case to demonstrate that hypnosis is not the only open way of treatment in such cases and that the variations must always be adjusted to the special conditions. The case gains importance by the fact that the patient was himself a physician well trained in mental observation.

The patient is a highly educated physician of middle age. He reports that he had been neurasthenic all his life with slight ever-changing symptoms. He has always been troubled by the " perseveration " of tactual images which had a strong feeling tone and which were associated with seen or heard reports of the experiences of others. For instance, when he read in a newspaper that someone had hurt his hand with a pin, or that someone had cut his foot on a nail, he immediately felt a not directly painful but uncomfortable sensation at the particular place in the hand or in the foot, together with a shrinking of the whole body and such tactual sensation usually returned during the following days in fainter and fainter form until it faded away. Most troublesome had always been the reading of any torture processes in historical books or in fiction. Yet there had never been a case in which the sensations really had the vividness of hallucinations and never a case in which the after effects had not disappeared at least in a few weeks.

This time the effect had already lasted four months and it became more and more troublesome. The patient had not the slightest fear of mental disease and no anxiety, but he felt a very serious disturbance by the instinctive effort to get rid of the intrusion. The place of the disturbance was the wrists. The starting point was a definite experience. On an unusually hot summer day the physician had listened for a long time to the complaints of a female patient who suffered vehemently from a nervous fear of scissors and knives and who was afraid that she would cut her artery at the wrist. He believes that it was the exhausting heat of the day which weakened him to a point where the story of his patient affected him very strongly and made him think of it all the time. Yet there was no sensation element involved. A few hours later, he sat in a hotel at his dinner. Just in front of him a butler started to carve a duck with a long, sharp knife. In that moment he felt as if the knife passed through the wrists of both arms. He felt for a moment almost faint; arms and legs were contracted and an almost painful sensation lingered in the skin, and did not disappear for hours.

From that day at the sight of knives or razors, not only in his hands or his direct neighborhood, but also in a store and finally in a picture, stired up at once the optical image of that carving knife cutting into the skin of the wrist, only with the difference that it seldom was found in both arms, usually in the one or the other. The sensation became a strictly tactual one with optical overtone, but there was no emotion in it. The pain element had disappeared. Also the shock, which still recurred in the first days slowly disappeared. The longer the symptom lasted, the more the optical factor faded away, and the tactual factor came into the foreground after three or four weeks. Perhaps seeing a razor in a store window or a pocket knife open no longer stirred up the image of cutting the wrist, but simply a strong tactual sensation, as if the skin of the wrist was scratched and pinched. Finally, after about two months, the association character disappeared to a high degree and the scratching and cutting sensation in the skin became independent and automatic. The patient awoke in the morning with a vivid tactual hallucination of being cut without associating with it any picture of a knife. Throughout the day, in the midst of work and in the midst of conversation, sometimes one and sometimes the other wrist became the center of the exasperating sensation, easily bringing with it involuntary reactions as if to withdraw the arm. This became more and more frequent and more and more vivid.

The doctor, fully aware of the borderland character of this experience, felt sure that his inner fight against the disturbance would get control of it. The usual tonics did not show any influence. On the other hand, there were no other nervous symptoms and, with his most acute analysis, he did not find the slightest trace of emotion any longer. When the symptoms reached a point at which they seriously interfered with his comfort, he asked me for psychotherapeutic treatment, under the condition that I was not to apply hypnotism. He was absolutely averse to the use of hypnotism in his own case because he was afraid that to be hypnotized would mean for him a certain disposition to fall into hypnotic sleep by auto-suggestion, as he knew the vividness of his imaginative sensations. He wanted to avoid that the more as his own professional work might sometimes demand hypnotizing in his own practice. In any case he had an aversion to it and asked for other means.

Under these circumstances, it seemed to me the most logical conclusion that the counter idea with its antagonistic reactions might be reënforced by direct perception. The abnormal tactual sensation forced on consciousness the idea of the cutting of the wrist. The necessary counter action would be to force to consciousness the idea of the uninjured wrist and the corresponding reactions. As the wrist can be easily made accessible to sight and as I anticipated that the visual sensations would be more forceful than the tactual ones, I told him to look straight at his own wrists for ten minutes three times a day after waking, after luncheon, and before going to bed. He had to hold his two forearms close in front of his eyes and stare at them, giving his full attention to the visual impression of the smooth, uninjured skin of the wrist. If during this process, the tactual counter-sensations were vivid, he had to go on with the staring at both arms, both held near together until the perception had crowded out the rival touch sensation. When this performance had been carried out six times, he did not notice the coming up of the tactual sensation with vividness any longer. From the third day it had disappeared entirely. I told him to go on with the process still every morning for some weeks. The physician himself considered the cure as complete.

Our first case dealt with hypnosis, our second case removed the intruding idea by a perception in a waking state. To point at once to the variety of methods which we sketched, we may turn again to a case of emotionless idea removed by the method of switching off and side-tracking the originating and physiological "complex."

The patient is a school-teacher in the Middle West, a nervous, thin-looking woman of about twenty-five. Her only complaint is a persistent idea that she may at any time get a child. She has had this idea " as long as she can remember," according to her first expression. She never had any intimate acquaintance with any man, she was never engaged, she hated bitterly every thought of immorality, she knows and has assured herself by much reading that it is entirely impossible that she might get a child without sexual contact. Yet this thought recurs to her all the time, even when she is talking with other people. It embarrasses her in school, in spite of her teaching only girls in a private institution. This thought keeps her away from company and the effect of its embarrassing occurrence depresses her, but she is sure that the thought itself does not include any emotion. It is a mere thinking of it with a full consciousness that it is absurd, and yet she cannot suppress it.

I began at once to try to find the origin of her queer obsession. After some efforts to pierce into her memories, we came to an experience of her youth. When she was about thirteen years of age, a young girl whom she had admired much for her beauty, living in the neighborhood of her parents, suddenly got a child which died after a few days. At that time no thought of immorality seems to have entered into that news. It was evidently mere sadness about the quick death of the child which gave to the experience its emotional tone. She was at that time completely naïve. She received an intense shock in the thought that an unmarried girl may suddenly get a child which would then quickly die. She cannot tell whether the thought that she herself would get a child had ever entered her mind before this occurrence in her neighborhood, nor can she say that it occurred immediately or very soon after it. She now knows only that she has always had that thought, but whether that means more than ten years, she does not know.

I considered it a justifiable hypothesis that this strong emotional experience early in life had become the starting point for that secondary absurd thought. I considered that primary experience as cause for a deep physiological brain excitement which had irradiated towards the ideas of her personality. It had stirred up there associations which kept their psychological character while the primary disturbance had long lost its psychical accompaniment. It worked its mischief in a physiological sphere but was probably still the starting point for the persistent obsession. My aim was to remove this cause. It would have brought little improvement simply to suppress the freak idea as long as that physiological source was active. On the other hand I should not have the means to stop the physiological after-effects of that real experience: I had to sidetrack it and to secure thus a reduction. I decided therefore to work on the basis of that hypothesis, to accept that physiological complex as existing, but to switch it off by linking it with appropriate associations, thus setting it right in the whole system of her thoughts.

For that purpose I brought her into a hypnoid state, bending her head backwards and speaking to her with slow voice until I saw that a slight drowsy state was reached. In this state I asked her to think back as vividly as she could of that experience of her youth, to fancy herself meeting that pretty girl, her neighbor, once more. She is to imagine that she speaks with her. Now I make her talk with me and she assures me that she sees the scene distinctly. She believes she sees the girl on the street. I ask her to tell the girl how indignant she feels over her behavior; she is to tell her that she understands now all which she did not understand in her childhood, that she knows now that she must

have lived an immoral life; that she must have had a friend
and that a pure girl like herself could never under any
circumstances come into such a situation, that no pure girl
could suddenly have a child. She is to express to the other
girl her deepest disapproval of such conduct and her own
feeling of happiness that anything like that could never happen to her. In accordance with my demands, she worked
herself entirely into the scene: without using audible voice,
she internally spoke with great vividness to her neighbor. When I awoke her from her drowsy state, she was
quite exhausted from the excitement. I repeated that scene
with her four times. She assured me that she felt it every
time more dramatically. The power of the obsession weakened from the first day. After the fourth time, it had disappeared. The subcortical complex had evidently found its
normal channels of discharge.

In discussing this method of side-tracking the complex, we mentioned that in other cases the result is
reached by bringing the memory of that first experience to a vivid motor discharge, without substituting
any other ideas. For that purpose no direct personal
influence is necessary. Treatment might just as well
be performed " by correspondence," provided that the
right starting point is discovered and that right suggestions are given. As an illustration, I may choose a
case which shows at least the maximum distance treatment by mail, from Boston to Seattle. This particular case presented no difficulty in getting hold of the
starting point as my correspondent, whom I have
never seen, himself at once pointed to the original
source of his obsessing idea.

The patient who lived with his family in Seattle wrote to me the following: " ———— I shall undertake to describe in a few words a condition which the writer has fought against for about eight years and which has subjected him to untold mental anguish. ———— I was backward in a social way but altogether happy. After working in a bank about a year, was discovered one evening by the cashier smoking a cigar in the basement, was unable to look him in the face at the time. Went home that night and thought very little about it, but on the following morning during the regular course of business, I stepped up to him to ask some question, and as usual, unconsciously looked him in the face. His glance was questioning and suspicious, and that was the beginning of a life of anguish for me. At first I could not look him in the eyes, then when looking at some other person, I happened to think of it and so on, until in two or three days it was impossible to look at anyone who came to my window. The cashier did everything he could for me. No use: I quit my position, lost most of my friends, had to leave a happy home and came to Seattle to work for an old school friend. In the first year, owing to new environments, I managed to conceal my mental condition to a certain degree. All of a sudden, I was again plunged into the depths of black despair. It took me about two years to (partially) forget it, when the same thing occurred again, and I lost my grip. The last time about eighteen months ago was almost more than I could stand. These three or four instances I speak of were cases of extreme despondency, but my usual mental condition is extremely unhappy. If occasions arise where I have to sit and talk to anyone for ten minutes, controlling myself is such an effort that it leaves me with a case of the blues. . . . I shall come and see you as the relief would give me a new lease on life."

This letter was written on the twenty-third of January, 1908. I replied to him at once that he certainly ought not to come from the Pacific to the Atlantic, but that I wanted him to write to me much more about that first occurrence. As he was evidently right in considering that episode as the starting point of his troublesome associations, I supposed that these associated ideas had not yet become independent but were still the effect of that first " complex." Therefore I wanted to bring that to complete discharge. Accordingly I wrote him to think himself once more into that happening of years ago, to pass through it with all the power of his imagination, to describe it to me then in as full a statement as possible and to express in the letter also his conviction that there was no reason to avoid the eyes of his superior, that he might have looked straight into his face. As soon as he got my reply, he wrote to me on the sixth of February a description of that first episode, filling nineteen pages, telling me all about his relations to those various men and every minute detail was brought clearly to consciousness again. I did not add anything further, but the expected occurred. On the eighteenth of February, he writes to me: " In the last week or ten days, the writer has noted a decided improvement regarding mental condition. The result is a new interest in life. If you can spare the time, would like to have you write me a few lines. Gratefully yours." At the end of the month he writes: " Received your letter about half an hour ago. Hasten to assure you with a great deal of pleasure that I am feeling much better. Since sending you the letter regarding the first case, I have noticed day by day an improvement." On the eighth of March: " Since writing you last I have noticed a gradual improvement. It has given me wonderful encouragement." On the tenth of March: " Just a line to say that I am still improving." On the twelfth of April: "I desire to say that since the taking up of treatment with you, life has had a far different appearance to me than it has had for the last ten years." On the twenty-first of April: "Since my first letter to you, there has been such an improvement that I have accepted a position which carries with it much responsibility."

This case leads over to the large group in which the obsessing idea involves the relation to a particular person. I find in such cases autosuggestion more liberating than heterosuggestion if the development has not gone too far. Of course autosuggestion can never take hypnotic character, but makes use with profit of the transition state before normal sleep. The type of these cases which are everywhere about us may be indicated by the following letter.

The writer is a young woman of twenty-four, whom I did not know personally. She wrote to me as follows: "I am a writer by profession and during the last year and a half have been connected with a leading magazine. In my work, I was constantly associated with one man, the managing editor. This man exerted a very peculiar influence over me. With everyone else connected with the magazine, I was my natural self and at ease, but the minute this man came into the room, I became an entirely different person, timid, nervous, and awkward, always placing myself and my work in a bad light. But under this man's influence, I did a great deal of literary work, my own and his too. I felt that he willed me to do it. The effect of this influence was that I suffered constantly from deep fits of depression almost amounting to melancholia. This lasted until last fall, when I felt that I should lose my mind if I stayed under his influence any longer. So I resigned my position and broke away. Then I felt like a person who, having a drug to stimulate him to do a certain amount of work, has that drug suddenly taken away, and without it I am unable to write at all. . . ." I wrote to the young lady that she could cure herself without hypnotism and without my personal participation. I urged her simply to speak to herself early in the morning and especially in the evening before going to sleep, and to say to herself that the man had never helped her at her work, but that she did it entirely of her own power, and that he had never had any influence on it, and that she can write splendidly since she has left the place, and much better than before. A few months later, she came to Cambridge and thanked me for the complete success which the auto-suggestive treatment had secured. She was completely herself again and was fully successful in filling a literary position in which she had to write the editorials, the book reviews, the dramatic criticisms, and the social news. As a matter of course, such treatment had removed only the symptom. The oversuggestible constitution had not been and could not be changed. Thus it was not surprising that in the meantime, while her full literary strength had come back, she had developed some entirely different symptoms of bodily character which I had to remove by hypnotism.

As soon as the obsessing idea of the influence of another person takes still a stronger hold and develops systems, the suspicion of insanity always lies near; especially when hallucinations are superadded, the probability is great that we then have to do with the delusions of a paranoiac, and thus no case for psychotherapeutic treatment. Yet it is always wise to keep a psychasthenic interpretation in view as long as the insanity is not evident. I may mention such an extreme case.

The patient, a man of middle age, highly educated, for years had heard voices calling his name. A man with whom he had some personal quarrel, had, as he believed, hypnotized him from a distance and made him act queerly or do things which he really did not want to do, by telepathic influence. It is a development which is found quite frequently. Abnormal organic sensations or abnormal impulses and inhibitions which the patient cannot account for by his own motives become connected with some vague ideas which are in the air, like wireless telegraphy or telepathy or hypnotism from a distance or electrical influence, or magnetism or telephoning, these then attached to an acquaintance who stands in a certain emotional relation. Here, too, some organic sensations evidently had been the starting point and the idea of the man with whom he quarreled had been secondarily attached. From this starting point more and more detail was reached. Every action was brought into connection with the powerful enemy who controlled more and more even the normal and reasonable doings of the patient. My first impression was decidedly that of a paranoiac. Yet in some ways the case suggested another view. There had remained an insight into the unreality of the obsession. The patient did not really believe the theory of the telepathic hypnotic influence. He felt it more as an idea which he could not get rid of and he did not know clearly himself whether he requested hypnotic treatment on my part for the purpose of counteracting the hypnotic power of his enemy or for the purpose of liberating him from his exasperating fixed idea. Moreover, I found that his voices had no hallucinatory character, but were merely sound images. I decided to make the experiment without great hope of success.

I hypnotized the man deeply and suggested that no one
can have power over his actions, that he is the responsible
originator of everything that he does and that no one can
influence him and that from that hour he would feel free
from any telepathic intrigue. The effect of the very insistent and urgently repeated hypnotic suggestion during the
first rather long treatment was such a surprisingly good one
that I decided to continue the psychotherapeutic cure. I
hypnotized him daily for two weeks. The belief in the
real wrong doings of an enemy disappeared entirely from
the first. It was at once apprehended as a mere obsessing
idea in the own mind and this idea itself began to be resolved. It lost its unity; the absurd impulses were still felt
but they became less and less connected with the idea of
another man, and as soon as they were rightly understood
as doings of the own mind, the opposite motives gained in
strength. A stronger and stronger appeal to his own power
made these motives more and more influential. Slowly the
association of the influence of the other man faded away
entirely. I intentionally had not given any attention to the
pseudo-voices, inasmuch as they had not taken any relation
to the ideational delusion. I therefore did not include them
in my suggestions, as I consider it wise to confine hypnotic
suggestions always to as few points as possible. Yet these
voices decreased too. At a certain point in the cure I substituted—to save my own time—an autosuggestive influence,
or rather a mixed one, inasmuch as I had him read ten times
a day a letter of mine which contained appropriate suggestions. After about six weeks, all the disturbances for which
he had sought my advice had disappeared.

Obsessing ideas of such personal influence involve
of course always a certain amount of emotional ex-

citement and they may lead us to the unlimited field of disturbances in which the persecuting idea is surrounded by emotional attitudes. Analysis shows easily that the emotion is an essential factor and that it persists in the disease while the ideas to which it clings may change. Central is the emotion of fear; nearest to it that of worry, but any emotion may give color to the particular case. Again any number of methods may be applied and a few illustrations with quite different ways of treatment may indicate more fully the character of the trouble. There is no doctor in the city and none in the remotest village who may not find such cases in his near neighborhood. Of course slight degrees are easily hidden by the patient's own inhibition of external expression. If such suppression by the own will secures a real overcoming of the unjustified emotion, this is surely better than to begin any medical treatment. But as the suppression usually means simply lack of discharge and thus offers all the conditions for an unhealthy inner growth of the trouble, the neglect of such disturbances is most regrettable, and frankness of the patient must be encouraged. Such situation demands a careful observation of the whole case and a subtle adjustment of the treatment to the individual needs. It may perhaps be helpful at first simply to indicate the varieties of the more frequent disturbances of this kind by quoting from various letters. Each case belongs to a type which can easily be removed by psychotherapeutic influence, generally even by a skillfully directed autosuggestion.

The writer is a young man.

"I have always, as long as I can remember, been very nervous and sensitive. When about seven years of age, I was attacked by St. Vitus' Dance. Before that I cannot say whether I was particularly nervous or not. Afterward it was impressed upon me by the remarks of relatives that I was nervous, so that I soon took note of this condition myself. The manner in which this weakness has been especially troublesome is that it has caused me to be very shy. I shrank from new acquaintances and disliked being observed. Often in walking along on the street, I imagined myself closely noticed by the passerby and I always felt uncomfortable.

About three years ago I suffered from typhoid fever and after recovering, a new form of the old trouble showed itself. This time I imagined that when eating I chewed my food in a manner that was ridiculous and which made people hardly keep from laughter in observing me. Often I had to leave the table when half through because I felt I could not bear having critical eyes upon me any longer. About three months ago I determined to be troubled no further by my own foolish fancies and by constantly schooling myself I have improved very much. Still, however, when I walk alone along the street, I must fortify myself mentally before passing each group of people. If once I allow myself to think that they are looking at me, I feel almost paralyzed, my feet seem too heavy to lift, my arms do not seem to swing naturally, and in attempting to look placid and unconcerned, I feel that I am failing utterly. Also when at table, I must still tell myself before each mouthful that I have no need for fear, that my manner at table is equal and perhaps superior to the others beside me. I have gone a certain length in my self-training, and have relieved myself of a great deal of the mental distress, but now I believe

I can advance no further. What seems needful now is to do away with the self-consciousness which brought on my worries, though whether this is possible is hard to say."

Here the letter of a young woman, the type which fills the army of the mind healers and faith curists.

" For years I have been seeking, or perhaps to be more accurate I should say waiting, for a mind to drift toward me; a mind that would understand my particular case of fear brought on by the constant bullying and nagging from my earliest childhood by those in my home. This fear of brutality has greatly depleted my nervous system and has unfitted me for the strong, useful, forceful life I should have expressed. If I could only rid my mind of the thought that I am always displeasing, or rather going to displease people, for I hardly do displease them; if I could get rid of the fear of caring what the attitude of other minds toward me is, I feel that I should then strike out into a strong life of helpfulness to others. In other words I have always felt behind me a great force pressing me out into public work. When I was a child, it was so strong that I was sat down upon brutally, to so great an extent that I feared to voice my convictions and that fear still clings to me like a neme-sis. It seems that every individual personality in a public or private audience rises up to overwhelm me, causing my tongue to grow heavy and my mind to become a blank. This enervating fear blends into every thought I have, whether sleeping or waking. I have fought with all my might to rid myself of it but so far in vain."

Here an expression of a very frequent variety. The writer is a middle-aged man.

"I am possessed of a fear that is constantly with me that something dreadful is going to happen and I do not seem to be able to overcome it. I am told by physicians that I am bodily sound, although very nervous, and that the fear is generated entirely by autosuggestion. When at its worst, it weakens and terrorizes me and in my better moments I am tormented with a fear of a recurrence of a bad spell. It is fear of a fear. A year ago at this time I had a very bad spell but got along fairly well through the summer, but I am afraid that I will soon again be in a bad condition and lose all that I may have gained."

The " fear of a fear " is indeed a symptom which the psychotherapist has to fight extremely often, but as soon as he has really recognized it and analyzed the whole mental condition, he will hardly have any difficulty in uprooting it. I add a letter of a school-teacher in New York. He writes:

"I am teaching in a high school. I am of a nervous temperament and constitutionally limited in endurance. Often my work is done in a condition of greater or less exhaustion. I find that I blush very easily in purely freak-ish ways, when there is no occasion for it. I find this blushing connecting itself with certain of the girl pupils of my classes in a conspicuous way. It occurs hardly ever except when my class is facing me and I seem to be powerless to overcome it. I have always tried to live a careful moral life, but my early life was very much secluded. I lacked entirely the free intercourse young people usually have together and I felt awkward with others for a long time. In the matter of the blushing, it sometimes occurs in the case of girls who are especially pleasing to me but also not infrequently in the case of some who are not at all so. The whole thing might be passed over were it not that it has considerable effect in causing constraint toward my students and in some cases affecting them very strongly in an emotional way at the very time of life when such things can do most harm. I regard the matter as being so serious that it brings directly in question my right to teach, but I do not feel at all sure I could find other work that I could do if I give up my present position. The very thought that on a particular occasion it would be extremely awkward to blush makes it almost impossible for me to avoid it."

But we have rather now to consider the therapeutic side, and we may begin again with a routine method of a simple hypnotic treatment.

The patient is a young university professor. His intellectual work is perfect in all directions. There are no nervous symptoms, though there are some slight disturbances of digestion. He suffers as soon as he comes into a crowd of people and as soon as he is on any high place, where he has to look down; the worst when both conditions are combined, as for instance, at a concert or a theatre in a balcony seat. But every meeting of many persons, even at church, produces all the symptoms of nervous excitement. He was easily brought into hypnotic state by verbal suggestions. When he was in hypnosis, I reënforced the conditions for an opposite attitude. I told him that as soon as he was in a crowd of persons he would feel especially comfortable, would enjoy himself, would fully enter into the spirit of the occasion and feel especially secure in their presence. Whenever he should be on a high place, he would enjoy the safety of the ground on which he was standing or the seat on which he was sitting. I assured him that he would neglect entirely whatever he saw and would rely completely on his safe feeling resulting from his tactual impressions. After having hypnotized him three times the disturbance disappeared completely, and even an evening at the theatre in an exposed box on the balcony was enjoyed without any discomfort. After about a year, at a period of fatiguing work, some traces of the anxiety appeared again. This time two hypnotic sittings were sufficient to remove the disturbance of the equilibrium, which as far as I know has not come back. The same hypnotic treatments were used in a secondary way to remove the digestive trouble.

I again quote the case of a teacher, a profession in which the psychasthenics are unusually frequent. It is a case of a young woman from the Middle West.

The young lady wrote me: "I come of a race of strong women and am not hysterical or easily frightened by many things that disturb women. Since my fifteenth year I have been seized by hallucinations of absurd or serious nature which no reasoning could explain away and which have gradually undermined my power of resistance to them. At the age of twenty-two, after a year of unusually hard work, my nervous endurance gave way, and with this breakdown came a sense of fear and a horror of crime that I have been unable to overcome. I have never felt the slightest inclination toward wrongdoing. It is a feeling rather that my shrinking from any mention of evil makes it impossible for me to listen or think rationally when such things are discussed. This feeling has seemed to change my whole attitude toward life and has left me without power to control my facial expression or carriage when it takes possession of me. I have been able to teach more successfully than I could hope, but it is only by cutting myself off from the friendships and pleasures incident to my life that I am able to accomplish my work. I have fought this trouble alone and will still do so if there is no help, but the thought that it is the source of great distress to those dear to me makes it very hard."

A few weeks later the lady insisted on coming to Cambridge. I found that there had never been any hallucinations and that she used the word in her letter only to indicate some insistent memory images which had never taken the vividness of real impressions. In the presence of her friend, I hypnotized her deeply and strengthened through urgent suggestions her consciousness of her having done the morally right thing at every situation in her life and her conviction that she never did and never would commit a crime. Here as always, if possible, I left alone the emotional idea but reënforced the opposite. The effect was an immediate one. She felt freer the next day than she had felt for years. I repeated the treatment a few times and she assured me that the feeling had disappeared entirely.

I take the rather severe case of a woman of fifty.

The highly educated and refined lady had lost her husband by an accident in Switzerland, which had been misrepresented by some of the newspapers as suicide. Two years later she wrote to me: " I feel as if I had received indelible photographs on my brain which have since greatly affected my health and from which I may never recover. This winter the symptoms I have been able to control returned and I have been ill. I unfortunately saw the newspaper headlines with my husband's supposed suicide. Though I exclaimed then, ' how outrageous,' I felt as if I had been struck and since then I can seldom read a paper without dread and apprehension, and the hearing of anyone's suicide fills me with terror. When I hurried to Europe, on the ocean a week from the day of my husband's death, I had a curious and overwhelming shock. On opening a drawer and seeing a pair of scissors, they looked to me like a dagger and suddenly the whole cabin seemed filled with implements of death. The doctors said that I would find it hard to get over such impressions but I told them I would, as I had courage and will. But I have been realizing in these two years that I may be suffering from something that may be beyond the control of will. I often become so nervously sensitive that scissors are unbearable for me to see, or a steel knife or anything that might express death. Our family physicians are still against hypnotism, and if I should go to a neurologist of my own selection, it might be to one who believed still only in nerve foods, baths, or a sanitarium."

The lady came from the South, with her nurse, to Boston and insisted on being hypnotized by me. I cannot say whether a really deep hypnotic state was produced at once as I refrained from testing it. There was certainly no amnesia. Probably it began only with a slight drowsiness but at the fifth treatment I found a relatively deep hypnosis. It was a capricious case in which the improvement was fluctuating but clearly setting in from the first day. I trained her in hearing and seeing words like death and suicide with a reënforced feeling of strength and calmness; I forced her to see and touch scissors with an artificial attitude of strength and indifference. At the same time I reënforced her good mood and her enjoyment in life. When she left for England a few weeks later, she felt herself mentally cured, and throughout the summer her letters testified the wonderful change which the treatment had brought about. Half a year later, as the result of an exhausting physical local treatment, the psychophysiological symptoms came back to a certain degree. She requested me by a letter from England to give her some help by suggestion to suppress again the recurring intrusions. As I had observed her strong suggestibility, I sent her over the ocean a little pencil of mother-of-pearl which she had seen in my hand, and advised her to look at it until she counted twenty slowly and then to close her eyes and simply to sleep. The autosuggestive effect was unusually strong. She writes from London: " When I saw the enclosure of your letter I felt as if it would burn through my hand and the feeling became so overpowering that I locked it away with my jewels, but as the days ran into a week I felt I could not live with it in my apartment any more, and I felt almost ill, until it occurred to me I could seal it and take it to my bankers. I felt as dreamy and absent-minded and paralyzed as if you had just treated me." Nevertheless the effect was on the whole the desired one and she returned to America with a wholesome freedom of mind. I hypnotized her twice again and she writes in her last letter: " I can never repay you for what you have done for me. You have given me back my courage and my love of life in its vividness and interest and color, all that through the last years I had so entirely lost."

Even in cases where the disease itself is inaccessible to psychotherapeutic treatment, the superadded grief and worry brought on by the disease might yield to the mental influence and the whole situation would to a high degree be transformed for the better by it. I have often been asked to hypnotize in such cases, where the depression was wrongly taken as a part of the nervous disease; sometimes I agreed to do it in spite of feeling sure that the disease itself could not be removed. I quote an instance.

A young woman afflicted with epilepsy was brought up in the belief that she had only from time to time fainting attacks from overwork, and with them secondarily neurasthenic symptoms, especially spells of depression colored by a constant fear of the next fainting. She had heard voices all her life and they frightened her in an intolerable way. I produced a very slight hypnotic state. I concentrated my effort entirely on suggestions which were to give her new interest in life, and diminished the emotional character of the voices without even trying to make them disappear. I proceeded for several months. The young woman herself believed that the fainting attacks came less frequently afterwards; yet I am inclined to think that that is an illusion. But there was no doubt that her whole personality became almost a different one with the new share in the world. The epilepsy remained probably unchanged but all the superadded emotions were annihilated and she felt an entirely new courage which allowed her to control herself between her regular attacks. She had been unable to undertake any regular work before for a long while, but all that improved. More than a year afterward, she wrote me: " I have really worked most of the time this past winter and spring and I think I can see a steady though slow gain. I am reading quite a little and doing it for the most part easily. To be sure I have, after I have read, hard times with the voices but their character is usually less determined and fearful than formerly. Several times I have thought I must come again to you but each time I have started again to fight it out for myself, but now, as I am gaining, I can better estimate the great help your influence was to me at a juncture when everything seemed so hopeless and helpless."

Even in slight psychasthenic disturbances, the psychotherapeutic influence is not always successful, especially if there is no time for full treatment. But it is very interesting to see how even in such cases the symptom is somehow changing, almost breaking to pieces. It becomes clear that a protracted effort in the same direction would destroy the trouble completely. Typical is a case like the following.

An elderly woman has been troubled her life long by a disproportionate fear of thunderstorms with almost hysterical symptoms. As she had no other complaint, I hardly found it worth while to enter into a systematic treatment and could not expect much of a change from a short treatment, considering that her hysteric response had lasted through half a century. As she begged for some treatment, I brought her into a drowsy state and told her that she would in future enjoy the thunderstorms as noble expressions of nature. The whole procedure took a few minutes. Yet after some summer months she wrote me a letter which clearly indicated this characteristic compromise between the habitual dread and the reënforced counter idea. "I have the same sick dread at the sight of thunder clouds that I have always had, but I seem to have gotten somehow a most desperate determination to control my fear. I have done this to the extent of keeping my eyes open and looking at the storm. Is that hypnotism or pride?"

Another thunderstorm case may lead us to other methods of treatment. Here again in the field of emotional response, we may consider the methods of going back to primary experience, known or forgotten.

A young married woman of the West had suffered always from hysterical attacks in response to any sharp sudden impressions, especially sudden loud noises. The banging of a door, but worst of all a thunderstorm, could produce hours of weeping and crying and desperate mental condition with all expressions of excitement. Her husband wanted me to hypnotize her but I preferred another way. I tried to get her memory back to the earliest case of which she could think of this hysterical response. As long as we were in ordinary conversation, she could not trace it beyond about her twelfth year. But when I brought her into a drowsy state, her memory revived older experiences and finally settled at a school experience in her seventh year of age. She then had an excitable country school-teacher who relied on whipping the children. Once her neighbor in the class did something forbidden. Her teacher mistook her for the culprit and began to whip her most· forcibly before she could explain anything; and while the punishment was going on and she began to bleed from a wound, she all the time felt that she wanted to express her innocence and could not speak. After that, evidently the first attack of hysteric character followed. From that time on any sudden impression released the same group of reactions. The suppressed emotion had evidently become a psychophysical " complex." As soon as I had reached this starting point of her pathological history, I asked her to bring back to consciousness as many details as possible of that first incident. She told me all the names and described the classroom and brought herself vividly into the whole situation.

Then I asked her to tell me the whole story once more and to express strongly her innocence and the wrongness of the punishment, and when she had completed her account, brought out with fullest indignation, I had her tell the whole thing once more and then a third and a fourth time, until she was quite tired out from it. That was all I did. ·Very soon after, the husband reported that there was a great improvement in every respect, no hysteric attacks, only slight discomfort. Most of the stimuli which had previously produced strong reactions now passed without any disturbance and even thunderstorms were experienced with relative ease. A year later they came once more to Cambridge, and she simply passed once more through the same process of discharge which seems now to have removed the symptoms still further.

By far more reliable, however, is the method of side-tracking the starting experience into a new associational track.

A gentleman with a decidedly psychasthenic constitution developed a tendency to hesitate in walking on the street. It was not a complete stumbling but a disturbing inhibition, which set in when he was walking alone and his attention was not absorbed by something on the street. He believed that it came on most strongly when he looked down at the pavement. He suffered from it vehemently and avoided going on the street alone. He was unable to connect it with any starting point. He interpreted it as merely a symptom of overwork. But going with him through all kinds of experiences which he had had on the street in previous years, we finally found that once he was running to catch a street car, when he suddenly saw almost immediately before him a big hole dug out for laying gas pipes. He was able to stop himself quickly enough not to fall into the hole but he got a strong emotional shock from the experience. He, himself, did not think that his walking troubles set in immediately after this shock. Yet the hypothesis seemed to me sufficiently justified that there existed a connection, even though some weeks lay between that first experience and the first observation of the abnormal inhibition in walking. On that basis I tried to train a new associative connection. I made him drowsy and asked him to think himself once more into the situation of his run for the car but as soon as he reached the hole to jump over it. He went through this motor feature on ten successive days with new and ever new energy and from that time up to the present the trouble on the street has disappeared entirely.

To mention at least one case of the large group in which suppressed sexual emotion was the evident source of an anxiety-neurosis, I mention the case of a woman who showed very strong symptoms of anxiety and oppression and who was cured by a simple advice.

The woman, aged thirty-two, was a saleswoman in a large store selling gentlemen's gloves and ties. She suffered from time to time by attacks of vague anxiety in which her heart showed vehement palpitation. There were paleness and perspiration and at the height a nervous trembling together with a feeling of despair. These attacks were not frequent, separated sometimes by weeks, sometimes by months, but troubling her exceedingly. She had been assured by a physician that her heart was normal and that she was probably overworked. She could find absolutely no source of the disturbance. After a long conversation, I was also unable to discover any direct or indirect causes until I worked on the basis of those theories which we have discussed, the theories which connect hysteric symptoms with chance intrusions which stand in relations to past suppressed emotions of sexual character. The patient absolutely denied any present sexual emotions. She had been engaged about eight years before and acknowledged that at that time there were strong sexual feelings connected with her fiancé, who broke the engagement. Psychoanalytic methods now brought it to full clearness that she had her first attack after selling a pair of gloves and fitting them to the hand of a male customer who had a certain similarity to her fiancé. It was not possible to trace this in the same way for later cases too, but it seems that bodily contact with a man by fitting gloves preceded every attack. All this was brought out partly by questions, partly by free ascending associations while she, herself, believed that she simply pronounced nonsense words as they came to her mind, and partly it was secured in a half-hypnotic state. I came to the conclusion that the suppressed sexual emotions at the breaking of the engagement were the primary cause of the disease. The similarity of the first customer together with the tactual sensations had evidently touched that complex and brought the suppressed emotion to an explosion which frequently takes the form of palpitation and similar symptoms. Later the mere tactual sensation alone produced by the contact with the hand of a man, possibly with a similar optical impression, perhaps also with the sound of the voice, brought back the reaction. Instead of giving treatment, I insisted that she change stores, and become saleswoman in a house where she would have to do only with women, and to sell articles which did not bring her into personal contact with customers. After more than six months of work in her new place, she reported that the attacks had not come back again.

Of course it may readily be acknowledged that this method does not allow a sharp demarcation line between its various factors. It cannot be denied that an element of straight suggestion may be included. The man whom I train in the forming of a new antagonistic motor response feels it of course all the time also as a silent suggestion to overcome the old disturbance. It is thus to a certain degree impossible to say where the effect of the discharge ends and where that of the hidden suggestion begins. Yet there certainly cannot be any doubt that this revival of the first experience and its improved discharge works directly towards the removal of the troublesome symptom.

Abnormal fear is also the essential factor in most cases of stammering. The patients usually know it themselves. For instance, a lawyer writes to me:

"I have been a stammerer the greater part of my life and have visited every stammering school in the country, but the relief obtained has been temporary and in most cases I was not benefited at all. I am convinced that stammering is due wholly to an abnormal mental condition, which consists of an unreasoning fear that takes possession of the individual when he attempts to utter certain sounds. It is simply a lack of confidence inspired by numberless failures to articulate properly and is not caused by any organic trouble, because, taking my own case for example, I can at times talk as fluently and easily as anyone. I am firmly convinced that stammering can be cured by hypnotic suggestion. If you could get me in the hypnotic state and suggest to me repeatedly that from thenceforth I would have easy fluent speech, I feel absolutely certain that such would be the case."

Or an engineer writes to me:

"At times I stammer very badly. In an ordinary conversation it is scarcely perceptible, but it is almost impossible for me to make an explanation or relate an incident or tell an anecdote. I began to stammer when I was about seven years of age—I am twenty-nine now—and continued until I was seventeen, when I broke myself of it by reading aloud. It came back on me about a year ago, at which time I was laboring under a very severe nervous strain on account of business matters. I have since tried to break myself of it in the way that I did at first, reading aloud, but have been unable to do so. Can it be cured by hypnotic treatment or suggestion? Can any hypnotist of ordinary ability do it?"

I should affirm this question, which is one of the most frequent put to the psychotherapist. And yet, if I myself have entirely given up the cure of stammerers in recent years, it was not only because there was little chance to learn anything new scientifically from it but also because it was ultimately disappointing, as the severe cases cannot be cured entirely. Every hypnotist can quickly secure a strong improvement. In even new cases I found an almost surprising improvement in the first two weeks, an improvement which stirs up the most vivid hopes of the sufferers. Then the improvement becomes slower and finally it stops before a complete cure is reached. The patient notices it and it easily works back on his emotion and thus begins again to disturb the speech, unless a very careful continuous counter-suggestion is given. Slight disturbances, to be sure, can be removed entirely. The essential point will always be to suggest to the stammerer the full belief that he is able to speak every word and that he is able to speak it in every situation. But where there is a limit for improvement, we must take for granted that the disturbing fear is only superadded to an organic trouble. In such cases, probably the inability of certain nervous paths was primarily irreparable. These inabilities then became the source of discomfort and of fear and this fear added greatly to the disturbance. Hypnotism then quickly removes that part of the disturbance which had been superadded by the mental emotion but it cannot remove that primary factor, the objective inability, and every cure thus finds its limit there.

Near the field of emotions stand also the many varieties of sexual abnormities and perversities. I abstain from discussing any special cases but it may be said that suggestive treatment is in this region powerful to an almost surprising degree. Even homosexual tendencies which go back to the beginnings of the memory of the individual yield, as my experience shows, in a few weeks, if again the suggestion is not so much directed towards the suppression as to the creation of the antagonistic reaction, that means in this case, of the normal sexual desire.

Both ideas and emotions, of course, lead to actions. Moreover we always insisted that the resulting action is an essential part of the psychophysical situation and that every mental experience has to be characterized as a starting point for action. Yet this factor of activity and of attitude sometimes stands in the foreground. The controlling idea is then the idea of an end of action, the predominant emotion, the emotion anticipated from a certain activity. Typical for that are those disturbances in which an abnormal impulse or an abnormal desire awakes perhaps a desire for ruinous drugs like morphine or cocaine or an impulse to criminal deeds, like stealing. But the disturbances of the psychomotor factor are not less present when the central complaint is a lack of energy, the most frequent symptom of the neurasthenic; and our whole discussion has made it clear that a mere lack of attention belongs to the same category.

Of course, the abnormal impulse is psychophysically not different, whether it leads to a legally important result like the impulse to kill or leads to an indifferent result. The subjective suffering may be the same in both cases. The starting point of the impulse may be any chance experience. The psychasthenic may pick up such impulses from any model for imitation or from any haphazard report. It may be entirely freakish and yet beyond conscious control.

A physician had read in a well-known book on hysteria about a case in which a girl was troubled by a constant effort to move the big toe in her shoes. This idea worked on him as a suggestion for several months. At my advice he fought it by auto-suggestion. He brought himself into a slightly drowsy state by staring into a crystal ball and assuring himself by spoken sentences with monotonous repetition for a long while that he has perfectly the power to hold the toe at rest. From the second day only a slight kinæsthetic sensation remained; the movement itself disappeared.

Or a more unusual case.

A young lady once noticed in a man a different color in the two eyes. It gave her an uncanny feeling, together with the natural impulse to compare the two eyes. Accordingly she shifted her own eyes from one eyeball to the other in the man's face. The accent which this shifting impulse had received by the disagreeable feeling evidently forced her to repeat this movement with everyone. At first it became half a play, but soon a disturbing habit and finally an intolerable impulse. Whenever she talked with anyone, she lost control of her eyes and was obliged to enter into a kind of pendulum movement from eye to eye. The situation became so unendurable that the thought of suicide began to occur to her. I hypnotized her four times, suggesting to her complete indifference as to the face of those with whom she spoke and at the same time certain new habits of fixation. The impulse lost its hold and when I saw her last, it had completely disappeared.

By far more frequent than such neutral impulses are the desires, for instance, of the alcoholist. On the whole it may be said that psychotherapy can gain its easiest triumphs in the field of alcoholism and a wide propagation of psychotherapeutic methods and of a thorough understanding of psychotherapy would be fully justified, even if no other field were accessible but that of the desire for alcoholic intemperance. The moral disaster and economic ruin resulting from alcoholic intemperance, the physical harm to the drinker and to his offspring is so enormous, and the temporary cure of the victim is so probable that the movement certainly deserves most serious interest. Yet I speak of temporary cure and I refer here especially to the restriction with which I introduced the psychotherapeutic methods in general. They do not deal with diseases but with symptoms; and they certainly do not deal with constitutions, but with results of the coöperation of constitution and circumstances. That the given constitution may be brought anew under conditions which again stir up similar symptoms is always possible, and just with alcoholism the danger lies near unless beneficial influences remain in power. Certainly no one has a right to neglect such psychotherapeutic aid simply because relapses are possible. Even a temporary relief can be a great blessing. Moreover, the temporary relief is the safest basis to work towards the prevention of a recurrence of the evil. Only in two directions is further restriction needed. Psychotherapeutic methods are in my opinion of very small avail in cases of periodic drinkers. Such periodic attacks of patients who have not even a desire for alcohol in intervals between the attacks, intervals which may last a quarter of a year, are related to epilepsy. It seems that constant hypnotic influence during the interval has a certain power to reduce the periodic impulse. I personally have not seen any special improvement from it. The second restriction would be that the drinker has to be under constant supervision during the first days of hypnotic treatment. No patient, not even the morphinist, is so skillful in deceiving his friends and even the physician. Even the most emphatic gestures of sincerity ought to be distrusted.

Only a short time ago I dealt with a young man whom his parents and a chauffeur had accompanied to Boston, exclusively for the purpose of watching him constantly while I was to attempt to cure him from excessive whiskey drinking. The chauffeur accompanied him from his room in the Boston hotel to the threshold of my laboratory. All through the day he was with his parents, and at the hotel the management had given the strictest orders not to sell any drink to the young spendthrift. He was an earlier student of mine and had attached himself to me with such an apparent sincerity as removed every possible doubt of his pledge. Intentionally I had not even asked him for a pledge not to drink but only for a pledge to confess to me the next day if he ever should take any alcohol. In a tentative way I suggested to him in a half hypnotic state on the first day that he would feel disgust for whiskey. I did not expect much of an improvement before at least three or four treatments. I was therefore most surprised when he most solemnly assured me the next day that he awoke in the morning with an assured feeling that he should never touch whiskey again and that he had not the slightest desire for it. Instead of a systematic development of suggestions, I confined myself therefore to a mere repetition of the treatment of the first day and as every morning the same assurance came forth, there seemed to be no need for any variation. It was not before the fifth day that I discovered that he had taken from the start a pint of whiskey every day. When he first arrived he had bribed a laundress of the hotel to bring to his room every day the whiskey hidden in the laundry and he drank it during the night. Then I declined any further participation.

The danger of deceit is of course less imminent when not the family but the patient himself takes the initiative. Yet even here distrust is wise. The patient has sometimes the most sincere intention to be cured, but under pressure of his craving he admits compromises which he hides from the physician. Having reduced the large quantity of alcohol to which he was accustomed, he hides the fact that he yet takes a few drinks, which he thinks cannot prevent the cure. Yet inasmuch as a complete cure has to rely on psychical factors, this consciousness of deceiving even with small transgressions interferes badly with progress and, inasmuch as the cunningness of the patient is itself a symptom of the disturbance, the strongest possible precaution is advisable at the beginning. For that reason it is also not best to begin at once with complete prohibition, but to lead to a total abstinence in about one week. But certainly in the case of every drunkard, total abstinence is the only desirable goal. A pronounced drinker ought never to be transformed simply into a moderate one. The return to intemperance would result rapidly. On the other hand it would be unfair to deny that psychotherapy has cured the symptom if the desire really once disappeared completely, even if, after years, new temptations develop a new desire. I myself had diphtheria three times in my life; my constitution is thus probably especially favorable to that disease but I do not estimate less the fact that I was perfectly cured the second time, in spite of the fact that I caught it a few years later a third time. To be sure, such experiences of relapse cannot be spared any psychotherapist. I may give a typical instance.

A well-known professional man of fifty years, through a long bachelorhood, was accustomed to close his work at four o'clock and then to sit comfortably in his study with a book and an unlimited supply of brandy. He took one cognac after another and every evening he was completely intoxicated. He married a young wife and felt the need of changing his habits, the more as he himself saw symptoms of his excess which alarmed him. When he came to me, I saw that he was seriously wishing to give up, and he understood himself that there was only the one way, namely, complete abstinence. He felt that he could not reach it by his own will power alone and sought my aid. I hypnotized him six times, suggesting at first a reduction to four drinks, then to two, then to one and then to pure mineral water. I concentrated my effort on stirring up the antagonistic attitude, the dislike of the smell of brandy and the aversion to its taste. The effect was excellent. After the fifth time the mental torture which he had felt in the first afternoons had completely disappeared. I considered further hypnotizing superfluous and felt sure after the sixth time that the man was cured. For about a year he remained abstinent, but in the meantime his professional life brought severe disappointments, and with cool consideration he decided that he might have at least some pleasure from life and forget its miseries. Accordingly after a year he determined again to take some brandy in his study, and of course, that led rapidly to an increase of the dose and today he is probably at the old point. And yet it may be said with correctness that psychotherapy had done its duty. If at the right moment before he took the first step again, even the slightest countersuggestion had been applied, the disastrous second development could have been easily avoided.

My experience indicates the best results where the suggestions are from the start directed as much against the unfavorable social conditions, with their temptations and impulses to imitation, as against the alcoholic beverages themselves. On the whole it is easier to break the vicious drinking habits of the social drinker than those of the lonely drinker, a point which ought to be well considered in settling the complex problem of prohibition versus the temperance movement.

The situation of alcoholism repeats itself in still more ruinous forms with morphinism and cocainism, vices which grow in this country to an alarming degree. The psychotherapeutic treatment of such drug habits demands much patience and much skillful adjustment to the psychological conditions. Its general difference from the treatment of alcoholism is given by the circumstance that any too rapid withdrawing of the drug is certainly dangerous, if the organism is adjusted to a relatively strong dose. On the other hand, I may say that I have not seen a single case in which a really patient and insistent treatment of morphinism has not been successful, even if the destructive dose of forty grains a day had become habitual. The condition is only that the patient himself have the best will, a will which yet is not strong enough to win the fight without psychotherapeutic help. But no one ought to expect that the psychotherapist can secure miracles like some of the pill cures which treat the drug fiend in three days. Moreover neither physician nor patient ought to believe that the worst is to come at the beginning. On the contrary, it is the end which is hardest, the reduction of the small dose to nothing. As illustration, I give an extreme case.

A man who was formerly station master on a railroad had been operated on in a hospital after an accident, and as some pain in the hip remained which disturbed his sleep, the physician of the hospital gave him some morphine and provided him with the material for morphine injection after leaving the hospital. Then began the usual story. He became more and more dependent upon his injection, the dose was steadily increased, he found unscrupulous physicians who yielded to his demand for morphine prescriptions; he lost his position with the railway by the growing effects of the morphine poisoning, he became divorced, sank lower and lower, his daily dose fluctuating between thirty-five and forty grains a day, and when he came to me, he presented a picture of the lowest type of hopeless manhood. He spent practically the whole day in bed and was only able to totter slowly along with a cane. He assured me that life was hell for him. He could not sleep, he could not eat, he could not think, he had made up his mind to commit suicide if I could not help him. I foresaw that it would in the best case demand months of insistent energy to make a man out of that unfortunate wreck. He had gone through three different morphine cures in three sanitariums and none had helped him, and every physician whom he had consulted had declared his case as beyond any physical cure. I decided to make the somewhat disproportionate sacrifice of time in order to study whether even such an extreme case of morphinism is accessible to psychotherapeutic treatment. Four months later, he left my laboratory looking like an athlete, strong and vigorous, joyful and energetic. For three weeks he had not received any morphine, had good appetite, slept well, and had happily married. As his wife was a trained nurse, she will take good care that no new slip shall ever occur.

There was nothing remarkable in those four months of treatment. He was easily hypnotized, and I hypnotized him at first every day, then every second day, then every week. It was without difficulty that I reduced the forty grains to about six grains a day. Then the struggle began. To test the case as a strictly psychological problem I left the effort entirely to his own will, that is, I did not deprive him of the morphine supply but left the regulation in his own hands. During that whole winter he had a bottle with a thousand morphine tablets standing on his desk. Thus he would have been entirely able to satisfy any craving, but by his own will he followed my suggestions and never took more than I permitted. It meant a terrible struggle. The tortures which he had to pass through were perhaps worse than those which he had experienced at the time of his lowest downfall. They came to a focus when he tried to go from five grains to three grains a day and then again when he approached half a grain. From there he had to move to a fourth of a grain, then to an eighth, and even that had still to be divided into four different doses which were then reduced to three, to two, and finally to one dose and ultimately to injections of warm water. A rapid increase in general strength and a return of appetite for food began when he had reached the five grain limit. I did not allow on any occasion the introduction of a substitute. On the other hand, I added every day suggestions covering the various secondary symptoms, especially the pains in the stomach and the feelings of faintness and the emotional depression.

There is no doubt that under favorable conditions, especially if the dose of morphine is not too strong, autosuggestion can bring about a similar effect. A reduction of ten per cent. every week can be carried through, if a pledge is given to one's self in a drowsy state. The great value of autosuggestion showed itself not seldom in the fact that morphinists who had applied to me by mail for a cure in the mistaken belief that I do work in a professional way for payment and who got from me a written reply that I could not receive them, but that they can help themselves, wrote to me that my letter gave them strength to reduce their dose considerably.

Quite similar is the situation with cocainism or with the combination of morphine and cocaine which is so frequent nowadays with young physicians. I have repeatedly seen cures where the case already gave the impression of insanity. Again I give a rather extreme case.

A physician had acquired the habit of using and misusing cocaine for the treatment of a disease of his nose. The habit grew to a craving for cocaine while the cocaine itself poisoned the brain. Acoustical hallucinations began; he heard voices from every corner of the room, and on the street the voices took persecutory character. He connected them with his brother living in Europe, heard his voice in the denunciations, and developed a pathological system of ideas around the central thought that his brother had a telepathic influence on him. His reason succumbed, he lost all consciousness of delusion, and believed himself really to be under the control of the absent brother. When he came to me he had been without sleep and without food for several days, and he was not seeking my help to get rid of the mental disturbance but to overcome the power of his older brother. He did not connect the fear at all with his misuse of cocaine. When I discovered the rôle which the cocaine played, I determined to try the suggestive influence, the more as I found that he was in a half-hypnotic state as soon as he had entered my room. I suggested to him to sleep and to take food and to reduce the cocaine dose by a fourth. The next day he was an entirely different man by the effect of ten hours' sleep and a large breakfast. Now I concentrated my efforts on the reduction of the cocaine. After ten days of hypnotic treatment he gave up cocaine entirely, after three weeks the voices disappeared and slowly the other symptoms faded away. The pathological idea of the telepathic influence lasted a while after the voices had gone until this idea, too, yielded to suggestion. It still took six weeks before he himself felt that he was entirely normal.

The way in which the average physician nowadays neglects the simple tool of suggestive treatment, when it can be used for the protection of society, is perhaps nowhere so reckless as in the case of the morphinist and cocainist. To give a typical case of this neglect I may mention that of a highly intelligent young man who had been in the habit of using both cocaine and morphine for ten years when at his own request he was sent to a New York hospital. He had been taking alternately morphine for a year or two, then cocaine for a year or two, and had sometimes alternated and sometimes combined both in an irregular way. When he entered the hospital in May, 1908, he was in a cocaine period and was taking the enormous dose of one hundred and eighty grains of cocaine every day. In the hospital they withdrew the drug altogether. During the first weeks, he was entirely sleepless. They energetically refused him any substitutes and after six weeks he began to feel comfortable. He gained steadily in weight and after three months, when he left, he had gained fifty pounds, felt entirely comfortable, and seemed in all respects normal again. Before twelve hours had passed after leaving the hospital, he had again taken thirty grains of cocaine and ten grains of morphine, and this dose rapidly grew until after a few weeks it again reached a hundred grains of cocaine and up to sixty grains of morphine a day. Then came the complete breakdown. If that man in the last two or three weeks of the hospital treatment, when he felt entirely comfortable and normal and had gained his normal weight, had received even a slight suggestive treatment suppressing any desire for cocaine or morphine, he would easily have been saved. To let such a man after a drug career of ten years go out again to the places of his old associations, where the desire had to be stirred up, is inexcusable at a time when psychotherapeutics has won its triumphs in this field. It might have been sufficient to give him preventive treatment at least for the first three days of his freedom. And such a case is typical of hundreds.

The overstrong impulse and overstrong desire finds its counterpart in the abnormal lack of energy and lack of attention. The patient—and it is especially the neurasthenic patient—has lost his usual strength, he shrinks from every undertaking, he cannot decide upon any action, he needs a disproportionate effort for the smallest task, and cannot concentrate his attention in spite of his best will. The varieties of this lack of power and inertia are familiar to every physician. They certainly often need much more than merely psychotherapeutic treatment, although on the physical side no schematic method is admissible. The laziness of the anæmic needs a different treatment from the laziness of the exhausted but in every case psychological factors can be of decisive influence, whatever the physical and chemical treatment besides them may be. A few letters may again illustrate the varieties. Here again there is no sharp demarcation line between the normal and the abnormal. Letters like the two following, for instance, are hardly letters of patients. They show a variation which is still entirely within normal limits and yet a source of suffering; it is a disturbance which usually can be removed by psychotherapeutic means.

"I do almost everything with effort, nothing spontaneously. I have been writing for five years but am a mood writer of the worst type. The mood comes at such uncertain times that I seem to be absolutely at the mercy of caprice. This might not in itself be a misfortune but writing is my only calling and I suffer the proverbial torments of lost spirits when I am idle. The necessity of driving myself to every piece of work, aggravated by the fact that my parents allowed my constitutional inertness to have full play, has hitherto prevented me from forming any regular habit of labor. I am now thirty-eight. Would you suppose that if I kept my nose to the grindstone for one, two or three years, I might yet hope to work with some ease and regularity? That is, if I compelled myself to write a certain number of hours every day as a discipline, regardless of the quality of matter I produce, is there any probability that I might ultimately overcome the fearful paralysis that so often grips my faculties? Can constitutional indolence be overcome by determination? I put in a little time on a couch every day. When worried I get neurasthenia and all kinds of phobias. Just now I am afraid to look at the newspapers on account of the cholera in St. Petersburg, and I have seen the time when I found it difficult to drink water after I had boiled it myself."

Also the next man is familiar to all of us.

"Plainly we are told every man is born into the world to fill some purpose, or at least be of some benefit to himself or his fellowmen. For some reason I do not make friends among men. I have not the zeal or ambition to carry or even begin a conversation that will interest the individual man. I worry a great deal. I have never been able to concentrate my mind to study and figure out problems. I can read them zealously but apparently do not get to the bottom and cannot retain what I do read. If I could just get hold of the power of thinking and dig out that tangible something that holds me back, I could go forward and make myself what I know I should be. But I feel that so far I am a total failure. If I only had that one great gift, the power of concentration and will power, I would make what I so much desire, a success of myself."

A similar effect and yet psychologically a different condition exists where the lack of energy results from the suggestive power of the opposite, producing a constant indecision.

" I am thirty years old and nearly all my life since childhood I have been fearfully troubled with the habit of indecision and regretting whatever I do. It has grown into a habit so fixed that at times I am fearful of losing my mind. I feel anxious to do something and decide to do it, then as soon as it is done, I nearly go wild with regrets until I have to undo it, if possible, and then only to regret that. I am this way about the most trifling things and about the most serious. I can't perform any duty well. In business and in social affairs, it is always with me. It has me in its clutches, a horrible monster dragging me down. My friends misinterpret me and wonder what I mean by doing so when all the time I want to do what is for the best and cannot for this tyrant who is ever present with me. I will plod for hours and hours at a time, and at every turn I am handicapped. I am intelligent naturally and appear a perfect fool."

From the report of such chronic cases we may turn to the acute ones. Here a characteristic letter of a typical neurasthenic young modern poet.

"These are my plans but I hardly think that I can carry them through, although perhaps you can help me by suggestion. I have the feeling that through the whole of last year my development did not go forward but backward. It is as if by a mental or physical overstrain, my whole personality has entered into a transition. I have no joy in life, no sensation in love, no satisfaction in labor. My will has become weak where it was strong. I am lazy, up to an absolute dislike of everything, while I have been energy itself. Often I have only the one desire, to end my life from mere fatigue. If there had been any external reason for ending my life, I should perhaps have done it long ago. I am so apathetic that I no longer take myself seriously. My successes do not please me; the idea of writing anything gives me anxiety. I have become less resisting, more sweet, more soft, I should almost like to say, more feminine. I became infatuated with a girl, simply because I knew that she hates all men. The inaccessible is still the only thing which can stimulate me somewhat. I have even written a poem on her, but nothing can satisfy me in love. I consider my state a disease of the will as a result of nervous exhaustion. I must find some one who, with kindly power, reënforces my will system. I need a strong mind— it may be a man or a woman. It would even be possible in the latter case that I might marry her.

Even the writing of this letter has fatigued me so much that I should like best to sleep. In moments like the present I should like best to throw myself down on the street or . . . quickly . . . sink . . . into the ocean. (I regret having made the little points. They look as if my expressions are a pose.) Yet there are moods in which I am entirely normal and no one fancies what I am passing through. I have even become superstitious lately. Are there perhaps beings which can absorb our energy? Perhaps another being has drunk up my energy."

Authors run easily into such states. Here is another.

"I am a neurasthenic, and I am beginning to believe, a professional one. My object in writing is to ask concerning the advisability of my visiting you for treatment. I am ready to take the next train if you say the word, if you believe you can help me. It seems that the regular practitioner, who is very irregular, cannot. If there is one good doctor I have not consulted, I would like to know his name. I was doing editorial work in X and broke down. Still the doctor said that if I liked my work, I should go back to it and pitch in. I did. It lasted a few days and then I had to give up altogether, couldn't grind out another word. Then to another doctor ———— also the best in the city. He told me to give up all work, which I did, and then I went on a farm for six months. That did not help me either. Later I went west and spent some time in the mountains. I felt no better there. Then I went to Arizona and lived in a tent out on the desert; that did not help me. There was always a sensation of exhaustion and any physical exertion put me on my back, even when it was light and pleasant exercise. Then I went to California; it did me little good. It is a perfect paradise for anyone who has not got neurasthenia. I still have not got myself in hand. I cannot do or say or write just what I wish, and cannot concentrate my thoughts. To try to read a book is punishment because I forget as fast as I read." And so on.

I answered him certainly not to come but tried to induce some autosuggestions. A few weeks later, he wrote me: "Ever since you wrote me, I am now feeling somewhat improved." Yet I cannot judge how far the improvement belonged to the psychical factor only, inasmuch as I had advised him also to take some bromides. The really effective treatment would have been heterosuggestion and I had no time to enter into the case.

Where direct suggestion is used, the effect is often surprising.

A young lawyer after a period of overwork had come to a state of complete lack of energy. He could not find strength to write a letter and he came to me at a day when he did not see any way but suicide open for himself. He complained that, as soon as he began to grasp a thought, it was evaporating. He stared absently about the room and felt sure that he would never again achieve anything. He had not even the energy to read the newspaper. I hypnotized him three times, each time waking in him the pleasure in a definite piece of work, at first simply in a novel which he was to read, then in some letters which he was to write, and then in his professional work. There was always an interval of three days. The fourth time he declared himself that the hypnotic influence was unnecessary, as he felt that he was again in the midst of his work.

As a rule the effect is a much slower one, but if all personal factors are well considered and especially physical disturbances are excluded, the result is usually satisfactory.

Very different from such neurasthenics, of course, is the lack of attention in the feeble-minded, and suggestion of the ordinary type is hardly advisable, but it is surprising how much can be reached by a systematic psychical régime. I give one typical instance, representative of many.

A boy of twelve years when he was brought to me showed the mental powers of a stupid child of four. In a silly way he repeated every question which he heard without answering it; he talked steadily to himself in a nonsensical manner, mostly repeating nursery rhymes without end, never holding his attention to anything in the room, giving the impression that there was no attention whatever. The boy was a child of rich parents; he had his own teachers, but was for a large part of the year under the influence of the parents only, who very naturally yielded to every desire of the unfortunate child. I insisted on a complete change of the education. It was my effort to build up the mind by a rigorous training and by development of the power of inhibition. I absolutely forbade any meaningless material like the nursery rhymes, insisted that the child should never be allowed to talk to himself, and whenever he began to speak to himself he was to be addressed sharply, and if he yet went on, to be slapped on his hands. In the same way he was not allowed to repeat a question, but the question was repeated until he answered it, the question always formulated in simple words. He was forced to go through simple reading and writing without being allowed to make his silly diversions. His whole life was brought under strict discipline and no parental indulgence was permitted. Six months later the child was completely changed. It seemed as if he had gone through an improvement of three years. I regulated the whole of his elementary studies in accordance with the successful principle. The training of inhibition stood in the foreground and every haphazard reaction was severely rebuked. The summer vacations spent with the parents in the fashionable surroundings, to be sure, had always a retarding influence, but the main part of the year in which it was possible to carry through the strict discipline showed such steady and inspiring progress that the boy, while of course feeble-minded for life, can yet live externally a harmonious life.

'A systematic training of the power of inhibition is indeed the fundamental factor in all psychotherapeutic treatment when the disturbance is in the volitional sphere, but the inhibition is secured most safely by reënforcement of the antagonistic attitude. From these volitional variations on the one side, from the ideational disturbances on the other, only a few steps lead to those dissociations of the personality which are characteristic of many graver cases of hysteria. But to give to them any adequate analysis, it would be insufficient to refer in this brief way to particular cases. Psychopathological literature possesses some excellent analyses of such complex disturbances. As I said before, I abstain entirely here from such complex phenomena, as they enter too seldom into the sphere of the practitioner and as the bewildering manifoldness of their symptoms does not allow us so easily to recognize the fundamental principles which alone were to be illustrated by our short survey of practical cases.

XI

THE BODILY SYMPTOMS

THE discussion of the bodily symptoms which may yield to psychotherapeutic treatment, naturally forms only a short appendix to our discussion of the mental symptoms. Our interest was from the beginning essentially a psychological one. I shall have to be the more brief as my personal experience in the treatment of bodily diseases through mental therapy is entirely secondary and accidental. The psychological laboratory would, of course, be an entirely unfit place to struggle with diseases of which the chief symptoms are not psychophysical. Yet in spite of frequent testimonies of well-known physicians to the contrary, I am still inclined to think that this is also the situation at large. I think that in medicine in general the psychophysical effect of mental treatment is by far more important and by far more extended than the healing effect on diseased peripheral organs. Of course these peripheral parts of the body may be favorably influenced in an indirect way by the mental treatment; we shall have to take notice of this important result but that is strictly not a therapeutic effect on the bodily symptoms. Moreover, purely

psychical effects may give an impression as if the
bodily symptom itself has been removed.

To begin with the latter case, it is especially the inhibition of pain which easily makes one believe that a
bodily disturbance is successfully treated. I have
repeatedly seen cases in which I tried by suggestion
to soften the pain resulting from a peripheral disturbance like inflammations, rheumatism, decayed teeth
and so on. The effect was often such a total disappearance of the pain that the patient himself was inclined to believe that the objective disease had been
ended, while in reality the state of the diseased organ
was not changed at all. It has often happened that
I tried to cure a person of certain mental symptoms
by suggestion, ignoring entirely the existence of some
pain resulting from a bodily disease with which I
had nothing to do. Yet the suggestion of improvement seemed almost to irradiate and the pain disappeared in spite of having been ignored by the
hypnotizer. For instance, I treated a woman who
suffered from psychasthenic obsessions, fearing all
the time that something would happen to her child.
I did not give any direct attention to the fact that
she had had for years a painful disease of the bladder
for which she was constantly treated by a specialist.
But while I did not mention the bladder in my hypnotic suggestion, yet the abdominal pain disappeared
together with the obsession and the situation might
easily have suggested that the bladder trouble was a
nervous one which had been cured by the hypnotic
sleep. The fact was that the bladder disease was

not influenced by the mental treatment at all, and needed a continuation of the same local treatment. It was only the psychophysical pain in the brain which had been inhibited.

Quite parallel to the disappearance of the organic pain sensation is the arising of a general feeling of improvement. This organic sensation of general betterment may again be a strictly mental occurrence without any objective reference to a real improvement in the bodily conditions. Yet again that easily gives the impression of an important change in the bodily conditions themselves. The miraculous cures of various diseases through mystic agencies generally belong to this category. There is no doubt that often the migrating charlatans who advertise themselves by a free treatment of the sick and invalids on the theater stage of small towns, produce momentary effects which are sufficient to deceive. The quack handles the diseased organ, perhaps a goiter or a leg crippled by rheumatism, with a cruel rudeness and overwhelms the suggestible mind so completely that the first autosuggestion is that of a complete change, and that means cure. The disastrous results follow later. But from such barbarisms we come by gradual steps to the suggestion of improvement where the feeling of betterment can be in itself an important factor for the cure. Yet even there we must not mistake the possible secondary effect of a mental change from a psychotherapeutic cure of the bodily disease.

Not seldom the removal of physical disability

seems secured as soon as certain mental disturbances
are removed. There is no reason to believe for instance that suggestion can have an important influence on a diseased sense organ, and yet hypnotic influence and even autosuggestive influence can under
certain circumstances greatly improve seeing and
hearing. Especially in the field of hearing the central factor is of enormous importance. Hyperæmic
and anæmic conditions in the brain centers of hearing
control the vividness of the received sound. The
patient who cannot hear a certain watch more than
one foot distant may be able to hear it after some
glasses of wine at a distance of three or four feet.
Thus it is only natural that a hypnotic influence can
produce similar changes on the psychophysical centers in such cases in which the source of the trouble is
a psychophysical laziness in the acoustical center.
Sometimes even this laziness itself is the result of
psychical autosuggestion which can be fought by
countersuggestion. I saw, for instance, a distinct
improvement in hearing in the case of a young
woman who had increasing deafness while the aurists
declared that the ears were in proper condition. I
found that she lived with a father who suffered from
a severe middle-ear catarrh and that she was simply
controlled by a hidden fear that she might have inherited the ear disease of her father. I removed
this fear, partly by reasoning, partly by suggestion,
and partly by tricks which surprised her, for instance,
making her hear her watch with unaccustomed
strength when she took it between her teeth and

closed both ears. The autosuggestive fear was up-
rooted by these and the central ear organs slowly
came to normal functioning.

The purely psychical character is still more evident in the frequent hysterical anæsthesias. No one
doubts that here the sensations are inhibited only
and that the mental influence removes this inhibition
without any influence on the sense organs proper.
Frequently also organic troubles like stomach diseases
appear cured when in reality hysterical disturbances
are at the bottom. The stomach may be sensitive to
any pressure and may produce severe pains and vomiting on taking any food and everything may indicate a serious local disturbance. Yet hypnotic
treatment may quickly remove the symptoms because
the whole reaction may have resulted from the
shock which perhaps a too hot piece of potato caused.
The removal of this mental starting point results in
a cure of the apparent stomach disease. Again in
other cases, the appearance of a physical cure is given
by the creation of psychophysical substitutes. I do
not believe that hypnotism or suggestive treatment
can influence the brain parts which have suffered
from a hemorrhage. Yet the paralysis of the arm,
for instance, which resulted from such a breaking of
a blood-vessel in the brain may be to a high degree
repaired by building up new motor images in the
psychophysical system, which become starting points
for a new learning of movements. The patient did
not understand how to make the most out of those
motor paths which had been left. The destruction

of the chief channels of discharge had inhibited in his mind the idea of possible movement. He no longer believes that he can move and it needs new suggestions to overcome this inhibition. The curative effect on bodily disabilities is thus often an illusory one.

That does not mean that the field in which psychotherapeutics may work directly on the body is not after all a large and interesting one. Theoretically it is still little open to real understanding. The explanation has essentially to rest on the acceptance of a given physiological apparatus. A certain psychophysical excitement produces by existing nerve connections a certain effect, for instance, on the bloodvessels or on the glands of a certain region, or on a certain lower nervous center. That such apparatus exists, the physiological experiment with persons who are hypnotized to a high degree can easily demonstrate. Their nose bleeds at a command; a blister may arise on a part of the skin which is simply covered with a penny, when the suggestion is given that the penny is glowing hot. With some subjects, the pulse can become slower and quicker in accordance with the suggestion; with some even the bodily temperature can change on order. Our understanding of these indubitable facts indeed does not go further than the acknowledgment that the paths for such central connections exist. That means we simply describe the facts once more in the terms of anatomy. But after all in the same way we rely on the nervous connections, if a thought makes us blush and ultimately if our will moves our arm or if our ideas move our speech apparatus. We do not choose the muscles of our arm, we hardly know them; we know still less in speaking, of the movements of our vocal cords, and in blushing of the dilated blood-vessels. That ideas work on the lower centers of our central nervous system, centers which regulate the actions of our muscles and blood-vessels and glands, must simply be accepted as the machinery of our physiological theory. The connection of such theories with purely physical facts is given by the experience that an electrical stimulation of the nerve may have the same influence as ideas. The electric current, too, can regulate the beat of the heart, or contract and dilate the vessels, or reënforce and relax the contraction of the muscles, or strengthen and weaken the functions of the glands.

Nearest to the psychophysical processes stands the bodily symptom of insomnia. There is no doubt possible that the work of the psychotherapist can be very beneficial in producing sleep by suggestion. That autosuggestions for sleep play an important rôle is popularly accepted. Next to the most immediate means such as lying down, or cutting off sense stimuli, or trying not to think, or avoiding movements, certainly the most well known factor is the expectation of sleep with the belief that sleep will come. This belief may be reënforced to strong autosuggestion which may then overcome other factors that hinder sleep. For instance, I have repeatedly received letters from strangers containing expressions of gratitude with news which under other circumstances would at least not flatter an author. They wrote to me that immediately after reading one or another essay of mine on hypnotism, they fell into deep sleep. Yet as they were always patients who had suffered from insomnia, I was pleased with this unintended effect of my writings. But in most cases a real cure demands heterosuggestion.

There is room for any variety of effects; often they enter immediately. The other day I gave sleep suggestion to a young woman who had overworked herself in literary production. For months she had not slept more than three or four hours a night and even that only after taking narcotics. I intentionally did not allow her to come into a hypnotic sleep but kept her fully awake, increasing her suggestibility while her eyes were wide open. I suggested to her to take a walk, then to eat her dinner, and after that to go to bed at once. She went to bed at seven o'clock and slept without waking until ten o'clock the next morning, and after fifteen hours' sleep she was like a different being. A regular eight hour sleep is sometimes secured, even where no immediate direction has been given for it. On the other hand, I cannot deny that I have sometimes been entirely unsuccessful in securing better sleep by the first three hypnotic treatments. When the first three treatments were unsuccessful, I always gave it up on account of lack of time. Yet the experience of others shows that in such cases, often after a long continued hypnotic treatment insomnia yields to suggestion.

One of the great factors which work against the mental treatment is the habit of so many sufferers of relying on their sleeping powders which, to be sure, remain effective only by increasing the dose and thus finally by making them dangerous. Every chemical narcotic has in itself suggestive power and strengthens the belief of the sleep-seeker that he cannot find rest without his dose. To overcome the monopoly of the opiates is one of the most important functions of psychotherapy.

It is not surprising that the relations of psychotherapy to sleep show such a great variety. The factors which coöperate in normal sleep are many and the disturbance can have very different character. We had to speak of the psychophysics of sleep when we discussed the theoretical relation of sleep to hypnotism and insisted that it is misleading to consider hypnosis simply as partial sleep. We claimed a fundamental difference between the selective inhibition in hypnotism and the general reduction of functions in sleep. To understand sleep, we have to recognize it as one of the fundamental instincts, comparable with the instinct for food or for sexual satisfaction. Every one of such instincts has a circular character. Mental processes, subcortical processes, and physical effects are involved in such a way that each reënforces the others. The physical effect of the sleep instinct, comparable with the pepsin secretion in the food instinct, or with the hyperæmia of the sexual organs in the sexual instinct, is a change in the cortex by which the sensory and motor brain centers are put out of action. What kind of a change that is, is quite indifferent. It may be a chemical one but more probably it is a circulatory one. Let us say it is a contraction of blood-vessels which by the resulting anæmia makes the sensory centers unfit for perception and the motor centers unfit for action. In this way the brain becomes protected by sleep against the demands of the surroundings. The mental reactions are eliminated and the central nervous substance has an opportunity to build itself up. This protective physical activity is now evidently itself controlled by a subcortical center, just as secretion and sexual hyperæmia are controlled. This center probably lies in the medulla oblongata.

Some theorists, to be sure, are inclined to think that the fatigued brain cells enter directly through their exhaustion into the protective sleep state. But that simplifies the situation too much. It is quite true, as these theorists claim, that monotonous stimulation of the senses produces sleep. But it is evident that the sleep occurs even then not only in the particular overtired brain cells. A monotonous stimulation of the acoustical center raises the threshold of perception for all the senses and brings sleep to the whole brain. This control of the whole apparatus is thus surely regulated by one definite center. But this lower center, which controls the anæmia of the cortex, is itself directly dependent again upon a mental condition, the mental experience of fatigue. The fatigue sensation, which is possibly the result of toxic processes, works on that lower sleep center, just as the appetizing impression or the sensual images work on the centers of the other two instincts. On the other hand this protective blood-vessel contraction creates again as in the other cases a characteristic organic sensation, the sensation of rest which arises when the threshold of perception and activity is raised. The world begins to appear dim and far away, no impulse for action excites us. This organic feeling of rest associates itself with the fatigue feeling. The fatigue sensation, the subcortical sleep center, the contraction of the vessels in the cortex, and finally the rest sensation form together the complete circle. The difficulty which arises in this case lies only in the fact that the cortex gone to sleep annihilates also, of course, the fatigue sensation and the rest sensation. For that reason the real circle can appear only in the preparatory stages of sleep. As soon as sleep itself sets in, the circle is broken. The circle character of every instinct must lead the physical effect upward to a higher and higher degree. Not to become excessive, the physical effect must be checked somehow. In all other spheres, it finds its end in satisfaction, for instance, by eating or by the sexual act. In sleep the circular process ends automatically by its own effect as soon as complete sleep is reached. Its causes, the fatigue and the rest feeling, are stopped, as soon as the effect, the anæmia, is secured.

We see now how widely different starting points can lead to sleep and can understand from it how widely different disturbances can prevent sleep.

Sleep must result when fatigue is coming, but sleep must also result when the elements of the rest feeling are produced, and as we saw that the components of the rest feeling were the sensations of decreased sensitiveness and decreased activity, sleep must result when either the sensations and associations are absent and actions are suppressed, or when monotonous sensations and automatic actions raise the threshold. Sleep must arise further if our will associates the mere idea of such rest, and finally physical or chemical means may produce a sleep bringing effect either on the lower center or on the bloodvessels and cells of the cortex. Correspondingly sleep may be prevented by disturbances in any one of these spheres. There may be no normal fatigue, there may be no fatigue sensation, there may be no rest feeling on account of perceptions, or on account of associations, or on account of impulses to action; there may be no normal response in the sub-cortical center, there may be no physical effect in the cortex on account of an existing hyperæmia or on account of an abnormal condition of the cells. The psychotherapeutic treatment must carefully analyze which element would be fit to supply the last link in the circular chain. Sometimes we need the suggestion of fatigue, sometimes the inhibition of ideas, sometimes the suppression of impulses, sometimes the suggestion of rest, and so on. A mere general suggestion of sleep is on the whole effective only in the cases of those persons in whom this idea in itself awakens those various components. Very often it is entirely ineffective in this general form. Sometimes it is possible to carry the hypnotic state itself directly over into sleep, but it seems more in the interest of the patient to separate those two states distinctly.

We are still confined to processes in the brain itself if we turn to headache. If it were only a question of inhibiting the pain by mental suggestion, the case would not be different from inhibiting the pain of a peripheral organ without attempting to cure the diseased organ itself. But in the case of headaches, it seems justified to claim that in certain varieties of this multifold symptom, not only the pain is suppressed but the disturbance itself is removed. Especially where the headache seems to result from hyperæmia, the trouble seems to be accessible to psychotherapeutics. On the other hand I have never seen any lasting effect on the so-called sick headache or migraine. While continuous headaches or headaches which occur daily yielded to my influence, sometimes completely, I was unable to prevent even by preparatory hypnotization any migraine which appears periodically, for instance, simultaneously with menstruation.

A few words only as to the general diseases and disturbances for which a very strong therapeutic effect has been claimed by masters of the craft like Wetterstrand, Moll, Dubois, and others. From my own experience I can affirm the often lasting effect in the disturbances of the functions of the digestive apparatus. The stomach and the intestines seem to a high degree under nervous influences which can be changed through hypnotic suggestion. If we consider what intimate connection exists between the functions of these organs and the normal emotions, it seems hardly surprising that mental factors can regulate their disturbances. Vomiting, diarrhea, and especially constipation, often yield to slight suggestions, even in a superficial hypnotic state. Here, too, I have seen repeatedly a complete regulation of a long-standing disturbance as an unintended by-product of hypnotic suggestion directed towards the cure of psychical troubles. Much value is claimed for hypnotic method in the treatment of anæmic conditions. It is said that anæmia improves after a few hypnotic treatments, the appetite becomes better, the cold hands and feet grow warmer, the headaches disappear, the capacity for work increases rapidly, and most surprising of all the leucorrhea ceases. As to heart disease, we ought to think in the first place of the disturbances of nervous innervation. I have seen repeatedly a remarkable decrease of nervous palpitation of the heart through direct mental influence, abstracting here from the secondary effect of suppressing mental excitement and fear. Where organic heart diseases are surely present, it seems that hypnotism can sometimes act beneficially if the heart trouble is accompanied by anæmia and general debility; of course a developed valvular disease cannot be removed. In the same way it seems that in Bright's disease, certain painful symptoms may be suppressed, but the kidneys certainly cannot be influenced. At

least open to serious suspicion are the insistent claims
that diabetes can be cured by suggestion. Dr. Quack-
enbos of New York, for instance, gives to some of
his diabetes patients a hypnotic suggestion by the following words: "If your pancreas be crippled in its
production of the natural ferment which is given off
to blood and lymph and which conditions the normal
condition of sugar in the body or restrains the out-
put of sugar from the liver tissues, you will see that it
forthwith pours into your blood or lymph the sufficient quantity of sugar oxidizing ferments." It
certainly transcends our present understanding if we
are to believe that a suggestion of this type will
change the action of the pancreas. It is hardly worth
while to enter into the still more extravagant claims
from other sides like those for curing cancer and
phthisis. On the other hand, in the light of all that
we have discussed, there is no difficulty in understanding the easily observable influence in the regulation of menstruation, in the cure of contractions, local
congestions, and incontinency of urine. I may mention finally the use of hypnotism for helping in a safe
and quick confinement.

But in addition to all this, we have the great help
which psychotherapy may bring indirectly in the
treatment of physical diseases. I said, for instance,
that I do not believe in a real help by mere suggestion
in cases of diabetes. But no one ought to underestimate the value which may result for the treatment
from a suggestion of a well-adapted diet. The patient who feels a craving for bread and potatoes and

perhaps sweets, and is too weak to resist it, is indeed brought into safety if suggestion liberates him from such desires. The same holds true for every other diet and for any medical régime of life which does not harmonize with the natural instincts of the patient. For not a few sufferers, reënforcement of the interdict against coffee and tea or alcohol and tobacco is more important than any medicine. Hypnotic suggestion can easily create dislike of the prohibited material and can build up new desires and inclinations. In the same way it is indirectly most important to stir up, for instance, the sensations and feelings of appetite and thus to make normal nutrition possible. Also in cases of anæmia or tuberculosis, such indirect assistance can produce some beneficial consequences.

The same holds true of the power of the psychotherapist to secure sleep. The fight against insomnia which we discussed referred only to that sleeplessness which is itself an expression of the disease. But as a matter of course, the loss of sleep can accompany most different diseases, as an almost accidental result. To secure sleep means then not to treat the symptoms of the disease but a by-product; and yet every physician knows how much is gained if the lost energies are restituted by a sound sleep. And finally we have the indirect help towards the cure by the suggestive removal of pain. We have no right to say that it is a pure advantage for the treatment of the disease if the pain is centrally inhibited. Pain surely has its great biological significance and is in itself to a certain degree helpful towards the cure, inasmuch as it indicates clearly the seat and character of the trouble and warns against the misuse of the damaged organ which needs rest and protection. To annihilate pain may mean to remove the warning signal and thus to increase the chance for an injury. If we had no pain, our body would be much more rapidly destroyed in the struggle for existence. But that does not contradict the other fact that pain is exhausting and that the fight against the pain decreases the resistance of the organism. As soon as the disease is well recognized through the medium of pain and the correct treatment is inaugurated, not only the subjective comfort of the patient but the objective interest of his cure makes a removal of pain most desirable. While it would be absurd to say that hypnotism can cure tuberculosis or cancer, it is fully justifiable to say that hypnotic treatment in tuberculosis or cancer is to a high degree beneficial, inasmuch as it can secure sleep, appetite, and freedom from pain, three factors which indirectly help to fight the disease. The elimination of pain may sometimes also play its rôle in slight operations where other methods of narcosis seem for any reason undesirable, and very frequently hypnotic suggestion has been used for this purpose at childbirth.

The same importance which belongs to the removal of bodily pain in the treatment of a peripheral disease may be given to its mental counterpart, to the worry, excitement, and emotional shock. They all stand in the way of a real success in any cure. Even the chances of a dangerous operation are entirely different for the patient who goes to it with free mind and a happy mood, with full confidence in its success, from those of a patient who has worked himself into a state of fear and anxiety. Here again the depression and the excitement are not in question as symptoms of a disease, as they were when we discussed the phobias and despondencies of the neurasthenic and of the hysteric. They are merely normal side-effects of the bodily disease, accentuated perhaps by a suggestible temperament. To eliminate all these emotions means to change most helpfully the whole atmosphere of the sick-room and to deprive invalidism of its saddest feature. This negative factor corresponds of course most directly to the positive feature of building up new hope and joyful expectation. He who creates confidence makes convalescence rapid and strengthens the power to overcome disease.

It would be medical narrowness if the physician were strictly to deny that the effect of such emotional change may sometimes lead far beyond the ordinary suggestive influences and that in this sense the miraculous really happens. When out of a despondent mood in a suggestible brain an absorbing emotion of confidence breaks through, a completely new equilibrium of the psychophysical system may indeed result. In such cases, improvements may set in which no sober physician can determine beforehand.

Central inhibitions which may have interfered a life long with the normal functioning of the organism may suddenly be broken down and in an entirely unexpected way the mental influence gives to the forces of the body a new chance to help themselves. The reasoning of the scientific physician may easily stand in the way there. He may be afraid of such overstrong emotion because he knows too well that such unregulated powers may just as well destroy the good as in another case the bad; in short, that ruin may result just as well as health. But that does not exclude the fact that indeed almost mysterious cures can be made without really contradicting the scientific theories. Such are the means by which the mystical cults earn their laurels. A chance letter of the type which often swells the mail of the psychologist may illustrate this effect. I choose it because it is evidently written by a skeptic. A short quotation from the lengthy epistle is sufficient.

" My condition was horrible in the extreme. I had consumption of the lungs and other supposedly fatal troubles, complicated by wrecked nerves. At the present writing, I am robust and splendidly healthy, looking twenty years younger than I did at the period previously described. The Christian Scientist saw my condition but appeared unconcerned and unafraid, I being absolutely hopeless, skeptical, and deeply contemptuous meanwhile. On the third day of her treatment I was desperate for sleep, she having forbidden drugs, and I deliberately took an overdose of chloral, thinking to die at once and end it. My condition justified the act. She brought me out of the coma of the chloral after three hours of mental work, and the next day I felt decidedly calmer and less afraid of the coming of night, should I live to meet it, which seemed doubtful. At noon she left me to go to her home to lunch. I was pondering seriously on her reiterated ' God is love and fills the universe and there is nothing beside Him,' when I suddenly had a sensation of being lifted up or rising slowly and becoming lighter in body. A rush of power that I have no way of describing to you filled me. I seemed to be a tremendous dynamo in the air several inches above the ground and still ascending. When I noticed everything around me becoming prismatic and more or less translucent, I could have walked on water without sinking, and I had distinct understanding that matters seemed to be disintegrating and dissolving around me. I was frightened but self-conscious and quiet. I remained in this state for about three hours, my consciousness seeming to have reached almost cosmic greatness. I could have cured, I felt, any human ill, was filled with an absorbing altruistic desire to help suffering. It was tremendous and totally foreign to my everyday attitude. At the end of the day, towards twilight, I became wearied of the tremendous throbbing and exalted state in which I still remained and gave utterance to the thought aloud. Almost before I had formulated it the condition left me, and like the sudden dropping of a weight, I struck the ground, the same dull, ordinary person of everyday experience, but with the vast difference of perfect health, radiant and lasting to the present writing. My father like myself is baffled and wondering. We are both pretty hard skeptics. I want the truth, whether it be terrible or otherwise. I am profoundly grateful to the Christian Scientist, if I regained my health through her ministrations, but I have not so far been able to label myself and rise in their church services to tell what has been done on me. The performance repels me as crude and rather bad taste. I swear to you on my honor as an American woman and a mother that what I have written you is true, absolutely. If you can give me any light or if my experience may perchance give you a helping ray, my renewed lease on life may have had some purpose after all, which I have often questioned in my cynical moods."

The unprejudiced psychotherapist will be perfectly able to find room for such cures and, if it is the duty of the scientific physician to make use of every natural energy in the interest of the patient's health, he has no right to neglect the overwhelming powers of the apparently mysterious states. Some of this power ought to irradiate from his eye and his voice whenever he crosses the threshold of a sickroom. Some of that power ought to emanate from him with every pill and drug which he prescribes. The psychotherapeutic energies which work for real health outside of the medical profession form a stream of vast power, but without solid bed and without dam. That stream when it overfloods will devastate its borders and destroy its bridges. The physicians are the engineers whose duty it is to direct that stream into safe channels, to distribute it so that it may work under control wherever it is needed, and to take care that its powerful energy is not lost for suffering mankind.

PART III

THE PLACE OF PSYCHOTHERAPY

XII

PSYCHOTHERAPY AND THE CHURCH

THE belief in supernatural energies has cured diseases at all times and among all peoples. Everywhere the patient sought help through the agents of higher forces and everywhere these agents themselves utilized their therapeutic success for strengthening the belief in their over-natural power. The psychologist would say that it was always the same story, the influence of suggestion on the imagination of those who suffer. Yet the variety of forms is abundant. Not only the special symbols but the whole attitude may take most varied character, and every special appearance is intimately related to the whole mystical background and to the religious, scientific, and social ideas of the time. If nevertheless, even at the same time in the same country, very different forms of religious suggestion are at work, it must not be forgotten that those who live together in any nation and are united in many common purposes represent after all different stages in the development of civilization. It has always been true that those whose minds are saturated with the real culture of their time are working together with those whose culture belongs to earlier centuries and with others whose minds are essentially of the type of the primitive peoples.

Let us glance at the life of the savages. In darkest Africa, we find a special caste with its professional secrets which accepts new members only after long tests. They are evidently persons with over-sensitive nervous systems and liable to hallucinations. As soon as they have their attacks of abnormal excitement, they are conceived to be agents of superhuman powers, and on account of this they are able to prescribe the cure of any diseases. In Australia, therapeutic power belongs to the koonkie, a man who as a child had a vision of a demonic god. From him he received the power to heal the sick. He goes to the patient, touches the painful parts and rubs them and after a few minutes, he shows a little piece of wood which he had hidden in his hand and which he claims to have extracted from the body of the sufferer. The native feels actually cured after such manipulation of the koonkie, who evidently believes himself in his power. In Siberia, we find shamanism. The shaman stands between man and the gods. These shamans are excitable persons with epileptic tendencies, or at least over-suggestible men or women who by autosuggestion and imitation can bring themselves into ecstatic convulsions. They alone know from the gods the means to treat diseases and their personal influence overcomes the ailment. In early America, before the European discovery, the cure of disease belonged in the same way to the middleman between the gods and human beings. In the Antilles, for instance, the bohuti heals the diseases which are regarded as punishments of the gods for human neglect. The priest by inhaling a certain powder brings himself into an ecstatic condition, then presses the painful organs of the patient, sucks at various parts of his body until he finally produces some little bone or piece of meat which until then he kept hidden in his mouth. The disease disappears, and the extracted bone is used as an amulet which secures good harvests. Other Indians had their piachas. They were selected from among the boys of about ten years old and were then sent to lonely forests where they had to live for years upon plants and water without any friends, seeing only at night the older priests from whom they learned the ceremonies for curing the sick. Here too their art consisted mostly in touching the painful parts of the body with the lips and sucking them to bring the evil saps out of the body by their supernatural power. In short, at the most primitive stages in Africa and Asia, in America and Australia, therapy was acknowledged to be a special power of men who had superhuman forces derived from good or evil gods.

All this repeats itself in the so-called half-civilizations. Among the masses of China, mental and bodily diseases were ascribed to the fox, which plays such a large part in the superstitions of eastern Asia. The priest has the power to banish the fox by mystical writings which he pastes on the wall of the sickroom, and the patient recovers, as the fox has to leave his body. In old Japan the mountain monks, who inherited their superhuman powers from a martyr of the fifth century, can remove the diseases which have magical origin or which are induced by the devil. They also supply the magical papers covered with writings and pictures of birds, to prevent the appearance of smallpox and pestilence and to cure a number of diseases. India, the classical land of suggestion and hypnosis, shows the most extensive connection between religious and magical powers among which the cure of diseases is only one feature. Such cure may be with medicaments or without, but the essential part always belongs to the prayers which make the good and evil spirits obedient to the healer. These prayers were often spoken in Sanscrit, which the people did not understand and which thus added to the mystic solemnity of the procedure. This suggestive influence of the use of older languages for religious solemnities, known only to the priests, repeats itself also at all times and among all nations. In Assyria and Babylonia, too, medicine was exclusively a branch of mysticism and essentially in the hands of the priests, who by words and magical beverages annihilated the influence of the malevolent demons. It is well known how the Old Testament reports the same traits of belief among the Jewish nation. We hear there that Miriam became leprous, white as snow, and Moses cried unto the Lord, saying: "Heal her now, oh God, I beseech thee." And after seven days Miriam was cured in consequence of Moses' prayer. And again, "The Lord sent fiery serpents among the people and they bit the people and much people of Israel died.—And Moses prayed for the people.—And Moses made a serpent of brass and put it upon a pole and it came to pass that if a serpent had bitten any man, when he beheld the serpent of brass, he lived."

Among the old Egyptians, it was especially Isis who discovered many remedies and had been much experienced in medicine, and after having become immortal, it was her greatest pleasure to cure the sick and to announce the right remedies in dreams to those who came to sleep in her temples. Many who could not be cured by any physician, and who had lost their sight and hearing or could not move their limbs, became well again when they took refuge in her temples. The same holds true for the Serapis temple; even the best known men go there to sleep to get from the goddess cures for themselves or for their friends. It is well known again that in other ways the old Greeks attached medical influence to temples and sacred springs and rivers and tombs. There were sacred springs which cured everybody who drank from them, there were statues which removed every disease when offerings were brought to them. Here again the most frequent is the cure of paralytic symptoms and of obsessions. The Orphic priests of old Greece most nearly resembled the shamans of the savages.

Those who are inclined to give to the life of Christ a rationalistic interpretation have often pointed out that the therapeutic effects described in the Gospels might also be understood as effects of suggestion by word and tactual impressions, produced especially on hysterics, epileptics, paralytics, and psychasthenics. Such rationalistic interpretations could also explain in the same way through the suggestive influence in the minds of the sick, those cures which Christ effected through others without being present himself. Here belongs perhaps the cure of the servant of the centurion in Capernaum or the cure of the daughter of the woman of Canaan. " And when he had called unto him his twelve disciples, he gave them power against unclean spirits to cast them out and to heal all manner of sickness and all manner of disease." The Acts give us the full details of how Peter and Paul cured the lame and how special miracles were performed by their hands. No doubt this belief in the curative effect of the disciples and their successors fills the first centuries after Christ. Eusebius tells us how they healed the sick by laying on of hands. The forms were frequently changing through the history of Christianity but the essence remains the same. Sometimes more emphasis is laid on the personal factor of the priest, sometimes more on the sacred origin of the symbol as in the case of the relics, sometimes more on prayer and godly works, but it is always the religious belief which cures. Typical are the therapeutic wonders of Francis de Assisi. He banishes devils, cures gout, lameness, and blindness. The traditional means of suggestion, prayer and the laying on of hands, had in the meantime been supplemented by the sign of the cross which the church had added. Moreover whatever he had only touched became a remedy for the sick. Protestantism brought no change in this respect. Martin Luther writes: " The physicians consider in the diseases only the natural causes from which a disease results and want to remove them by their medicines, and they are quite right in it. But they do not see that the devil often sends to one a disease which has no natural causes. Therefore there must exist a higher medicine, namely, the religious belief and the prayer through which the spiritual medicine can be found in the word of God."

The broad undercurrent of religious cures, especially in the Catholic Church and in the Greek Church, but with fewer symbols also outside of them, has up to the present time never ceased to flow. But independent of it the therapeutic belief has again and again been focused on certain individuals or certain sects or certain schools, in the midst of the steady progress of scientific medicine and sometimes synthesizing the religious claims with new-fashioned scholarly ideas. In the seventeenth century, for instance, the Irish nobleman Greatrakes became a famous center of attraction. He felt himself to be the bearer of a divine mission and healed the sick, appealing to their belief by laying on of hands and by movements which we nowadays call passes. Much more influential in the eighteenth century was Pastor Gassner in Germany. Gassner succeeded in producing with his religious psychotherapy such a tremendous stir that many thousands who needed cure from functional diseases, and thousands of curious people, too, streamed to his church in Ellwangen, and his methods of cure spread almost contagiously among the ministers of the country: an Emmanuel Church Movement of the eighteenth century. Gassner, too, discriminated between the diseases which have natural causes, that is the organic diseases, which he did not treat, and the functional ones, which were obsessions of the devil. To determine to which group the disease belonged, he ordered the devil to produce the symptoms of the sickness. When in this way the obsessional character of the disease was recognized, the minister began with his suggestive influences to banish the devil. He demanded firm confidence in the name of Christ, reënforced his effectiveness by narration of the cures he had perfected, used further certain manipulations such as the rubbing of the skin and passes on the head, and finally gave his suggestions with authoritative firmness. Many ministers who became his pupils treated like him with skillful combination of religion and hypnoid influences the spasms, catalepsies, neurasthenias, paralysis, and deafness, of neurotic patients.

There is no need to follow in detail the frequent similar occurrences between Gassner's time and our own. We all know where we are to-day. The medical profession and the medical science with its bacteriology and serum therapy, its Roentgen rays and its organic chemistry is far away from the church and without concession to religious aspects. On the other hand there are the yearly processions of thousands and thousands who make their pilgrimage to the sacred waters of Lourdes, guided by the Catholic priests, half-hypnotized by the hope that the Virgin will cure them. In every niche of the Catholic churches in all Europe, there are kneeling before the burning candles those who pray for nothing but their health; and their belief will sometimes yield almost miraculous cures. In England the Society of Emmanuel was founded by men and women to whom it seemed necessary to bring back to the minds of Christians the undoubted fact that Christ taught and worked for physical heath and to revive this sense of power over disease. Thousands were treated and the results have been "most encouraging." Among the cases successfully treated may be mentioned "one of cancer in which case the specialist called in had given the sufferer only three months to live while by means of the laying on of hands in prayer, a complete cure was effected."

Not dissimilar in its proceedings, though much more elaborate in its metaphysics than this movement in the midst of the Church of England, we find in America the Christian Science movement started by Mrs. Eddy. It was new as a therapeutic system, however old its philosophic elements. Mrs. Mary Baker Eddy writes: "In the year 1866 I discovered the Christ science or divine laws of life and named them Christian Science. God had been graciously fitting me during many years for the reception of a final revelation of the absolute divine principle of scientific being and healing." The disease is cured for the Christian Scientist by the belief in God because a true belief in God includes the insight that God is all reality and that reality therefore cannot include the ungodlike, that is, error and sin and disease. Disease is thus recognized as unreal and if it has become unreal, of course it has disappeared as part of our real life. Thousands and thousands have been cured under this symbol. And as the latest chapter of this history of five thousand years, we find the movement which Dr. Worcester has started in Boston and which, too, spreads rapidly over the continent and awakens the ambition of many a minister in every denomination in the land. The aim is to cure the patient by reënforcing in him through religious persuasion, through the contact with the symbols of the church and with godly men and through religious suggestion, a confident belief which gives new unity and through it new strength to the mind of the sufferer until it overcomes the functional disease of the body. The physician at first examines whether or not an irreparable organic disease has attacked the body, but if he does not find such organic destruction, then the patient is to be handed over to the minister, who will take care that through his religious belief and inspiration the mind will triumph over the weakness of the body.

Whoever looks in this way over the history of mankind can no longer doubt that belief in supernatural powers is really an agency for the overcoming of disease. We may be interested in it from the standpoint of religion or from the standpoint of psychology or from the standpoint of ethnology. In every case we have to acknowledge that he who believes may be cured. If we abstract first from the religious point of view and consider the problem as a scientific one, we have to interpret all those curative effects of belief as results of suggestion. The attitude of the one who gives the suggestion has gone in the history of mankind through all possible variations. He may have been filled with fervent belief, rejecting any interpretation except the religious one, or he may have produced the suggestion of belief almost with the intentions of a physician who simply relies on the physiological effects of any suggestion; and between these two extremes any number of steps is possible. Moreover the suggestion may have been detached from any personality and may have belonged to any symbol of religious energies, like the relics of the Catholic Church. Even the most skeptical of ethnologists ought to acknowledge that very little in this history of religious psychotherapy points to a conscious fraud. Those shamans of the savages from Siberia to South Africa, from Australia to Mexico, are in ecstasies which make them really believe in the mysterious power of their manipulations. The ethnologist finds indeed as most common characteristics of all those primitive movements that those who cure are chosen from among neurotics who by epileptic attacks or hallucinations and obsessions are predisposed to feel themselves as bearers of a higher mission.

Yet whether the attitude of the transmitter is religious or half-scientific, is inspired or insincere, the receiver of the suggestion is always in the same condition: he is believing in his cure through religious influence and through his belief he is helped, if he is helped at all. This uniformity does not exclude the fact that the patients too may show a manifoldness of mental states. They may remain in a completely waking state with reënforced suggestibility, or they may go over into a drowsy or hypnoid state or deeply into a hypnotic state, or may receive the suggestions as we saw even in sleep. Further their minds may be entirely filled with fine religious emotions and the therapeutic effect be only an appendix or, on the other hand, this confident expectation of the relief from pain may be their central content of consciousness and may control the whole mental interplay. The practical problem of the scientist is to consider how far these religious energies ought to be used today in the interests of the cure of diseases.

From a scientific standpoint such a discussion can hardly be fruitful with those who consistently take the religious point of view only. A view of the world which demands the faith that religious belief moves an almighty power to cure a diseased organ, or that the disease has no reality for one who lives in God, is invulnerable to merely scientific arguments.

The sick woman who kneels between the candles before the picture of the Virgin, praying that her heart, which the physicians declare incurable on account of a valvular disease, be cured, moves in a sphere of thought which lies entirely outside of the medical study of causes and effects. The same holds true, for instance, of Christian Science. This statement is in itself no criticism and no argument; it only acknowledges that any possible exchange of opinions has to be carried over from the scientific psychological ground to that of metaphysics and philosophy. It is quite different with modern movements of the type of the Emmanuel Church Movement, where the religious thought is intertwined with the psychological theory and where an actual coöperation of physician and minister is sought. Here church and science really meet on common ground, and it is important to examine objectively whether it is wise and beneficial to encourage the spreading of this tempting enterprise. The movement has reached the large cities between the Atlantic and the Pacific and is beginning to captivate the ministers of the small towns and villages. It seems as if an epoch has come for the church—the church which too long has ministered only to the spiritual needs of the community will at last remember again that Christ healed the sick, that mind and body are one, that the personality must be understood in its unity, and that endless fields of blessed influence may again be opened to the church when the minister becomes the physician of his congregation. Whoever knows the suggestive power of such a social movement, and considers the ease with which triumphant successes may be reached in this field and the disappointing and discouraging reduction of power which the church shows everywhere in its purely spiritual hold on the community, can foresee that all the conditions are favorable for a rapid spread and that the church clinics will become the American fashion of the near future.

It cannot be denied that the Christian church takes in hand there once more a work which belonged to it through centuries. But they were centuries in which the priest was in a certain degree the physician, just as he was the educator and teacher, simply because in the church there was centered all cultural influences which the community knew. The complexity of modern times has for centuries demanded the opposite system. Centralization is allowed only to the purely administrative influence of the state, while all the active functions are divided among specialists. We rely on the expert in education, we demand the expert in medicine: is more gained or lost if the religious leader now again suddenly undertakes a part of the functions which belong to the physician? It is true that the ministers of this school do not propose to undertake the physician's work to its full extent. They leave to him the first and in some respects most important step, the diagnosis, and abstain from the treatment of such cases as the physician declares inaccessible to psychical influences. They do not heal cancer and phthisis like the Em-

manuel Movement in England or like the mental
healers in America.

But is not perhaps just this compromise dangerous in another direction, inasmuch as it awakens a
feeling of safety in those who feel in sympathy with
scientific medicine? They have passed the hand of
the physician and believe accordingly that because
their illness is recognized as functional, the minister
can really perform all that ought to be done. Is this
belief justified? At the threshold, it occurs to every
one that such a diagnosis by physicians may be er-
roneous and that the chances for such error are under
the conditions of the church clinic much greater than
under the conditions of a regular medical treatment.
The diagnostician who treats the patient himself has
ever new chances to remodel his diagnosis and to
correct it under the influence of therapeutic effects.
The danger is great that under the proposed conditions, the activity of the physician will be superficial, because he is deprived of his chief means, the
constant observation. But we may abstract from
this possibility of error. Does the fact that the disease is one the symptoms of which may yield to psychical treatment really make it advisable that the
further treatment be handed over to the clergyman?
To begin at the beginning, the usefulness of psychical
treatment does not at all exclude the strong desir-
ability of physical treatment at the same time. The
emphasis which is laid on religious persuasion and inspiration, on prayer and spiritual uplift practically
excludes the use of baths and douches, of massage

and electricity, of tonics and sedatives. And yet it
is not caprice or sham when every well-schooled
medical specialist applies such means in the treatment
of these so-called functional diseases of the nervous
system. The minister applies and can apply only
one of many possible methods for cure and yet, if we
really want to make use of the resources of modern
knowledge, we have to adapt most carefully all possible means to the individual case. If we take the
strictly religious standpoint the situation is of course
different, but if we speak of psychophysiological effects, we may acknowledge the healing influence of
prayer and yet rely in the special case still more on
bromide or strychnine. Yet the religious psychotherapists not only neglect the physical help but
usually emphasize the antagonism. Some of the
strongest supporters proclaim it as a non-drug healing, thus deciding adversely about a medical method
regarding which they have no means at all to judge.

Parallel to this neglect of physical theory goes, of
course, the neglect of the physical factors in the disease. The physician may have justly diagnosed that
the case is "merely" neurasthenia or hysteria and
not a brain tumor or paralysis of the brain. Yet that
does not mean in the least that a real treatment which
remains in harmony with the progress of modern
medicine ought to ignore the hundred physical elements which enter daily into the disease. There are
the most complex digestive problems involved which
demand a thorough understanding of chemical metabolism, there are still more complex problems of the

sexual organs which the minister certainly ought not to discuss with his female parishioners, there are bacteriological questions, there are questions of the peripheral nervous system and sense organs; in short, questions which belong to a world into which the minister as minister has never looked. Even if he believes he might gather in an amateurish way some information as to those questions which lie so far from his experience as student of divinity, how can his half-baked knowledge compare with the experienced study of the regular physician? Such physical questions cannot be settled by the preparatory examination of the physician; they come up every day during the treatment and what the spiritual diet which the minister offers may help, may at the same time be ruined by the physical diet about which the minister without chemistry cannot judge.

But let us abstract from the bodily aspect. Is the situation really very different for the mental one? The appeal to the religious emotion, the reënforcement of religious faith is from the religious point of view certainly the one central effort from which everything has to irradiate. The unity of this controlling thought is the glory of such inspiration. But as soon as we handle this thought as a psychotherapeutic remedy, destined to restitute the disturbed psychological equilibrium, it becomes evident that the very uniformity of it makes it a clumsy, inadjustable pattern. If there is anything which impresses the careful student of psychology, it is the over-rich manifoldness, the complexity of mental life. Even the

simplest content of consciousness is a tissue woven
from millions of threads and any stereotyped influence means crudeness and destruction. The minister's attitude towards inner life is there directly
opposite to that of the psychologist. He cannot
enter into those endless interplays of associations and
memories, or inhibitions and sensations and impulses,
he cannot examine from which remote psychological
sources those ideas have arisen, how the feelings become disturbed and the judgments sidetracked. He
should not analyze even if he could, because his
whole aim is to synthesize. He asks for the meaning
and not for the structure, for the aims and not for
the elements. His therapeutic effort is therefore not
even directed towards a careful rebuilding of the
injured parts of the mind, but it is nothing more than
a general stimulation to the mind to help itself. By
touching on one of the deepest emotional layers of the
mind, the layer of religious ideas, the minister gives
to the soul an intense shock and expects that in the
resulting perturbation, everything will be shaken and
may then settle itself by its own energies in a healthful way. It is a fact that that can sometimes happen
and under certain conditions the chances for it are
even favorable. Under many other conditions the
chances are unfavorable and the result does not happen at all.

But whether or not a cure results, in any case it is
certainly not an effort which can be said to be in harmony with modern science. The idea of science is
always to understand the complex from its elements

and to restore the disturbed complex object by recognizing the disturbances in the elements and by bringing those disturbed elements into right shape again. Certainly the psychologist, too, in examining carefully the injured mental mechanism may discover emotional injuries which might be cured by the introduction of religious ideas, but he will not give to them a value different from the introduction of any other ideas and emotions, for instance, those of art and music and poetry, those of social company or civic interest, of travel or sport or politics. Each may have its particular value and to cure every mind with religious emotion would be from a psychological point of view as onesided as it would be to cure every disturbed stomach by milk alone. Moreover in very frequent cases, for instance, of neurasthenia or hysteria or psychasthenia, such wholesale remedies can form only the background of the treatment, but all the details have to be furnished with reference to a most subtle analysis of the special symptoms, and a particular organic symptom or a particular memory idea or a special inhibition by a well-selected counter-idea will do much more than any great emotional revival.

Stereotyped religious appeal is not only insufficient in an abundance of cases—it must never be forgotten that those who nowadays go to the minister for their health are already selected cases more open to religious suggestion than the average—but can easily be decidedly harmful. Of course that holds true for every physical remedy too, and the judgment of the exact limit is one of the chief duties of the physician. It holds also for the other mental factors like sympathy. A certain amount of sympathy may save a neurasthenic from despair, and only a little more may make his disease much worse and may develop in him a consciousness of misery which makes him a complete invalid. Still more is it true for the religious emotion, from the standpoint of nervous physiology the strongest next to the sexual emotion, that it can be the healing drug or the destructive poison. Everything depends upon the degree of the intrusion and upon the resistance of the psychophysical system. From a purposive point of view there cannot be faith enough, from a causal point of view there can easily be too much of the faith emotion. Religious fervor has at all times helped to create hysteria and to develop psychasthenias. It cannot be otherwise. A group of ideas which has such tremendous power over man must easily be able to produce inhibitions and exertions which become dangerous to a nervous system the constitution of which is pathological. To leave such a dangerous and powerful remedy entirely in the hands of men who by their profession must aim towards a maximum dose of religious influence can certainly not be in the interests of the patients or of the community.

Even the whole technique of this movement awakens the fear of possible harmful consequences. On the one hand we have the movement itself as a popular suggestion for the suggestible masses. The patient who seeks the help of a scientific neurologist hardly becomes a center of psychical contagion, but the church services for the sick offer favorable conditions for an epidemic development of hysterical symptoms. But more important are the influences on the individual patient. The whole purpose of the treatment demands the highest possible degree of suggestibility brought about by the ministerial persuasion. But it is evident that this degree of suggestibility means at the same time the most fertile soil for every chance suggestion and for influences which are perhaps entirely unintended. The physician and the psychologist, considering the mental state with reference to its elements, will make most careful use of those accessory influences. The minister, who necessarily has his spiritual aim in mind, cannot even become aware of all the involuntary influences which reach the mind in its most suggestible state. There can be no doubt that it would often need psychological art to avoid the creation of new pathological symptoms in such half-hypnotized patients. Yet the minister even goes so far as to make use of the sleeping mind without any consideration of the possible damage which may be done to his subject. He goes to the bedside of a sleeping girl and whispers his suggestions and is satisfied when they show their effects the next day. It does not lie in his horizon to consider the grave consequences which such suggestions during sleep may produce during future years in the brain the sleep of which has been transformed into such half-somnambulic relations. Hysterias may be created by such methods. No one can blame the minister for his remoteness from such doubts and problems, but the physician is to be blamed if he encourages the belief that all this still belongs to the proper sphere of the ministerial worker in abnormal psychology.

Those engaged in such work were not long in finding out that the mere emotional inspiration is often no sufficient remedy, and the development went along the same lines in which it has gone everywhere for some thousands of years. Not to disappoint the sufferers, the religion had to become in very many cases simply an inactive side issue and the real cure was performed by the same methods with which any worldly neuropathologist would go to work. If the woman who cannot sleep is cured from her insomnia by being made to listen to the beats of a metronome, it may sometimes be effective, however crude, but it is certainly no longer religion, even though the metronome stands in a minister's room. The more the movement spreads to those who have no psychological training and knowledge, the more it must be necessary for them to import the whole claptrap of the quack hypnotist and soon the minister may discover that in certain cases physical means and drugs help still better. Thus he simply enters into competition with the regular physician, only with the difference that he has never studied medicine. The chances are great that in his hands even such remedies and drugs may do harm and finally, even if they were effective, is not the question justified: will not religion suffer?

Indeed we have so far considered the question from one side only. We have confined ourselves to the question of how far such a movement is sound for the interests of the patient; but can we be blind to the other side and overlook the not less important problem of whether it lies in the interests of religion and of the church to amalgamate its spiritual work with a medical one? We are not thinking of those widespread, unfair arguments to the effect that this whole movement is undignified because it is instituted by the desire to fill the empty pews or to make competition with the success of Christian Science. That is utterly unjust. But there are intrinsic factors in the movement which interfere with the true aims of religion. First of all it cheapens religion by putting the accent in the meaning of life on personal comfort and absence of pain. The originators of the Emmanuel Movement stand well above such error, but their national congregations do not. Certainly the longing for pleasure and a well feeling and the abhorrence of pain and illness pervades our practical life and keeps in motion all our utilitarian efforts. But if there is one power in our life which ought to develop in us a conviction that pleasure is not the highest goal and that pain is not the worst evil, then it ought to be philosophy and religion. It is only the surface appearance if it seems as if the religious therapeutics minimizes the importance of pain; in truth it does the opposite. It tries to abolish pain, but not because it thinks little of pain; on the contrary, because it thinks so much of pain that it is willing even to put the whole of religion into the service of this strife for bodily comfort. The longing for freedom from pain becomes the one aim for which we are to be religious. In a time which denies all absolute ideals, which seeks the meaning of truth only in a pragmatic usefulness, it may be quite consistent to seek the meaning of religion in its service for removal of pain, and personal enjoyment. But in that case the ideal of both religion and truth is lost. It is finally not less undignified for religion to seek support for the religious belief in effects which it shares and knows that it shares with any superstitious belief on earth. Granted that the church can cure: the shaman of Siberia can cure too, and the amulets of Thibet not less. The psychologizing church knows, therefore, that it is not the value of the religion which restores the unbalanced nervous system; and yet it wants to provide for the spreading of true belief by the miraculous cures which it exhibits.

This situation naturally produces the desire of the church to substitute a religious explanation for a psychological one. It is claimed that after all it is not the mental effect of the prayer, but the prayer itself, not the psychophysical emotion of religion, but the value of religion which determines the cure. Yet in that moment the whole movement in its modern shape comes into a still more precarious position. If the cure results from the inner value of the religion how can we confine it to the so-called functional diseases and abstain from any hope in organic diseases?

Luther, from his religious point of view, still had the right to separate the two groups because only those functional diseases were effects of the devil, obsessions which could be banished by the minister and by prayer, while the other diseases did not result from the devil, but merely from natural causes. Such a definition does not fit into the modern system. To-day from a really religious point of view, both groups of diseases must be acknowledged to be natural or with Mrs. Eddy, as the work of the unholy spirit. Christian Science is indeed by far more consistent. If the cure results through the meaning and value of religion, there is no reason whatever why cancer and diphtheria and paralysis should not be cured as well as psychasthenia. And if, on the other hand, organic diseases cannot be cured because the psychophysical process of the religious emotion has no influence over diphtheria bacilli, then the whole process is removed to the causal sphere and it is acknowledged that the purposive meaning of religion is not in question at all. The whole system of such religious psycho-therapeutics is therefore in its inner structure contradictory. It contains causal and purposive elements without any possibility of unifying them. They are loosely mixed, and the power of prayer means on one page something entirely different from what it means on another. In these respects Christian Science is by far more unified and in harmony with itself; its therapeutics is really anchored in a system.

From a scientific point of view, its dangerousness

is of course much greater inasmuch as it extends its methods over every organic disease and thus applies merely psychical treatment where from a standpoint of scientific medicine, physical treatment would be absolutely necessary. Moreover its philosophy is after all only a pseudophilosophy; its tempting equations of disease and error and sin and unreality are ultimately a mere playing with conceptions. If we were to point to the root of the misunderstanding in Christian Science, we should say that everything depends on the philosophical commonplace that the objects with which we deal in our life are ideas and that our whole experience is mind. " Christian Science reveals incontrovertibly that Mind is All-in-All, that the only realities are the divine mind and idea." But now silently this mental character of the real world is identified with the mental experience which stands in contrast to the physical experience. There results the impression that physical experience therefore, does not belong to the world of reality. It is evident, however, that mental in contrast to physical means something entirely different from mental in the philosophical sense. In the latter meaning of the word, we all agree that the world is mental; the word mental indicates there that the world has reality not in itself but only as experience of subjects. In the second sense, mental or psychical means that it is experience for one particular subject only and not for every possible subject. The physical thing, for instance this table, is indeed different from my mental memory idea of a table, inasmuch as every possible subject can experience this table while my mental memory image belongs to me alone. The physical table and the mental memory image of it are both equally mental in the philosophical sense, inasmuch as the physical which is object for every possible subject and in this sense not mental is therefore not less given to subjects. Every physical body with its disease is thus in one sense taken as something not mental while in another sense as mental; if we use the same word in two entirely different meanings, it indeed cannot be difficult to demonstrate any metaphysical consequences.

But we do not have to deal here with the metaphysics of "Science and Health." If it is brought down to the concrete application, we stand before the same confusion which characterizes all compromises. Causal effects are sought in a sphere which belongs to purposive values. The psychological effects of the emotion of faith are sought and are misinterpreted as the emanations of religious powers. Religious psychotherapeutics in all its forms seeks to demonstrate to us the triumph of the soul over the body, while in reality it deals only with the mental mechanism which as such belongs to the chain of causal events in the same natural way as the organism. The soul, as spiritual agency in its sphere of purposes and ideals, does not enter the machinery of psychotherapy, and the psychological material on which psychotherapy is applied is not freer and not better and does not stand higher than the material of the bodily cells and tissues. The Emmanuel Move-

ment deserves the highest credit for bringing about a
systematic contact between religious faith cure and
scientific medicine, but the time in which the minister
himself undertook the medical treatment had to be a
time of transition.   It had to lead to a new relation
in which the ministerial function is confined to the
spiritual task of upbuilding a mind while the therapeutic function remains entirely in the hands of the
physician.   Where the physician believes that the
psychomedical treatment demands a new equilibrium
of the patient to be secured by religion, there the
minister should be called for assistance.   Psychotherapeutic hospitals would offer the most favorable
conditions for such coöperation.   But the minister
ought to enter even such a hospital with a strictly
spiritual aim, and he should never forget that the
task of the church stands much higher than the
utilitarian task of removing pain from the sick room.
But if those psychotherapeutic hospitals will flourish
and the physicians will at last make use of psychical
factors in their regular practice, they ought not to
forget on their part that the important step forward
was taken under the pressure of popular religious
movements.   The ministers first saw what the physicians ought to have seen before, but the physicians
will see it more fully and more correctly.

XIII

PSYCHOTHERAPY AND THE PHYSICIAN

EVERY thought of the physician moves in a world the structure of which is determined by the thought forms of cause and effect. He knows the effect which he wants to produce; it is the restitution of the organic equilibrium. He studies the causes which can secure that end. And again the disturbance of the equilibrium itself, the disease, is for him an effect which he seeks to understand by an analysis of the preceding causes. The means which he applies can therefore be valued only in reference to their efficiency; no other point of view belongs to his world. The religiously valuable may be indifferent or even undesirable in the interplay of causes, and the morally indifferent may be most important for the physician's interests. The religious emotion accordingly has to stand in line with any other mental excitement or with a hundred physical means which the laboratory and the drug store supply. The physician will welcome the methods of treatment without reference to metaphysical systems or to religious beliefs. To him it is an empirical fact that many disturbances of mind and body which interfere with the equilibrium of life can be repaired by influences on certain psychophysical organs. A part of these repairing influences he finds in the sense stimuli, for instance, of spoken or written words which reach the brain and awaken associative and reactive processes. He finds further that these influences can be reën- forced in their effectiveness by certain general condi- tions of the nervous system and again finds that these can be secured partly by sense impressions, and once more especially by words.

It is a matter of course to the physician that appli- cation of any sense influence on the brain demands a most subtle analysis of the psychophysical situation. Therefore he gives no less attention to the disen- tangling of the whole history of the individual brain, to its stored-up energies and to its mental possibili- ties. If he knows the psychophysical status, and finally if he knows the means of influencing those psychophysical organs which stimulate or inhibit the disturbed central parts, he can foresee the psycho- physical effects with a certain definiteness. Thus everything depends upon the sharpest possible, almost microscopic, mental analysis, together with a most thorough examination of the whole nervous system and the most careful calculation of the mental in- fluences applied. The vagueness of the religious ap- peal transforms itself into an exact calculation and the unity of the soul which seeks spiritual uplift trans- forms itself into a mental mechanism of bewildering complexity, and yet not more complex than the phys- ical organism, to which for instance, the chemical

means of the physician administer. Today medical
science is certainly only in the beginning of this great
movement. Especially the analysis of the psychophysical conditions still lacks a sufficient refinement
of method. But at least the causal principle is now
fully recognized and the scientific man of today no
longer doubts that this whole play of psychotherapeutic processes goes on as a causal process in the
psychophysical system of the individual without any
mysteriousness, without any magnetic influences, without any miraculous interference, without any agencies except those which are working in our ordinary
mental life in attention and reaction, in memory and
sleep.

It is surprising how late this recognition appeared
in the history of human knowledge. It occurred here
as in so many places in the history of human civilization that the simple is the late outcome of the complex. Just as in technique the apparatus often began
in a complex, cumbersome way and then became steadily simplified, so it is with explanations. The complex machinery of cosmic influences and obsessions
by demons and magnetic mysteries was at first necessary until the simple explanation was found that all
the results depend upon the working of the mind itself. Yet in technique and explanation alike, such
progress to the simpler means always at the same time
the making use of much richer knowledge. To explain an obsession or a sleep state by the agencies of
evil spirits or magnetic fluids is certainly an unnecessary side conception. But to understand it from the

working of the mind presupposes after all the whole modern physiological psychology, and thus had to be the latest step.

The effects themselves were certainly observed in all times. Even the phenomena of hypnotism date probably back some thousands of years, however difficult it may sometimes be to discriminate between the artificial hypnotic states and hysteric or hystero-epileptic occurrences in the past. Certainly it may be acknowledged that the Yogi in India cultivated in the most remote times the methods of autosuggestion which evidently led to hypnotic states, and everywhere around the Mediterranean, antiquity knew the hypnotizing effect of staring on polished metals and crystals. So in Egypt, so in Greece and Rome; and it has often been claimed that the priestesses of Delphi and the sibyls of the Romans were in states of hystero-hypnotic character. As to the therapeutic use, especially the Greek physicians applied hypnotic means. Excited patients were brought to repose by methods of stroking. The efforts to explain scientifically the mysterious powers which men can gain over the mind and will of another begin at the end of the Middle Age and were developed quite naturally from the prevailing astrological doctrines. Astrology worked on the theory that the human fate depends upon the stars. These stars have an effect on the human organism. That proves that an influence can exist between distant bodies. It is, therefore, not more surprising that one organism can also have an influence on another organism. Well known since antiquity were such influences from one object to another, as in the case of the magnet. Thus there may be a kind of magnetic power which creates relations between all objects in the universe.

Pomponnazi explained thus at the end of the fifteenth century the therapeutic effects of the human soul by the mutual influence which stars and men have on each other. This theory comes to much more important development in the writings of the physician Paracelsus. One individual by the power of his effort can influence the will of another individual, can fight with it, and suppress it; and all through energies which are analogous to the magnetic power which binds stars and men. In the middle of the seventeenth century, Helmont connects this power of magnetic attraction and repulsion with an ethereal element which penetrates all bodies and keeps them in motion. Through it man, too, can by his mere imagination work on other men. This will can also be effective on drugs which get through it a special therapeutic power. Somewhat different was the theory of a Scotch physician, Maxwell, in the second half of the seventeenth century. The ethereal spirit, which is identical with light, can be artificially cumulated in any organism and that secures its health. As one man can influence this vivifying ether in any other man, he can produce cures even from a great distance. All diseases are merely reductions of this ethereal spirit in the organism.

But the general stream of the explanation continued in the direction of the magnetic doctrine. It was especially Mesmer in the eighteenth century who, in a long life of fantastic mysticism and yet of universal serious study, surely contributed much to the development of the theory. He had started to use, like others, the magnet in his medical practice. But he discovered that the same therapeutic successes could be gained without applying the magnet itself, but by simply using his own hands. The patients became cured when he moved his hands slowly from their heads to their feet. The magnetic power was therefore evidently in man himself. It was an animal magnetism in opposition to the mineral one which belonged to the magnet and to the stars. He believed further that he was able to infuse this magnetic power into any lifeless thing, which would then have curative influence on the nerves. There can be no doubt that, whatever may have been the value of his theories, he cured a large number of patients, evidently producing a state which we would call today a hypnoid state and often simply appealing to the natural suggestibility of the impressionable minds. Among his pupils, usually called mesmerists, was Puysèyur, who discovered, in 1784, the state which was called artificial somnambulism, a kind of sleep in which the ideas and feelings of the magnetized can be guided by the magnetizer. Here evidently was the first recognition of the psychotherapeutic variation which we call today hypnotism. There followed a period in which the scientific interest of the physicians was somewhat sidetracked by an unsound connection of these studies with mystic speculations and with clairvoyance. But especially in Germany animal magnetism in Mesmer's form and in the form of artificial somnambulism grew in influence through the first decades of the nineteenth century and succeeded in entering the medical schools. The reaction came through popular misuse. At about the third decade of the century, interest ceased everywhere.

The Portuguese Faria insisted in 1819, practically as the first,. that all those so-called magnetic influences, including the delusions, the amnesias after awaking, and the actions at a command, did not result from a magnetic power but from the imagination of the subject himself. He believed that the effect depended upon a disposition of the individual which resulted from a special thinness of blood. He abstained therefore from the magnetic manipulations and produced the somnambulic state by making the patients simply fixate his hands and by ordering them to sleep. Thus he is the first who understood these changes as results of mental suggestion. The next great step was due to the English surgeon, Braid, who in the forties studied the magnetic phenomena and like Faria insisted on the merely mental origin of the abnormal state. He proved that a person can bring himself into such an artificial state and that it is therefore entirely independent of energies from without. He examined especially the influence of staring at a shining object, a method which not seldom was called Braidism. He also introduced the word hypnotism. In America mesmerism was generally known under the name of electrobiology; and Grimes in par-

ticular came to results similar to those of Braid. Yet
the influence of these movements on the medical
world remained insignificant until a new great wave
of psychotherapeutics by means of suggestion began
in France in the sixties.

Of course this development from astrology to magnetism and from magnetism to hypnotism represented
only one side of psychotherapy. Parallel to it goes
the progress in the treatment of the insane. In the
first half of the eighteenth century, they are still on
the whole thrown together with the criminals but the
more the disease character of the disturbance is acknowledged, and the more special hospitals for the
insane are created, and finally the more the humane
treatment in them supersedes the brutal, the more
psychotherapy enters into the work. England showed
the way. Especially Arnold, Crichton, and Perfect
became influential; and soon Pinel and Esquirol followed in France; and Reil and Langermann in Germany. Reil recognized clearly at the threshold of
the nineteenth century that " Both psychical and physical diseases may be cured by psychical means, but
at the same time psychical diseases may also be cured
by physical means." And in his " Rhapsodies,"
rhapsodies on the application of psychical methods
in the treatment of mental disturbances, he declared,
" that the medical Faculties will soon be obliged to
add to the two existing medical degrees still a third,
namely, the doctorate in psychotherapy." This
stream became broader and broader and every new
development of psychiatry in the last hundred years

did new justice to the influence of psychological means in the treatment of mental diseases; to be sure, without allowing up to the present day the hope that mental factors as such can cure the grave forms of insanity. The borderland cases and the incipient mild forms alone allow the hope of a cure. Outside of them the work of psychotherapy in the insane asylum meant essentially improvement and relief only. Again, in another direction, the general dietetic influence of sound mental life may be called a part of psychotherapy and this engaged not a few of the leading medical thinkers in all countries during the last century, especially the nerve physicians who gave serious attention to the wholesome engagements of the mind. Finally, might not much be attributed to psychotherapy, which offically belongs to the doctrines of homeopathy?

But we may return to the new heralds of suggestion. Liébeault's book on the artificial sleep in 1866 became the starting point of the new great movement. Yet at first it remained unnoticed. It is claimed that for a long time only one copy was sold. But he continued to make his hypnotic experiments on the poor population of Nancy and they finally attracted the attention of some of the leading medical men there. Bernheim became convinced and Dumont, the physiologist Beaunis joined the movement, and in the eighties we find Nancy the center of hypnotic interest to which medical men from everywhere made their pilgrimage. This latter phase was paralleled by Charcot's studies in Paris, who brought hypnotism into nearest neighborhood with hysteria. And also the later development of the Paris school by Richer, and especially the brilliant work of Janet, kept hysteria in the foreground of the therapeutic interest. Liébeault's experiment had brought the psychology of suggestion entirely into the center of this whole circle of phenomena and this view controlled the development of the last few decades, which was essentially an elaboration of the special treatment of diseases. Forel in Switzerland, Moll and Vogt in Germany, Wetterstrand in Sweden became the chief exponents of therapy by hypnotism. Others, like Dubois, in Switzerland, emphasized more the suggestive treatment through persuasion. In England at first Carpenter, later Hack-Tuke gave serious attention to hypnotism, in Russia Bechterew, and in the last few years the literature on therapy by suggestion became developed in practically all countries. In America Beard, Hammond, and others belong to the older school; Osgood, Prince, Peterson, Putnam, Sidis, and others to the most recent years. At the same time, under the leadership of Kraepelin, Ziehen, Sommer, and others, the methods of the psychological laboratory, especially the reaction and association methods, were made useful for the purposes of psychopathology.

But interest in suggestion does not represent today the last step of psychotherapy. The latest movement, which is entirely in its beginning, the development of which no one can foresee, but which promises wide perspectives, is connected with the name of Freud in Vienna. The entirely new turn of psychotherapy is given by the fact that his aim is not to overcome a symptom by suggestion but to make it disappear by removing the ultimate mental cause. He found that large groups of mental disturbances result from a psychical trauma, a disagreeable idea which, inhibited in the mind, becomes the source of mischief and produces phobias and obsessions and hysterical motions. The cure of the symptoms demands the recognition of this first mental accident, which may lie back for years and which may no longer be in the memory of the patient. As soon as this earlier experience is brought to consciousness again, it needs only a natural discharge and a normal expression and the symptoms which it brought about will disappear. Thus the cure itself needs no hypnotism and no persuasion or suggestion but the reawakening of forgotten situations, and only in the service of this effort hypnotism may be used to reënforce the memory. Yet this represents only the first period of Freud's activity, in which he collaborated with Breuer, a phase which is represented by their book on hysteria, in 1895. But there followed a further development which is still more essential. The hysterical disturbance may indeed have started with such an accidental traumatic impression but that does not explain why just this impression had such a strong effect. Other impressions of equal strength and emotional vividness may have passed without leaving any damaging result. And therefore there must be some prior cause in the subject which makes just this particular impression so injurious; and here is the point of

Freud's fundamental discovery, which for the layman appears on the surface to have little probability but which has proved of greatest consequence for clinical work. It was found that only those situations become injurious and become starting points for hysterical symptoms which touch on repressed and artificially inhibited ideas of the sexual sphere.

Entirely new perspectives have been opened by these studies. Above all, now for the first time there is in sight a psychotherapy which not only aims to remove symptoms but which really uproots the disease itself. That earlier method of bringing the trauma to consciousness and making it discharge, the so-called cathartic method, removes only the particular group of disturbances but the patient remains a hysteric, and if ever new accidents should happen which would touch again those inmost repressed ideas, new hysterical symptoms would develop. But if we can go back to that starting point, if we can discover those first suppressions of desired gratifications which often most indirectly are related to the sexual sphere, and if we can liberate the mind from those primary strangulated affections, then the patient is really cured. Freud himself practically abstained from the help which hypnotism can give for the reawakening of forgotten experiences, while some of his pupils still prefer this short way to the forgotten memories. His way is, on the whole, to let the imagination bring up any chance material of associated ideas and then to study their connections and follow the hints they give. He calls it the psychoanalytic method. Others prefer the methods of association tests, again others tap the lower layers by automatic writing, but the chief problem remains always to discover those repressed desires and to understand through them the injurious effects of accidental experiences. The whole field of hysteria, and perhaps still more that of the anxiety neurosis, has come into new perspective through this pioneer work which men like Bleuler, Jung, and Stekel have developed in various directions.

Thus in recent decades the thorough work of scientific physicians has developed a psychotherapy of considerable extent and of indubitable usefulness, far removed from the simultaneous efforts of the churches and of the popular mental healing cures. A number of eminent men in all countries have tested the methods and have published the results. But the curious side of it is that all this is essentially a movement of leaders while the masses of the profession hesitate to follow. It is a set of officers without an army. Every large city has one or another specialist who applies suggestive therapy, one or another nerve specialist who hypnotizes, but the average physician moves on without any serious effort to utilize psychotherapy. It is as if the prescription of the modern chemical drugs were confined to some leading scholars in the country, while the thousands abstained from it in their office work and in their family practice. In reality psychotherapy ought to be used by every physician, as it fits perfectly the needs of the whole suffering community. Its almost exceptional use in the hands of a few scholarly leaders deprives it of its true importance. It is the village doctor who needs psychotherapy much more than he needs the knife and the electric current.

Why does the medical profession on the whole show this shyness in the face of such surprising results? In other fields they do not show any reluctance in taking up the newer developments of method. Even the Roentgen ray apparatus has quickly won its way, and psychotherapy is less expensive. To be sure, the most important reason is probably one which is most honorable. The physicians do not like to touch a tool which has been misused so badly. Psychotherapy has come too much into the neighborhood of superstition and humbug. Where miracles are performed, the man of science prefers to leave the field. The less one knows about those groups of problems, the less one is able to see the sharp demarcation line between true scientific studies, for instance, in hypnotism, and the pseudo-scientific fancies of psychical research. Experiments in suggestibility are then easily mixed with experiments in telepathy, and those go over by gradual degrees to clairvoyance and premonitory apparitions, and from there the way is not far to the reappearance of the dead and the routine performances of the spiritists. It seems to many as if there is no point where they have a reason to stop. If they begin with such abnormal phenomena at all, it seems as if they are necessarily carried over to all the mysteries of supernatural energies. Even the competition with Christian Science, and other mental healers whose judgment is not hampered by any previous study of medicine, might seem rather unattractive to the serious physician.

Further not a few have the impression that such suggestive treatment directly demands from them that they also begin to humbug their patients or to throw out suggestions which they themselves do not believe, in short, that they be brought down to the level of the miracle performer. Yet, however much all that speaks in favor of the conscientious instinct in the physician, it is ultimately based upon a misinterpretation. The line between real science and its counterfeit is here as everywhere a distinct one, and the true man of science ought not to hesitate in doing his duty from fear that he might not be discriminated from the charlatan. A well-conducted psychotherapeutic treatment as a scientific physician ought to carry it out, is entirely different in meaning and appearance, from the first step of diagnosis to the last treatment of after-effects, from every unscientific faith cure. It is also in no way necessary that the psychotherapist ever leave the path of complete sincerity. There is no reason at all for promising that the patient will be entirely cured if the physician believes that a real cure through suggestion is impossible. The more the true physicians undertake psychotherapeutic work, the more it will carry with it that dignity which is now too often lost by the predominance of those who treat without diagnosis and cure by mere appeal to superstition.

All that does not mean that other motives do not

hold the physician back. Not seldom he is afraid of unfavorable consequences. He does not feel sure that, for instance, a deep hypnosis is without dangerous results or that he will be able to produce it in the technically correct way. But all these objections mean nothing but insufficient acquaintance with the facts. Of course every technique needs its period of preparation for the task, but it is now sufficiently demonstrated that hypnotism carried through in a scientific spirit will never have any injurious consequences. The morphine injection and the Roentgen rays are by far more dangerous. Those who think that for hypnotizing especially inborn power is needed stand, of course, outside of a serious discussion. They do not even know the elements of the modern theories. Every physician has in himself the necessary means for a psychotherapeutic treatment in every form.

More scientific insight belongs to the argument that most of these psychotherapeutic schemes are essentially for treatment of symptoms. We have acknowledged that throughout. The possibility of a relapse or of a new obsession is thus to a high degree open, and that is certainly a discouraging feature. Yet we have seen sufficiently that as soon as the symptoms are removed, there is no lack of means, also by psychotherapy, to prevent the recurrence. Moreover, to remove the present symptoms is in any case a great gain and in many cases a decisive gain. And whatever can be secured by such methods is of such a character that hardly any other method could have been substituted. It can be said with certainty that hundreds of thousands leave the offices of their doctors every year without relief where relief could be secured by psychotherapeutic means.

To be sure, one reply of the physicians is not infrequent and carries some weight. Psychotherapeutic methods demand much time and patience and skill. To relieve a cocainist of his desire by mere suggestion may demand an assiduity which the average physician simply cannot afford; and nothing requires more time than a real use of Freud's psychoanalytic method. Hours and hours of conversation about the most trivial occurrences have to be spent to relieve the repressed ideas and to give them a chance for a free ascension. It cannot be denied that most of the really illuminating work in all these fields has been done by scholars who combine a strong theoretical interest with their effort to cure the patients, and who therefore examine and treat the individual case primarily from the wish to get new insight into the laws of nature. The average physician whose time is his income may be the less willing to enter into such time-devouring schemes, as the patients too easily may think that the physician did not do much for them when he simply was sitting down and gossiping with them.

Yet after all, behind all of it stands one motive which has held back the development of psychotherapy in the medical profession more than anything else. The physician feels instinctively that a real success can be reached in every one of these fields, only if he possesses a reasonable amount of knowledge of psychology. He feels that wherever he touches the patient's body, examines his lungs or his heart or his reflexes, that a large background of anatomical knowledge and of general pathology gives meaning to every single observation. But in the field of mental abnormities, in the whole world of ideas and emotions and volitions, he simply lacks that background. Everything seems to him without reference to real knowledge. He feels as amateurish as if he were to operate on the abdomen without knowing its anatomy. He is instinctively aware that even the simplest mental life represents a bewildering complexity and that to stimulate ideas or feelings or to suppress emotions, to inhibit volitions, must demand always a most subtle disentanglement of the most widely different components. He abstains from approaching that ground at all rather than to blunder by his ignorance of psychology. And after all, he is right. But is he right in allowing that ignorance? Can the medical profession afford to send into the world every year thousands of young doctors who are unable to use some of the most effective tools of modern medicine, and tools which do not belong to the specialist but just to the average practitioner, simply because they have not learned any psychology?

Indeed the times seem ripe for a systematic introduction of psychological studies into every regular medical course. It is not a question of mental research in the psychological laboratory where advanced work is carried on, but a solid foundation in empirical psychology can be demanded of everyone. He ought to have as much psychology as he has physiology. Moreover the psychological study ought not to be confined to the normal mental life. Again we do not speak of psychiatry. What is needed is abnormal psychology, entirely independent of the therapeutic interests of the alienist. The mental variations within the limits of normal life and the borderland cases ought to be studied there as well as the complete derangements. The ideal demand would be that the future physician should spend at least a year of his undergraduate time on empirical psychology, especially on experimental and physiological psychology. He would take perhaps half a year's lecture course on the whole field of psychology as covered in the English language by the well-known text-books of James, Wundt, Titchener, Judd, Royce, Calkins, Angell, Baldwin, Kuelpe, Ebbinghaus, Thorndike, Stout, Ziehen, Ladd, and so on. In the second half-year the course ought to be either advanced psychology entering into the more complex phenomena or a practical training course in elementary laboratory psychology as indicated for instance by Titchener's " Experimental Psychology. A Manual of Laboratory Practice." If the undergraduate can possibly afford the time in his college course, he ought to add courses which either lead him towards the philosophical problems of psychology or towards the comparative aspect of psychology. If he can find time for a year of post-graduate work between college and medical school, he could hardly spend it more profitably than by a year of research in a well-conducted psychological laboratory to become really acquainted with an independent analysis of mental states. On the other hand in the medical school, room must be found for a course in abnormal psychology, which of course presupposes a thorough knowledge of normal psychology and, if possible, follows the courses on nervous diseases and precedes the course on psychiatry.

For the average future physician, it would be wiser to omit even the psychiatry studies than those in abnormal psychology. The latter ought to lead him far enough to discriminate early between a mere neurasthenia, for instance, and a beginning of insanity. As soon as the discrimination is perfected and insanity is found, he has to give the case out of his care anyhow and hand it over to the specialist and to the asylum. The knowledge of psychiatric treatment is, therefore, not essential for the average practitioner. But no one can relieve him from the responsibility for those borderland cases, for the hysterias and psychasthenias and neurasthenias, and he can never master them without normal and abnormal psychology. Moreover it must not be forgotten that mental factors may enter into every disease. The psychology of pain, for instance, and of comfort feeling, the psychology of hunger and thirst, of nausea and dizziness, the psychology of the sexual feelings, the psychology of hope and fear, of confidence and discouragement, of laziness and energy, of sincerity and cunningness play their rôle in almost every sick room. And if the physician haughtily declares that he does not care for the methods of suggestion, it might justly be asked whether he can be a physician at all if he does not apply some suggestions; yes, if his very entrance into the sick room does not suggest relief and improvement from the start. The introduction of a serious study of psychology is the most immediate need of the medical curriculum. Instructorships in abnormal psychology must be created in every medical school; institutes for psychotherapy should soon follow. But in all this, there is nowhere to appear any artificial antithesis between mind and body, any more than between organic and functional diseases; we have discussed all that with full detail. Only the physician who has a thorough psychological preparation can fulfill the manifold demands which modern life must raise; he alone is prepared to coöperate with the other factors of the community in the development of a sound and healthful nation, to work towards the hygiene of the nervous system and of the mental life; and to correct the injuries which the perversities of our civilization inflict.

In all that he will not avoid the comradeship of the clergyman. He will, of course, not forget the fundamental difference of attitude between them, he will not forget that the minister seeks for the meaning and values of inner life while he, the physician, has to consider that same inner life from a causal point of view and thus has to work with it as with natural material for the normal functioning of the organism. But the interrelation between them can be intimate in spite of the difference of their standpoints. The minister, to be sure, ought not to consider health as such as the greatest good, but he will not forget that a wholesome devotion to ideals cannot be carried through when the attention is absorbed by the sufferings of the body and the mental powers are debilitated. Only in a sound mind the full ideal meanings of life can be realized. The minister must therefore seek the health of his congregation not because health is the ideal of life but because the true ideals cannot be appreciated by the mental cripple. On the other hand, the physician from his standpoint should in no way feel it his duty to play the amateur minister and to put emphasis on the spiritual uplifting of his patients. But he knows well that not a few of the suggestive influences which are needed for the relief from disease are most effective when an emotional emphasis can be given to the suggestions and that this emphasis is for large numbers most powerfully supplied by the religious emotion. Thus the minister will be a very important assistant to him and the church will most successfully do for many patients what for other patients perhaps travel or music or the theatre, sport or social life, may do.

Just in the relation to the church, the physician will need subtlest discrimination, and he will not forget that while even a strong religious emotion may be without damage for a normal man, it may well be injurious to the unstable brain. But if the physician uses tact and wisdom, he will be surprised to find how often the religious stimulation can indeed be helpful for his purposes and the division of labor demands that this be supplied not by himself but by the minister. He will advise the consulting sufferer to seek the influence of a godly man who awakens in him upbuilding wholesome emotions and volitions. The minister may in this way very well become the assistant of the physician. But whether this coöperation is looked on from the one or from the other point of view, in every case it needs absolute clearness. Nothing is gained and too much is lost if the two functions are carelessly mixed together. It is never the task of the minister to heal a mind and never the task of a physician to uplift a mind. One moves in the purposive sphere, the other in the causal sphere. Their friendship can seriously endure only as long as they remain conscious of the fact that they have two entirely different functions in the service of mankind.

XIV

PSYCHOTHERAPY AND THE COMMUNITY

BOTH the physician and the patient find their place in the community the life interests of which are superior to the interests of the individual. It is an unavoidable question how far from the higher point of view of the social mind the psychotherapeutic efforts should be encouraged or suppressed. Are there any conditions which suggest suspicion of or direct opposition to such curative work?

Of course society has to be sure that no possible misuse and damage are to result from such practice. Fears in that direction have been uttered repeatedly, but from very different standpoints. One which is perhaps most often heard in popular circles results from an entire misunderstanding and deserves hardly any discussion after our detailed study of the processes involved. It is claimed that suggestive power, especially in the form of hypnotization, may be secretly misused to make anyone without his knowledge and against his will a passive instrument of the hypnotist's intent. Often this is coupled with telepathic fancies. The hypnotist is believed to have mystic power to bring any person in a distant region under his mental control and thus to be able to carry out any sinister plans by the help of his innocent victim. All hypnotizing therefore ought to be interdicted by the state. The presuppositions of such a view are, as we know now, entirely absurd. We know that hypnotism is not based on any special power of the hypnotizer; there is no magnetic fluid in the sense of the old mesmerism. The imagination of the hypnotized person is the only hypnotizing agency. Thus no one can be hypnotized without his knowledge or against his will. The story of telepathic mysteries which is often brought before the public is probably always the outcome of a diseased brain. It is indeed a frequent symptom in paranoia and other insanities that the patient who feels abnormal organic sensations and abnormal unaccountable impulses interprets them as influences of a distant enemy. Whole pamphlets have been written with elaboration of such insane misinterpretations and requests to legislatures have been made in that spirit, but the physician recognizes easily throughout the whole argumentation the well-known phenomena of the mental disease.

To be sure, while no one can be hypnotized against his will, many a person is liable to accept suggestions from others and thus to carry out the wishes of others almost without knowing and certainly without willing that the other mind interfere with the interplay of the own motives. But if we were to strike out all suggestive influences from social life, we should give up social life itself. Suggestion is given wherever men come in contact; in itself it is neither good nor bad. The good resolution and the bad one can be suggested, the good example and the bad can be effective; both encouragement of the noble and imitation of the evil may work with the same mental technique. Certainly there are some persons who have a stronger influence than others on the imagination of those with whom they come in contact; their expression awakens confidence, their voice and their words reach deeper layers of the mind, their calmness and firmness overwhelm more easily the antagonistic ideas. But the chief difference lies after all in the different degrees of suggestibility among those who receive such impressions. The easily suggestible person cannot be protected by any interdict; he may catch suggestions everywhere, any advertisement in the newspaper and any display in the shop-window may overrun his own intentions. What he needs is training in firmness. The application of reënforced suggestion or even of hypnotism in the doctor's office is even for him no possible source of danger.

On a higher level are objections which come from serious quarters and which are not without sympathy with true science. In recent times this opposition has repeatedly found eloquent expression. It is an objection from the standpoint of morality, belonging therefore entirely to the purposive view of the mind, but we have now reached a point where it is our duty to do justice to this purposive view too. As long as we discussed the problem entirely from the standpoint of the physician, no other view of mental life except the causal one could be in question. As soon as we look at it from the standpoint of the community, it becomes our duty to bring the causal and the purposive view into harmony, and it would be narrow and shortsighted simply to draw the practical consequences of a naturalistic view of the mind without inquiring whether or not serious interests in the purposive sphere are injured. If there is moral criticism against suggestive therapy, it is the duty of the community to consider it. This opposition argues as follows: Hypnotic influence brings the patient under the will control of the hypnotizer and thus destroys his own freedom. Whatever the patient may reach in the altered states is reached without his own effort, while he is the passive receiver of the other man's will. His achievement has therefore no moral value, and if he is really cured of his drunkenness or of his perverse habits, of his misuse of cocaine or of his criminal tendencies, he has lost the right to be counted a moral agent. It would be better if there were more suffering in the world than that the existence of the moral will should be undermined.

No one ought to take such arguments lightly. The spirit which directs them is needed more than anything else in our time of reaching out for superficial goods. No one can insist too earnestly that life is worth living only if it serves moral duties and moral freedom and is not determined by pleasures and absence of pain only. Those who set forth this argument are entirely willing to acknowledge the profound effect which suggestive therapeutics may create. More than this, they have to acknowledge it to gain a basis for their attack. Just because the hypnotizer can entirely change the desires and passions, the habits and perversities of the suffering victim, he seems to them a moral wrongdoer who negates the principle of human freedom. A forcible book of recent days calls the suggestive power of the psychotherapist "The Great Psychological Crime." It says to the hypnotist: "By your own testimony, you stand convicted of applying a process which deprives your subjects of the inalienable right and power of individual self-control. In proportion as you deprive him of the power of self-control, you deprive him of that upon which his individual responsibility and moral status depend. In proportion as you deprive him of the free control and exercise of those powers of the soul upon which his individual responsibility and moral status depend, you thereby rob him of those powers upon which he must depend for the achievement of individual immortality."

But this censure too is entirely mistaken, not because it urges the purposive views against the causal but because it is in error as to the facts. Such critics are fully under the influence of the startling results which are reached; they do not take the trouble to examine the long and difficult way which has had to be traversed with patience and energy. It is quite true that if I hypnotize a man and suggest to him to take up after awaking the book which lies on my table, he follows my suggestion without conflict and in a certain sense without freedom. He feels a simple impulse to go to the table and lift the book and, as no stronger natural desire and no moral objection stand in the way, he carries out that meaningless impulse and perhaps even invents a foolish motive to explain to himself why he wanted to look at that book. But after a long experience, I have my doubts as to whether a man was ever cured in such a way by hypnotism of serious disturbances and of those anomalous actions which the critics want to see overcome by the patient's own moral efforts. On the contrary, every suggestion has to rely on the efforts and struggles of the patient himself and all that the psychotherapists can give him is help in his own moral fight. His own will is presupposition for being hypnotized and for realizing the suggestion. If again and again I hesitate to undertake new cases, it is just because I have to see during the treatment too much of this daily and hourly striving against overpowering impulses. The joy of removing some obstacles from the way of the patients is too much overshadowed by the deep pity and sympathy with their suffering and craving during the whole period of successive treatments. To make a man fight where despair is inevitable, and where the enemy is necessarily stronger than his own powers, can certainly not be the moral demand. Morality postulates that everyone find conditions in which he can be victorious if he puts his strongest efforts to the task.

In our discussion of the mental symptoms I reported as an illustration of the suggestive treatment of the drug passion the case of a morphinist. To make clear this purposive side of the case as against the causal one which alone interested the physician, I may add a few features to the short report as a typical example. When that man left my laboratory for the last time to go out to work and happiness, you might well have believed from his joyful face that it had been an easy and pleasant time in which hypnotic influence smoothly removed from him the dangerous desire for morphine. In truth it was the result of four months of the most noble and courageous suffering and struggling. He had been for years a slave to his passion. To quote from his little autobiography: " When I realized that I was addicted to morphine, I was at first not at all worried as I did not then understand the real horror of the thing, and did not then realize all the future suffering and misery that is coming to anyone who is the user of opium or any of its alkaloids. For the first few months, I found great relief after every injection of morphine, but soon I could not get the same easy feeling and could eat but very little and what sleep I got was in the daytime. I finally went to the sanitarium of a doctor but it was simply a money-making business for him; if he ever cured anyone, I never heard of it. I then tried another one; it was the same kind of a place as the former. When I first went to see the professor in the Harvard Psychological Laboratory, I was using between thirty-two and thirty-eight grains of morphine daily. He put me under his treatment October 6th and that day cut me down by hypnotic treatment to nine grains a day or three doses of three grains a day. I took my hypodermic as directed, but on the following day I lay on the bed too exhausted to get up even to get around the room, and I could not eat and only drank a very little water. The desire for the drug was something terrible. But in about four days I got used to the loss of so much morphine and stayed on this amount for a week, seeing the professor every other day for hypnotic treatment and then returning to my room where I spent twenty-two hours of the twenty-four on the bed, but did not sleep more than two or three hours a day. At the end of the week I was cut off by hypnotic suggestion half a grain and this put me to fighting the desire again. This lasted two or three days and then I began to feel better and began to sleep a little more. But at the end of the week I was cut off another half grain, and the whole fight would have to be begun over. These reductions of the dose were made a week apart and sometimes only two days. The worst time of all was a cut from four injections of a fourth of a grain each to four of one eighth of a grain each, which was about January 10th. At this time I had the worst two days of my life. I tried whiskey, but it gave relief only for about half an hour and then the desire was worse than ever."

In this way every few days I gave the poor fellow under hypnotic influence the suggestion to reduce the dose of morphine in a prescribed way, and with enormous effort he withstood his craving for more, in spite of the fact that he had during all this winter a bottle with a thousand tablets of morphine, prescribed by an unscrupulous physician, in his writing desk. He was thus at every moment during the day and night in full possession of the deadly poison with which he could have fully satisfied his craving. It was a moral victory when he finally reached the point at which he went for several weeks without any desire for morphine and finally presented the remaining tablets to a hospital. And yet there would not have been the least chance for his winning this ethical victory without the outer help of the hypnotist. We do not eliminate the moral will but we remove some unfair obstacles from its path. We have no mystic power by which our will simply takes hold of the other man's will, but we inhibit and suppress by influence on the imagination those abnormal impulses which resist the sound desires. If that were immoral, we should have to make up our minds that all education and training were perverted with such immoral elements. Every sound respect for authority which makes a child willing to accept the advice and maxims of his elders is just such an influence. If it were really a moral demand that the will be left to its own resources and that no outside influence come to strengthen its power or remove its hindrances or smooth its path, then we ought to let the children grow up as nature created them and ought not to try to suppress from without by discipline and training, by love and encouragement, the willful impulses and the ugly habits. Even every good model for imitation is such a suggestive influence from without and every solemn appeal to loyalty and friendship, to patriotism and religion, increases the degree of suggestibility. That is the glory of life that the suggestive power may belong to moral values instead of mere pleasures, but it is not the aim of life to remain untouched by suggestion. And he who by suggestion helps the weak mind to overcome obstacles which the strong mind can overthrow from its inborn resources works for the good of the individual and of the community in the spirit of truest morality.

Much more justified than such ethical objections are the fears which move entirely in the causal sphere. It must be acknowledged that a method which has such powerful influence over the mind that it can secure ideas and emotions and impulses which the own will of the patient cannot produce, ought to be allowed only to those who are prepared for its skillful use. To hypnotize or to perform any persistent psychotherapeutic treatment may thus be dangerous, if it is done by the unfit. We have discussed before the injuries which might result from the administration of such powerful psychotherapeutic effects through the best meaning minister, but we can extend this fear to anyone who has not systematically studied medicine and to a certain degree normal and abnormal psychology. The possibilities of overlooking symptoms which ought to suggest an entirely different treatment, or of adjusting the treatment badly to the special physical conditions, or of ignoring the desirable physical supplement by drugs, or of creating unintentionally by suggestion injurious effects, are always open when medical amateurs undertake such work. Certainly there is no physician who is not liable to make mistakes, and a physician who has never given any attention to psychology and psychiatry would also be a rather poor agent of psychotherapeutic methods, but the probability is that such a physician would simply abstain by principle from all psychotherapeutic methods; his mistake only begins if from his lack of acquaintance with the subject he draws the conclusion that the method itself is undesirable. That his real preparation ought to include psychological studies we have pointed out before, and the time seems ripe for the community to urge such a reform of the studies.

All that involves the conviction that even the experimental psychologist as such is not prepared to enter into medical treatment; and a " Psychological Clinic," managed by a psychologist who is not a doctor of medicine, is certainly not better than a church clinic. I cannot even acknowledge the right of psychologists to make hypnotic experiments merely for the psychological experiment's sake. Nobody ought to be brought into a hypnotic or otherwise abnormal state of mind if it is not suggested by the interests of the subject himself. Science has the right to make hypnotic experiments, or experiments with abnormal mental states, only under the one condition that a physician has hypnotized the subject in the interests of his health and that the patient has agreed beforehand to allow in the presence of witnesses certain psychological studies. Needless to say that any hypnotization for mere amusement and as a parlor trick ought to be considered as criminal.

On some other objections which interest the community as such we had to touch before, and there is no need of returning to them with any fullness of argument. We spoke of the danger which the mental cures carry with them when they are based on any particular creed, and especially when they are tied up with a semi-religious arbitrary metaphysics. What is gained if some nervous disorders are helped by belief, if the belief itself devastates our intellectual culture and brings the masses down again to a view of the world which has all the earmarks of barbarism? That is indeed one of the central dangers of all non-medical suggestive cures, that while any belief may cure through the mere emotional power of the act of believing, the content of the belief gains an undeserved appearance of truth. Any absurd superstition can become accredited because its curative value may be equal to a truly valuable suggestion. The intellectual life of the community would have to suffer greatly if the way to be freed from bodily suffering had to be the belief in the metaphysical doctrines of Mrs. Eddy's " Science and Health." From a cultural viewpoint, too, suggestive therapeutics must stand the higher, the more sharply it is separated from special philosophical or religious doctrines. No theory of the world and of God ought to gain authority over the mind from such an external motive as a belief in its curative effects. Freest from such implications is certainly the hypnotic method of the physician who does not need the strong religious reënforcement of the suggestion because he reënforces instead the suggestibility of the patient by slight influences on his senses.

Even where sound religion without superstition and without pseudophilosophy stands behind the therapeutic work, the community will not give up the question whether the church does not necessarily neglect by it the interests which are superior. The community becomes more and more strongly aware that too many factors of our modern society urge the church to undertake non-religious work. Social aid and charity work ought to be filled with religious spirit, but to perform it is not itself religion. Still more that is true of the healing of the sick. Whether or not such expansion of church activity in different directions saps the vital strength of religion itself is indeed a problem for the whole community. The fear suggests itself that the spiritual achievement may become hampered, that in the competition of the church with the other agencies of social life the particular church task may be pushed to the background, and that thus the church in imitating that which others can do just as well or better loses the power to do that which the church alone can do. The final outcome is therefore practically in every way the same. From whatever starting point we may come, we are led to the conviction that the physician alone is called to administer psychothera-

peutic work, but that he needs a thorough psychological training besides his medical one.

But the interest of the community is not only a
negative one. Society does not only ask where psychical treatment can be dangerous, but asks with not
less right whether the scheme and the method might
not be fructified for other social ends besides the mere
healing of the sick. If psychotherapy demonstrates
that for instance hypnotism makes possible the re-
shaping of a pathological mind, it is a natural
thought to use the same power for remodeling perhaps the lazy or the intemperate, the careless or the
inattentive, the dishonest or the criminal mind.
Both educators and criminologists have indeed often
raised such questions, and social reformers have not
seldom seen there wide perspectives for social movements in future times.

There can be no doubt that the possibility of such
remodeling activity is given, but as far as education
is concerned certainly grave misgivings ought to be
felt. When we spoke of the treatment of the sick,
we had always to emphasize that the suggestion cures
symptoms but not diseases. In the same way hypnotic suggestion might reënforce a single trait but
would not reform the personality of the child. Yes,
the artificial reënforcement of such special features
would deprive education of that which is the most
essential, namely, the development of the power to
overcome difficulties by own energy. Wherever a
reasonable amount of own will force and attention
can be expected to overcome the antagonistic influ-

ence, there artificial hypnotic influence ought to be avoided. Everything ought to be left in that case to suggestions within normal limits, in the form of good example and persuasions, authority and discipline, love and sympathy. That holds true even for very slight abnormalities which seem still within the limits where the own energies can bring about the cure. For instance, I have steadily refused requests of students and others to use hypnotism for the purpose of overcoming merely bad habits, such as the habit of biting the nails. A child who finds some difficulty in sticking seriously to his tasks might learn now this and now that under the influence of hypnotic suggestions but he would remain entirely untrained for mastering the next lesson. In the same way some naughty traits might be artificially removed but the child would not gain anything towards the much more important power of suppressing an ugly tendency by his own effort. All that finds its limits where the inhibitions or obstacles in the brain of the child are too strong possibly to be overcome by the own good will, but in that case we already stand in the field of abnormal mental life and then of course psychotherapy has its right. The feeble-minded and the retarded child, the perverse child and the emotionally unstable child, belong under the care of the physician, and in such a case he ought not to hesitate to use the whole supply of psychotherapeutic methods which are at his disposal.

Still more complex is the criminological problem. It sounds like an easy remedy for the greatest social calamity, if it is proposed simply to hypnotize the criminal and to supplant his antisocial will by a moral one. And if the absurdity of such a proposal is recognized it seems to many justified to demand such an intrusion at least in the case of the born criminal, even if the occasional criminal cannot be reached. But the conception of the born criminal is also only a label which is superficially used for a great variety of minds. That men are born with a brain which necessarily produces criminal actions is not indicated by any facts. The varieties which nature really produces are brains which are more liable than others to produce antisocial actions. We recognized from the start that the abnormal mind never introduces any new elements but is characterized only by a change of proportions. There is too much or too little of a certain mental process and just for that reason there must be a steady and continuous transition from the normal to the entirely abnormal. Here again we have not a special class of brains which are criminal; but we have an endless variety of brains with a greater or smaller predisposition for antisocial outbreaks. The variations which produce this criminal effect may lie in most different directions.

The brain may be for instance inclined to overstrong impulses, so that any desire rushes to action before the inhibiting counter-idea gets to work. Or, on the other hand, the brain may have unusually weak counter-ideas so that even a normal impulse does not find its normal checking. The fact that selfish and thus antisocial desires awake in the mind is not abnormal at all; only if they are not normally inhibited, the disturbance sets in. Furthermore the associative apparatus of the brain may work especially slowly; it may thus bring it about that the counteracting ideas do not arise in time. Or the emotions of a person may be unusually strong. Or there may be strong suggestibility, by which a bad example or a strong temptation has especially easy access. Or there may be negative suggestibility, by which a moral admonition stirs up a vivid idea of the opposite. In short, there may be a large number of factors, sometimes even in combination, each one of which increases the chances that the individual may come in danger in the midst of developed society. Yet no one of those factors involves just the necessity of crime. The same kinds of brains might simply show stupidity or credulity or inconsiderateness or brutality or stubbornness or egotism, and might by each of those factors decrease their chances in the community without directly running into conflict with the law. The criminal is therefore never born as such. He is only born with a brain which is in some directions inefficient and which thus, under certain unfavorable conditions, will more easily come to criminal deeds than the normal brain.

With the idea of a stereotyped born criminal there disappears also the idea of a uniform treatment against criminal tendencies. That men are different in their power of resistance or in their power of efficiency or in their intellect or in their emotions, we have to accept as the fundamental condition with which every society starts. It would be absurd to remodel them artificially after a pattern. The result would be without value anyhow, inasmuch as our appreciation is relative. No character is perfect. The more the differences were reduced, the more we should become sensitive even for the smaller variations. All that society can do is, therefore, not to remodel the manifoldness of brains, but to shape the conditions of life in such a way that the weak and unstable brains also have a greater chance to live their lives without conflicts with the community.

The situation is different as soon as the particular surroundings have brought it about that such a brain with reduced powers has entered a criminal career. The thought of crime now becomes a sort of obsession or rather an autosuggestion. The way to this idea has become a path of least resistance, and as soon as such an unfortunate situation has settled itself, the chances are overwhelming that a criminal career has been started. If such cases should come early to suggestive treatment which really would close the channels of the antisocial autosuggestion, much harm might be averted. Yet again the liability of the brain to become antisocial would not have been removed, and thus not much would be secured unless such a person after the treatment could be kept under favorable conditons. With young boys who through unfortunate influence have caught a tendency, for instance, to steal, and where the fault does not yield to sympathetic reasoning and to punishment, an early hypnotic treatment might certainly be tried. I myself have seen promising results. But if the impulse has irresistible character in such a way that the good will is powerless, we are again in the field of disease and the point of view of the physician has to be substituted for that of the criminologist.

Whether pedagogy and criminology are to make use of the services of psychotherapy is thus certainly an open question. It would be short-sighted to overlook the serious obstacles which stand in the way. But while the social life outside of the circle of real disease may better go on without direct interference by psychotherapeutic influences, it is certainly the duty of the community to make the underlying principles of psychotherapy useful for the sound development of society. The artificial over-suggestions which are needed to overcome the pathological disturbances of mental equilibrium may be left for the cases of illness. But we saw that every mental symptom of disease was only an exaggeration of abnormal variations which occurred within the limit of health. To reduce these abnormalities means to secure a more stable equilibrium and thus to avoid social damages, and at the same time to prevent the growth of the abnormality to pathological dimensions. To counteract these slighter variations, these abnormalities which have not yet reached the degree of disease, will demand the same principles of treatment, only in a weaker form. It is in a way not psychical therapy but psychical hygiene. And this is no longer confined to the physician but must be intrusted to all organs of the community. And here more

than in the case of disease, the causal point of view
of the physician ought to be brought into harmony
with the purposive view of the social reformer, of
the educator and of the moralist.

The ideal of such mental hygiene is the complete
equilibrium of all mental energies together with their
fullest possible development. To work towards this
end does not mean to aim towards the impossible and
undesirable end of making all men alike, but to give
to all, in spite of the differences which nature and society condition, the greatest possible inner completeness and outer usefulness. The efforts in that direction have to begin with the earliest infancy and are
at no age to be considered as finished; the whole
school work and to a high degree the professional
work has to be subordinated to such endeavor. Society has further to take care that those spheres of
life which stand less under systematic principles, such
as the home life of the child and the social life of the
man, his family life and his public life, are steadily
under the pressure of influences which urge in the
same direction.

Harmonious development without one-sidedness,
and yet with full justice to the individual talents and
equipments, should be secured. That means from
the start an effort to secure balance between general
education and particular development. The latter
has to strengthen those powers by which the boy or
girl by special natural fitness promises to be especially
efficient and happy. It has to be supplemented later
by a wise and deliberate choice of such a vocation as

brings these particular abilities most strongly to a focus. Yet this alone would mean a one-sidedness in which the equilibrium would be lost. More important, it would leave undeveloped that power which the youth especially needs to acquire by serious education, the power to master what does not appeal to the personal likings and interests. An equilibrium is secured only if at the same time full emphasis is given to the learning and training in all which is the common ground of our social existence. From the multiplication table to the highest cultural studies in college, the youth is to be adjusted to the material of our civilization without any concession to the emasculating desire to adjust civilization simply to the particular youth. He has to learn learning and not only to play with knowledge, he has to learn to force his attention in adjustment to those factors of civilization which are foreign to his personal tendencies and perhaps unsympathetic. Free election of life's work and unyielding mental discipline in the service of the common demands should thus steadily coöperate. The one without the other creates a lack of mental balance which is the most favorable condition for a pathological disturbance.

The mere learning is of course on both sides only a fraction of what the community has to develop in the youth. Mental hygiene begins with physiological hygiene. The nourishment of the child, the care for the child's sense organs, the recesses and the rest from fatigue, and especially the undisturbed sleep are essential conditions. The interferences with sufficient sleep are to a high degree responsible for the later disturbances of the mental life. It must not be forgotten that the decomposition of the brain molecules can never be restituted by anything but rest, and ultimately by sleep. Physical exercise is certainly not such restitution. In the best case it brings a certain rest to some brain centers by engaging other brain parts. The child needs sleep and fresh air and healthful food more than anything else, if his mind is active. The careful examination of the sense organs and of the unhindered breathing through the nose is most important. Even a slight defect in hearing may become the cause of an under-development of attention.

More important than mere physical hygiene is the demand that a sound character and a sound temperament are also to be built up, at the side of a sound interest. Here again everything depends upon a wise balance between the development of that which is given by nature to the particular individual and the reënforcement of that which society demands and which belongs therefore to the common equipment. The emotional stability and emotional enlargement of the mind is perhaps most neglected in our educational schemes. On the one side it demands a systematic discipline of the emotions, on the other a healthy stimulation of emotions. Here is the place where imagination in play and later in art come in. The biological value of play always lies in the training for the functions of later life, and especially for the emotional functions. The play of our children is too little adjusted to this task. For this reason it leaves too many unprepared for the world of art and for the emotional experiences of real life. Both lack of emotional discipline and narrow one-sidedness of emotions interfere with the harmonious development. Destructive emotions like terror ought to be kept away and not needlessly brought near by uncanny stories and mystic superstitions. It is the healthy love and sympathy of the home which contributes most strongly to the normal development of emotions. Again in the field of will, we want the strong, spontaneous, independent will which is not frightened by discomfort and not discouraged by obstacles, and yet we want the will which is not stubborn and selfish but which subordinates itself to the larger will of the social group and to the eternal will of the norm. There is no balance where independence and subordination do not supplement each other. A wide education not only trains for both but also secures habits which work as autosuggestions in both directions.

But all this harmonious development of intellect and temperament and character has to go on when the school days are over and just here begins the duty of the community as a whole. The special functions of the teachers have to be taken up by the public institutions. The whole social life must shape itself in such a way that everyone finds the best possible chances to perfect this harmonious growth. In the field of the intellect, the community must take care that thoroughness of training and accuracy of information is rigidly demanded and not thrust out by an easygoing superficiality. The expert ought to replace the amateur in every field. Every society which allows successes to superficiality diminishes its chances for mental health. Yet while thoroughness demands concentration in one direction, society must with the same earnestness insist on well-rounded general education and continuity of general interests through life. Literature and the libraries, the newspapers and the magazines play there a foremost rôle, and again the mental health of the community has to pay the penalty if its newspapers work against general culture. In the emotional field art and music, fiction and the theater on the one side, the church on the other side, remain the great schools for a development of sound emotions. Where literature becomes trivial, where the stage becomes degraded, and where the church becomes utilitarian and uninspiring, great powers for possible good in emotional education are lost. But with this enrichment of feelings the disciplinary influence too has to go through the whole social life. Where art is sensational and the church hysterical,—in short, where the community stirs up overstrong feelings,—the wholesome balance is lost again. In a similar way the public demands should throughout stimulate the energy and ambitions and initiative of the man, and yet should keep his desires and impulses in control.

Few factors are more influential in all these directions than the administration of law. Sound sober lawmaking and fair judgment in court secure to the community a feeling of safety which gives stability to emotions and feelings. The disorganization which results from arbitrary laws, from habitual violation of laws, from corruption and injustice works like a poison on the psychophysical system. A similar unbalancing influence emanates from overstrong contrasts of poverty and comfort. A poverty which discourages and leaves no chances and a wealth which annihilates the energies and effaces the consciousness of moral equality, create alike pernicious conditions for mental balance.

Unlimited furthermore are the influences which depend upon the sexual ideas of the society. It is the sphere in which it may be most difficult to indicate the way towards a development without dangers. There is no doubt the arbitrary suppression of the sexual instinct must be acknowledged as the source of nervous injury while indulgence may lead to disease and misery. But in any case frivolous habits and easy divorce contribute much to the unbalanced life which ruins the unstable individual. Not less difficult and not less connected with the mental hygiene is the alcohol problem. For normal adult men mild doses have through their power to relieve the inhibitions undeniable value for the sound development of the community. Its intemperate use or its use by young people and by pathological persons is one of the gravest dangers. Whether intemperance ought to be fought by prohibition or rather by an education to temperance is a difficult question in which the enthusiastic women and ministers, backed by the well justified fears of psychiatrists, will hardly be on the same side as the sober judgment of scientists, unprejudiced physicians, and historians. In any case the saloon and its humiliating indecency must disappear and every temptation to intemperance should be removed. Above all, from early childhood the self-control has to be strengthened, the child has to learn from the beginning to know the limits to the gratification of his desires and to abstain from reckless over-indulgence. With such a training later on even the temptations of alcoholic beverages would lose their danger. Not less injurious than the strong drinks are the cards. All gambling from the child's play to the stock exchange is ruinous for the psychophysical equilibrium. The same is true of any overuse of coffee and tea and tobacco, and as a matter of course still more the habitual use of the drugs like the popular headache powders and sleeping medicines. The life at home and in public ought to be manifold and expansive but ought to avoid overexcitement and over-anxiety. A good conscience, a congenial home, and a serious purpose are after all the safest conditions for a healthy mind, and the community works in preventive psychotherapy wherever it facilitates the securing of these three factors.

For that end society may take over directly from the workshop of the psychotherapist quite a number of almost technical methods. Suggestion is one of them. The means of suggestion through education and art, through the church and through public opinion, through example and tradition, and even through fashion and prejudices, are millionfold, but not less numerous are the channels for antisocial and antihygienic suggestions. No one can measure the injury done to the psychophysical balance of the weaker brains, for instance, by the sensational court gossip and reports of murder trials in the newspapers for the masses. But while the influence of suggestion is on the whole familiar to public opinion, the community is much less aware of another factor which we found important in the hands of the psychotherapist. We recognized that mental disturbances were often the result of suppressed emotion and repressed wishes. For the cure the psychotherapist has to aim toward the cathartic result. The suppressed ideas had to be brought to consciousness again and then to be discharged through vivid expression. Society ought to learn from it that few factors are more disturbing for the mental balance than feelings and emotions which do not come to a normal expression. It is no chance that in countries of mixed Protestant and Catholic civilization, the number of suicides is larger in Protestant regions than in the Catholic ones where the confessional relieves the suppressed emotions of the masses. This is also the most destructive effect of social and legal injustice; emotions are strangulated and then begin to work mischief. The community should take care early that secret feelings are avoided, that the child is cured from all sullenness which stores up the emotion instead of discharging it. Certainly all education and social life demands inhibition and also the child has to learn not to give ex-

pression to every passing feeling.   To find there the
sound middle way is again the real hygienic ideal.
Too much in our social life and especially in the
sphere of sexuality forces on the individual a hypoc-
risy and secrecy which is among the most powerful
conditions of later mental instability.

Of course the background of a hygienic life of the
community remains the philosophy of life which gives
unity to the scattered energies and consequently
steadiness to the individual through all his hazards of
fate.   It might seem doubtful whether society could
get the prescription for such a steady view of the
world also from the workshop of the psychotherapist.
To the superficial observer the opposite might seem
evident, as every word of our psychotherapeutic study
indicated that that is a view of life which makes
man's inner experience simply an effect of foregoing
causes.   All life becomes a psychophysical mechanism
and from that point of view man's thinking and acting become the necessary outcome of the foregoing
conditions.   Nothing seems more unfit to give a
deeper meaning to life and a higher value.   And yet
if there was one thought which controlled our discussion from the beginning, it was certainly the conviction that this causal view itself is only an instrument in the service of idealistic endeavors; the reality
of man's life is the reality of will and freedom directed towards ideals.   One of these ideals is the
reconstruction of the world in the thought forms of
causality.   In the service of our ideals we may thus
transform the world into a mechanism: out of our

freedom we desire to conceive ourselves as necessary products. Whenever we aim to produce changes in the world, we must calculate the effects through the means of this causal construction, but we never have a right to forget that this calculation itself is therefore only a tool and that our reality, in which our duties and our real aims lie, is itself outside of this construction. The psychotherapist wants to produce effects inasmuch as he wants to cure disease. He is therefore obliged to adjust his work as such entirely to the causal aspect of man, as soon as he wants to seek the means by which he can reach the end. But even the fact that he decides in favor of those ends, that he aims towards their realization, binds him to a world of purposes, and therefore, he, too, with his whole psychophysical work, stands with both feet in a reality of will which is controlled not by causes but by purposes, not by natural laws but by ideals.

INDEX

399

INDEX

Printed in Great Britain
by Amazon

THE SIEGE OF BRADFORD

An account of Bradford
in the Civil War,
together with the text of
The Rider of the White Horse
a rare pamphlet of 1643

Compiled and edited by staff of
Bradford Libraries and Information Service

© 1989 Bradford Libraries and Information Service and P. R. Newman.
British Library Cataloguing in Publication Data
THE SIEGE OF BRADFORD: an account of Bradford in the
Civil War, together with the text of *The Rider of the White Horse,*
a rare pamphlet of 1643.
1. English Civil War. Siege of Bradford
I Bradford Libraries and Information Service
942.06'2
ISBN 0-907734-17-0

Printed by Bradford Metropolitan Council Printing Unit

Published by Bradford Libraries and Information Service 1989.
Second impression 1992.

Contents

Illustrations

Illustrations on pages 12, 13, 17, 18, 22, 38 and on the cover provided by courtesy of the Bradford Art Galleries and Museums Service.

Acknowledgements

Ros Cooper (formerly of Bradford Libraries and Information Service) for the idea and initial groundwork.

Andy Parkes (formerly of Bradford Libraries and Information Service) for transcription and introductory essay.

Dr. P. R. Newman (Castle Museum, York) for the main essay.

Anthea Bickley (Bradford Art Galleries and Museums Service) for advice and assistance.

Konrad Ronkowski, for photography.

Bob Duckett and Lesley Norton (Bradford Libraries and Information Service) for editorial work.

4

BRADFORD IN THE 1640s

West Yorkshire in the 17th century bore little resemblance to the area of today. The region consisted of small towns and villages. York, Wakefield and Pontefract were the most important settlements at this time; Leeds and Bradford were about half the size of Wakefield; while the smaller towns and villages were little more than hamlets. The population of the township of Bradford in 1602 has been estimated at 2,560, a figure which would not have increased much by 1640.

Bradford Dale — the valley of the Bradford Beck — which is now almost entirely urbanized, was then sparsely populated. It contained cloth-making settlements and some small-scale coal pits *(bell-pits)*. The inhabitants were mainly small-holding crofters who included cloth-making as a secondary activity. In the Bradford area itself, because of the poor quality of the land, people had to rely on cloth production as their primary source of income. This was essentially a cottage industry spread over a wide area supplemented by subsistance farming.

Physically, the appearance of Bradford Dale was considerably different to modern rural areas in that it was almost entirely open common land. Only the lands of Bradford Manor (the area immediately surrounding the town of Bradford) had been enclosed into fields by the middle of the 17th century.

John Leland, the Antiquary of Henry VIII described Bradford as a busy market town, economically based on the clothing trade, and this description would still have been applicable during the reign of Charles I. But with a population of less than three thousand, Bradford would be considered little more than a village by modern standards.

The three main streets in the 17th century were Westgate, Ivegate and Kirkgate, all of which survive in more or less the same location today. The centre of the town was the junction of the three streets where the market cross once stood. Further out from these streets (or *gates*) was open countryside.

The roads at this time were merely muddy tracks, which were frequently impassable. The streets within the town were usually better maintained since the people who lived alongside were legally responsible for their upkeep. However, Kirkgate was in poor condition in 1607 when 17 of its inhabitants were fined 10 shillings each for neglecting its repair. The pavement in Kirkgate was not continuous and the roadway was very soft and muddy, with rubbish and other household waste, together with ashes, all being thrown onto it from the houses lining the street. The Courts were kept busy issuing orders that sewage, rubbish and ashes should be removed from the streets.

The only buildings which survive today from the time of the Civil War are the Cathedral, Bolling Hall and the Paper Hall. It is probable that the houses in

Bradford at the time of the Civil War were of stone construction similar to the older houses that survive in more outlying districts today. Most of the houses had two stories, but were considerably cramped as regards living space since many would have been inhabited by merchants of various trades.

Bradford Beck was the chief source of water and was frequently in danger of pollution. There were two bridges over the beck at Bradford, one at the bottom of Ivegate and the other joined Kirkgate to Church Bank. The latter bridge was called Church Bridge and was wide enough for pedestrians and single horses, but carts and carriages would have had to ford the beck.

Bradford was relatively important during the War because of its strong support of the parliamentary cause due to its chiefly puritan population. In other respects it was a relatively insignificant place. Despite the fact that the cloth-trade was of considerable importance to Bradford, the town did not occupy a position of any great importance as regards the textile industry in Yorkshire. It was, indeed, well behind York, Halifax and Ripon in terms of production. The three small streets on the slope of the hill above the curve of the Bradford Beck formed a small but busy trading centre, relatively wealthy for its size, but had only a localised commercial importance.

SOURCES

Empsall, Thomas Thornton. *Some social aspects of Bradford in the 16th century.* (Unpublished typescript — No date).

Fieldhouse Joseph. *Bradford.* 2nd ed. 1978.

James, John. *History and Topography of Bradford.* 1841.

Law, Margaret. *The story of Bradford.* 1913.

Richardson, C. *A geography of Bradford.* 1976.

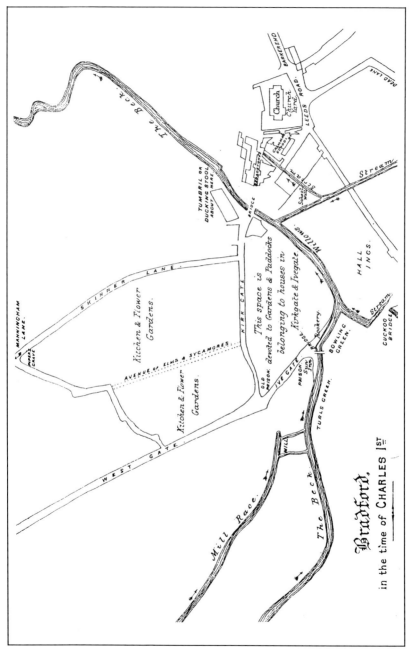

Bradford,

in the time of CHARLES 1ST.

Plan of Bradford in the time of Charles I drawn by Mr. W. Claridge and first published in his *Origin and History of the Bradford Grammar School.* 1882.

7

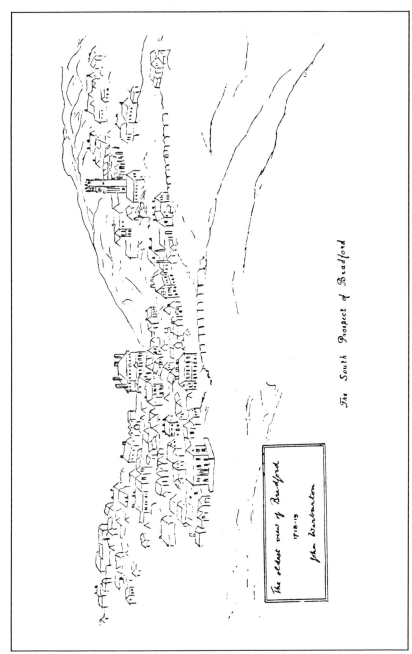

The oldest view of Bradford
1718-19
John Warburton

The South Prospect of Bradford

Drawing of Bradford 1719 by Samuel Buck for John Warburton.

8

THE CIVIL WAR AND BRADFORD

An essay by Dr. P. R. Newman

The pamphlet *The Rider of the White Horse,* published in London early in 1643, introduced to a wider public the parliamentarian hero, Sir Thomas Fairfax. Although parliament's successes in Yorkshire were due to active local men like Sir Thomas, the actual command of the parliament's army lay with Sir Thomas's father. Ferdinando, Lord Fairfax was an elderly man: although he occasionally took the field, it was to his son that he turned for the man of action.

The pamphlet celebrated parliamentarian triumphs in Yorkshire in the early part of the winter of 1642/3: that is, within only a few months of the outbreak of civil war in August 1642. Although for much of the spring and summer of 1642 the King, Charles I, had held his court at York and gathered about him supporters from within the county and from elsewhere, royalist organisation in the county was poor. When Charles I rode away on the journey that was to take him to Nottingham, where he raised his standard, and to Edgehill where the first major battle of the civil wars was fought, he left behind in Yorkshire a ramshackle military command. Headed by the somewhat passive Earl of Cumberland, the Yorkshire royalists proved unable to do much else than to hold York and the routes north. Even these were under threat from parliamentarian forces at Scarborough. The Fairfaxes and their fellow commanders, the Hothams in Hull, seemed to be able to move around the southern, western and eastern parts of the county with impunity. They even raided up to the very walls of York itself. The more active Yorkshire royalists, led by Sir Marmaduke Langdale and Sir William Saville, in despair at Cumberland's ineptitude, secured sufficient support to organise a coup against Cumberland. The old earl stepped down from command in November 1642, and was replaced by the far more energetic Earl of Newcastle and his military staff, virtually to a man tried and tested commanders. Newcastle's army was derided in London and elsewhere as a 'popish army', but it was a very real menace. The victories which Sir Thomas Fairfax, the Rider of the White Horse, was able to score against it were inflated out of all proportion as a consequence. Fairfax became a household name far beyond Yorkshire, and much was expected of him. His ultimate failure did not diminish the respect with which his earlier exploits surrounded him.

The Earl of Newcastle entered Yorkshire from the north in early December 1642, with an army of from 8 to 9,000 men. The existing royalist forces in Yorkshire were far fewer, and the parliamentarians had few men in arms. When Captain John Hotham took Cawood Castle in October, he had less than 1,000 men to call on. In that same month, when royalists from York established a

9

base at Leeds and launched an attack on Bradford on October 23rd, their 800 or so were driven off by less than half that number, and were so well beaten, that Leeds was abandoned and fell into parliamentarian hands. Thus it was the size of the Earl of Newcastle's relief army that caused the greatest concern to parliament's friends in the county. They would have to rely upon superior generalship to hold their own.

Within a week of arriving at York, the Earl of Newcastle struck at Tadcaster and Wetherby, seizing the bridges and driving out the enemy garrisons. Sir Thomas Fairfax drew his forces together at Selby, whilst Newcastle's troops advanced south and linked up with the small royalist garrison in Pontefract. An attempt by Fairfax to push through to the West Riding had to be given up. There were brisk cavalry actions at Monk Fryston (December 10th) and at Sherburn in Elmet (December 12th/13th) which Fairfax won, but these were fought against small royalist outliers.

The Earl of Newcastle decided to strike at the West Riding, and his primary target was Bradford. Against this minor town he launched a massive army, and it was Sir Thomas Fairfax's triumphant resistance that generated the legend of the *Rider of the White Horse*. Royalist forces occupied Leeds and Wakefield commanded by Sir William Saville. At about 10 in the morning of December 18th, the royalist vanguard under Colonel William Evers appeared outside Bradford. The garrison, we are told, had only 80 muskets amongst them, but there were a large number of local irregulars or 'clubmen' armed with scythes and pitch-forks. Chains and barricades were used to block the streets. It was rumoured that royalist sympathisers within Bradford would hand the town over, as they were said to have done in Leeds and Wakefield, but if this was true, they made very little effort to interfere with the defence. From various sources, it is possible to piece together the sequence of events of this battle for Bradford.

Conditions within Bradford, for the civilian population at least, must have bordered upon panic. There was no senior parliamentarian commander present in the town: the local militia were away on active service with Lord Fairfax, and although help was expected from Halifax, the decision to fight in face of so threatening an army was a brave one. Nevertheless, when the royalists appeared before the town, the houses must have been heavily shuttered and barred, and the inactive majority of the townsmen cowering nervously within doors. Sir William Saville had commanded the town to surrender: by the laws of war, if it did not, and it was stormed and taken, the royalist army would probably sack it. It was an unenviable predicament.

The royalist army approached the town without the usual caution. Perhaps they anticipated that Bradford would offer only light resistance, if any, at the last hour. They were fired upon by marksmen on the church steeple: "Our steeple had a notable advantage of them, which our musquitiers there especially improved against them, for when any buffe or skarlet coat appeared, they laid 2 or 3 of their peeces in one hole, and discharged at once upon them".

10

Saville's advance was halted in its tracks. He at once occupied houses near to the church, positioned a cannon, and sent Captain Goodricke with a troop of horse to the west of the town. Goodricke's men were driven off by musketeers. From the houses near the church the royalist gunners opened fire up Kirkgate, and the marksmen on the church replied with volleys of concentrated fire.

At this point, the men from Halifax arrived under Captain John Hodgson, and launched an attack on the royalist positions. It is likely that further reinforcements from Bingley had also reached the town. The onslaught of the Halifax troops distracted the royalists from their attack on the church, and in the lull, the defenders poured out to counter-attack. The royalist forces thus engaged, abandoned their position, and withdrew into hedged fields close by, where the fighting became hand to hand. The royalist officers "manifested great courage, but they smarted for it; our scythes and clubs now and then reaching them, and none else did they aim at". The royalist cavalry counter-attacked, but the defenders rallied, and eventually drove them off with heavy loss. In this action, most, if not all, royalists wounded or taken were killed out of hand, a barbarity that was to give the people of Bradford great cause for fear later in the war.

From the cover of the hedgerows, royalist musketeers now opened fire on the victorious defenders and "rained such a shower of lead upon our men, as forced them to retreat". They took with them a few prisoners, including Captain Goodricke and a Major Carew who had commanded the attack on the church. The royalist main body drew back, although it had been only partially engaged. The bitterness and savagery of the action, and the courage displayed by the men of Bradford, Halifax and Bingley, does not obscure the fact that they had encountered only a fraction of the enemy army.

The specific feature of the battle for Bradford must be the unwillingness of the defenders to show quarter to fallen royalists, particularly officers. One source notes "a stout gallant officer, commanding a company of foot, came running down a field, shaded with a hedge, intending to come running into the church .... two of the townsmen met him, and struck him down; he cried out for quarter, and they poor men not knowing the meaning of it, said — 'aye, they would quarter him' and so killed him .... they sent a trumpeter to request his corpse, which was the next day delivered to them". This must be the same man as "one ... in a skarlet coate, our club-men had got hold of ... and were spoiling him", that is, stripping the body. The excuse that the defenders did not know the meaning of quarter is interesting: for it may be held to exemplify the difference between the experienced, professional soldier whom they killed out of hand, and their own raw, inexperienced response to war. Such killing is done more out of panic and in hot-blood rather than cold, but the royalists never forgot nor forgave what had happened.

The pamphlet *The Rider of the White Horse* gives in graphic detail the events of the battle for Bradford. The most significant aspect of that tract, however,

Sir Thomas Fairfax
Portrait at Bolling Hall

12

Helmets of the Civil War period on display at Bolling Hall.

13

is that whereas the victory is clearly attributed in its title page to Sir Thomas Fairfax and his army, neither he nor his field army were involved. The defenders of Bradford were irregulars, supported by irregulars from nearby: they overthrew a somewhat half-hearted royalist assault, on their own, and with startling success. The basis of the published account must have been a letter or letters written from Bradford shortly after the action, and the London press and propagandists gave the attribution to Fairfax on the narrow grounds that the irregulars were nominally at least, under his authority as his father's second-in-command. In this way, the courage of the townsmen was utilised in the general interests of parliament. There were two consequences of this. The first was, that to the reading public of England, Bradford and the action there assumed a momentary importance out of proportion to what actually happened. Secondly, the reputation both of Sir Thomas Fairfax and of his small army was boosted in the public eye: the battle for Bradford provided encouragement for parliamentarians everywhere, which was the point and purpose of the tract. Even so large and potentially dangerous an army as that of the Earl of Newcastle could be beaten by ordinary men with such a leader. That was the message. The truth was, that the royalists were over-confident, employed but a small part of their strength, and were beaten by men who, leaderless, were desperate.

The Earl of Newcastle's advance into the West Riding was temporarily halted. He withdrew his troops, and Bradford breathed again. All, however, must have known it was not the end, unless events elsewhere came to Bradford's aid. One of the purposes for which the Earl of Newcastle's army had been raised, was to provide an escort for the Queen, who was expected to arrive from Europe with men and materials for the royalist war effort. Her appearance at Bridlington in February 1643 temporarily distracted Newcastle: he was obliged both to guarantee her safety, and to either march south with her to join King Charles at Oxford, or at least to let her have some of his regiments as an escort. Either way, her presence in Yorkshire created some kind of hiatus in royalist military strategy.

Nevertheless, Parliament's efforts could not be abated. They suffered a major loss when the commander of their garrison at Scarborough, changed sides and declared for the King. The royalist left flank was thus secured, although Hull was still a potential threat, and it was in Hull that Lord Fairfax had made his headquarters, with an advance base at Selby to help communications between the West Riding and the port. Newcastle's army, once the Queen was safely lodged in York, was set free to turn its attention against the West Riding again. On March 28th 1643 General Goring marched to Wetherby with 1,600 men, Sir Thomas Fairfax abandoned Selby, and prepared to defend Leeds. Fairfax, however, hovered around Tadcaster too long, and was out-marched by the royalists, who launched an attack on that important bridge over the Wharfe. The parliamentarians withdrew in disorder, and there was a complete breakdown in their command as a consequence. The two armies were barely 800 yards apart when Fairfax began his march towards Leeds.

14

The two armies were probably equal in numbers, although General Goring knew that the Earl of Newcastle's main army was near Wetherby and well within reach. The fact that he did not attack Fairfax caused the parliamentarian troops to relax what discipline they had, and the march came to a straggling halt on Seacroft Moor. It was then that Goring struck. The parliamentarian army disintegrated utterly, the foot fleeing in all directions, many taken prisoner. Sir Thomas Fairfax and his cavalry made good their escape and reached Leeds, where Lord Fairfax was waiting for them, but they were in a fearful predicament. Sir Thomas marched straight to Bradford with 700 men and positioned himself there, whilst the royalists occupied Wakefield. By late March/early April of 1643 the royalist army was probably 21,000 strong, 18,000 of them infantry-men, and skirmishing was constant. Royalist troops raided Barnsley, a parliamentarian infantry unit changed sides at Elam, and there was constant killing in the vicinity of Leeds. Newcastle, however, posting a strong garrison in Wakefield, decided to march south to take Rotherham and Sheffield, and gave the parliamentarian commanders in the West Riding cloth towns a breathing space.

The main royalist army quit York, though leaving it garrisoned, and with the Queen in attendance moved towards Pontefract. With the Earl of Newcastle's attention thus concentrated to the south, the parliamentarians struck at Wakefield, capturing the town on May 21st after hard fighting in the streets. They were driven to this by the success of the Wakefield garrison in cutting off supplies from Bradford, Halifax and Leeds: the attack was a response to the pleas of local people, suffering privations, rather than part of any carefully deliberated strategic manouevre, but it was nevertheless successful because it was so unexpected. Over 1,500 prisoners were taken, among them General Goring, and the royalists suffered a severe blow to their prestige. The *Rider of the White Horse* and his army had won a major tactical victory, forcing the royalists to fall back again towards York, and opening the trade routes into the West Riding.

Nevertheless, it was a victory of no great significance. The Earl of Newcastle in early June sent the Queen off to Oxford with an armed escort under General Cavendish, and once she was safely on her way, the Earl was free to turn his attention again to the West Riding. The hour of Bradford's reckoning had come.

On June 22nd the Earl of Newcastle's forces took Howley House and its governor Sir John Saville of Lupset. Saville had refused a demand to surrender, and Newcastle had ordered that he in particular was to be slain on the spot. But when the house was stormed — it was certainly not tenable — Saville's life was spared. Word of Newcastle's order, however, spread into the West Riding and there can have been few in Bradford who did not fear his approach. Before the Earl reached that town, however, he had to fight a major battle, that of Adwalton Moor, on June 30th. This battle broke the back of parliamentarian resistance, and threw Bradford wide open to the royalist army.

15

The battle of Adwalton Moor was brought on by Lord Fairfax himself. The Earl's army was weakened by the despatch of 7,000 men with the Queen, and the parliamentary commanders were prepared to gamble on a confrontation. Fairfax and his son had been reinforced by 2,000 troops out of Lancashire, although these reinforcements seem to have played little part in the battle itself. The precise strength of the rival armies is difficult to estimate. Newcastle may have had between 7 and 10,000 men in the field, parliament's army perhaps numbered between 3 and 5,000, including the reinforcements. The parliamentarians lost the battle, and lost it decisively, not because they were outnumbered, but because their organisation was again at fault. Major General Giffard was late in rallying the troops to take the field, by which time the royalist army was already in battle order, its main body drawn up on level ground on Adwalton Moor, five miles south west of Bradford. To attack this position, the parliamentarian troops had to advance uphill. They made steady progress, whilst the royalist cavalry were hindered by the walls and hedges of the enclosed fields bordering the moorland. Two royalist colonels were killed in the discharge of musketry fire from parliamentarian infantry lining hedgerows.

The sources suggest that for a time the battle hung in the balance, but that Newcastle himself tipped it in the royalist favour by snatching up a pike and leading a counter-attack. The parliamentary army was divided, Sir Thomas Fairfax fled towards Halifax, and those that were not killed, were rounded up in large numbers. It was a major royalist victory and at a stroke destroyed the field army of the parliament in Yorkshire.

"It was observed by some" wrote Captain John Hodgson who fought at Adwalton Moor with his Halifax irregulars, "that the land was like Eden before him (i.e. Newcastle), and behind him as a barren wilderness". The horror expressed by Hodgson was the horror that gripped the inhabitants of Bradford, nurtured for long on tales of the wickedness of the 'popish' army, and remembering too well their refusal of quarter in the fight of December 1642. Bradford was crammed with fugitives from the battle. "What a sad discouraging day was that!" wrote Joseph Lister. "All the Lancashire men, horse and foot, ran away home, and could by no means be persuaded to stay in Bradford." Lord Fairfax had rapidly abandoned the town and made for Leeds, thence towards the security of Hull. He left behind him about 800 men.

With little apparent hurry, Newcastle laid his siege lines around Bradford and positioned cannon on the hills. The fire from the cannon demoralised the defenders, and feigned royalist attacks caused them to waste their precious ammunition. Sir Thomas Fairfax, who had slipped into Bradford, parleyed for the surrender of the town, but both sides were suspicious of each other, and nothing came of the talks. Under cover of darkness, the royalists launched two larger assaults, both of which were beaten off, but at the cost of what was left of the defenders' powder and shot. In the dark hours of early morning, Sir Thomas Fairfax gave orders to his officers and cavalry to try to break out, and abandoned Bradford to its fate.

16

The Earl of Newcastle
Portrait at Bolling Hall

17

Pieces of 17th Century Armour on display at Bolling Hall

Sir Thomas Fairfax himself make good his escape, taking a royalist picket by surprise, but the cavalry following him were set upon and badly handled. Sir Thomas's own wife fell into royalist hands. As for the parliamentarian infantry, they too tried to make a break for it, but were forced back inside the town where they had surrendered with daylight.

The Earl of Newcastle at Bolling Hall, seat of the royalist Colonel, Richard Tempest, must have known of the circumstances prevailing in the town. The civilian population having stood so resolutely by the *Rider of the White Horse* and his army, had been left to their fate. The church steeple, with wool packs tied to it to resist cannon fire, stood unmanned. "Oh what a night and morning was that in which Bradford was taken! what weeping, and wringing of hands! none expecting to live any longer than till the enemies came into the town, the Earl of Newcastle having charged his men to kill all ... and to give them all Bradford quarter". There is no evidence that Newcastle ever gave such an order, although technically, since the town had resisted his army, he was entitled to exact retribution if he could take it. Joseph Lister, an eye-witness, later noted that Newcastle retracted this order after his dreams were disturbed at Bolling Hall by a ghost pleading Bradford's cause. Yet the terror in Bradford, which Lister graphically described, was real enough. The phrase 'Bradford quarter' had taken on an ominous meaning in the war in Yorkshire, and there is no doubt that Lister and his fellow townsmen truly waited in terror.

In reality, the townsmen and their families got off lightly. When the royalists marched in "some desperate fellows wounded several persons, that died of their wounds afterwards; but I think not more than half a score were slain". These were probably some of the town irregulars, perhaps even men involved in the killing of the royalist officer in December 1642. Lister himself fled to Colne in Lancashire as the royalists entered, but ventured to return to Bradford a few days later. He "found few people left, but most of them scattered and fled away. I lodged in a cellar that night, but oh! what a change was made in the town ... nothing was left to eat or drink, or lodge upon, the streets being full of chaff and feathers, and meal, the enemies having emptied all the town of what was worth carrying away, and were now sat down and encamped near Bowling Hall, and there kept a fair and sold the things that would sell'.

Newcastle's triumph at Adwalton Moor, coupled with the capture of Bradford and Halifax and the dispersal of the parliamentarian army beyond immediate recovery, was rewarded. Later that year he was created Marquess of Newcastle, and his second in command and military adviser, James King, created Baron Eythin. From Bolling Hall, overlooking the desolation of Bradford, the royalist armies were poised to sweep south towards London. For the supporters of the parliament in the south, and particularly in the capital city, the immensity of Newcastle's achievement could not be ignored. Out of the fear which it aroused, emerged the alliance between parliament and the Scottish Covenanters that would ultimately undo all that Newcastle had achieved. But the fact was, that English parliamentarians alone could not do that.

It remains surprising that after the enormous victory of Adwalton Moor, the royalists did so little to turn it to full account. As late as July 5th, the Earl of Newcastle remained at Bolling Hall, sending out summonses to enemy garrisons to surrender to him. Some of his troops made threatening moves towards Lancashire, but the Pennine passes were heavily defended. Middleham Castle in Wensleydale may have yielded to the royalists at this point, but the Earl's primary concern was to be with Lincolnshire and the counties that immediately bordered Yorkshire to the south. It is unlikely that he garrisoned Bradford: he certainly withdrew his troops immediately after the sack, and although he kept a garrison in Leeds, so thorough had been his victory that he felt no pressing need to maintain a strong military presence in the West Riding towns.

For the rest of 1643 Bradford remained quiet, securely in the territory controlled by the royalists, and returning to some kind of normality. Trade would have picked up swiftly, with fighting now more or less unknown in Yorkshire except around the Lancashire border or in the area threatened by the parliamentary garrison at Hull. The parliamentary army of Yorkshire had been broken: part lay in Hull with Lord Fairfax, part had left the county with Sir Thomas. Newcastle bent his strength to subdue Lincolnshire and adjacent counties, and proved time and again how potent an army he now led. But the projected great march on London came to nothing. The Earl allowed himself to be drawn back into Yorkshire in the autumn of 1643 to deal with the problem of Hull. It was his most serious strategic error. The Yorkshire royalists that were not attached to the marching army, had an inordinate fear of the Hull garrison, and under their pleas for help, Newcastle returned and wasted his army in an abortive and, in the end, disastrous siege of the port. The royalist army went into winter quarters at the end of 1643 with its morale low, and facing the threat of Scottish invasion to their rear.

In January 1644 there was still military stability in the county. Although Hull remained securely parliamentarian, its capacity for mounting anything other than nuisance raids was limited. Sir Thomas Fairfax was occupied in Cheshire with most of his Yorkshire army. Sir William Saville, a leading West Riding royalist, had died in office as Governor of York, and had been replaced by John Belasyse, a Yorkshireman who had been serving as a colonel with the royalist army at Oxford. It was into John Belasyse's hands that the security of the West Riding fell when the Scottish army finally invaded, and in the late winter of 1643/4 Bradford was once again dragged into the fighting.

Clashes between royalist troops and local or Lancashire irregulars became more frequent in January, as the promised Scottish invasion began to bolster the courage of the parliamentary commanders. On January 4th a royalist quarter at Sowerby was raided by unidentified parliamentarian irregulars from Heptonstall. These same irregulars were later badly beaten up at Mixenden. Sir Francis Mackworth, Newcastle's commander in the West Riding, hanged two prisoners taken there who were identified as deserters from the royalist army. There may have been skirmishing at Farnley around this time, but on

Musketry drill

21

Bolling Hall, Bradford. Temporary HQ of the Earl of Newcastle

22

January 28th Mackworth was recalled to York to participate in the war to the north, against the Scots, who had already occupied the whole of Northumberland.

John Belasyse, whose secretary has left a comprehensive account of his master's activities as Governor of York, was faced with an enormous task. He had to hold York, maintain the routes north for ferrying supplies and wounded men between the city and the field army; he had to recruit fresh troops; and he had also to contain the enemy in Hull and preserve the West Riding from incursions. Although a man of courage and resource, Belasyse found himself unable to handle all these tasks successfully. More than that, he had to deal with rivalries and enmities within the royalist faction in Yorkshire. The old Earl of Cumberland, who had been replaced by Newcastle as commander in chief in 1642, had died in 1643. His death meant the loss of a restraining hand, and the critical moment of the war created tensions that resulted in a decline in morale amongst officers of the Yorkshire army and civilian committee men. What probably added to Belasyse's difficulties was the fact that he was a Catholic, and there were many royalists whose attitudes to Catholics were not far different from those of parliamentarians everywhere. Nevertheless, Belasyse made considerable efforts to fulfill his onerous responsibility.

He established three headquarters for his army. At Malton he placed troops to overlook the East Riding, maintained a considerable garrison at York to safeguard the North Riding, and put into Leeds troops to overawe the cloth towns of the West Riding. There were also major infantry garrisons in Halifax and Doncaster. There were also roving cavalry units on the borders with Lincolnshire and Lancashire, keeping a constant watch. The first challenge, however, came from Hull. Lord Fairfax put cavalry into the field in mid February, and they won several actions — at Kilham near Driffield, at Bridlington where they took the town, at Driffield itself, and at Whitby where the town was occupied briefly. Belasyse, however, appreciated that however galling these victories were, they were of nuisance value only. His eye was fixed on the West Riding, and upon any attempted conjunction between enemy troops from Hull and those operating in small bands in the West Riding. As a consequence of this watchfulness, on March 3rd 1644 Bradford was again the scene of fighting.

Captain John Hodgson, the Halifax commander of irregulars who had fought at Bradford in 1642, had been detached from Sir Thomas Fairfax's army in Cheshire and had returned to Yorkshire. He came in a column of troops commanded by Major General John Lambert, one of parliament's better commanders. "We marched out of Cheshire to Sowerby, and from thence to Halifax, and back to Kighley, and so to Bradford" Hodgson wrote. At Bradford they found a small royalist force occupying the town, with musketeers in the church. The parliamentary cavalry were driven off in confusion, but Hodgson and the infantry charged home and scattered the royalists. They pursued them a little way, and then "retreated to Bradford, and quartered there a while". Advance detachments of the parliamentary force actually succeeded in seizing Tadcaster and holding on to it. From Bradford, other units on the night of March 5th/6th won a brief action at Hunslet near Leeds, where they spoiled a royalist cavalry regiment and took prisoners. There was further fighting at Kirklees near Huddersfield. In the East Riding, raiders from Hull stormed and took and occupied Stamford Bridge. A net was being drawn around the royalists at York, and Belasyse resolved to break it by a decisive action. He moved his main army to Leeds.

The events that were about to take place were critical for the war in the north of England as a whole. Belasyse thought sufficient of the parliamentarian threat to launch a major campaign away from his base at York. If he were to fail, the whole of the royalist war effort further north in Durham against the Scots would be placed in jeopardy. So he took with him to Leeds the bulk of his army, leaving a small garrison in York itself, and virtually abandoning the East Riding for the time being. This is a true measure of the threat posed by General Lambert. The royalist cavalry had been weakened since the fight at Bradford, by the despatch of 1,000 horse to join the army fighting the Scots. The size of the army at Belasyse's disposal was therefore not in excess of 6,500 men, of those about 5,000 were infantry. His choice of Selby as an operational base was sound. It enabled him to adopt a flexible posture, able to drive into the West Riding, but able also to deny any link-up between the troops from Hull and those operating to the west. He also had control of the river between Selby and York to ferry supplies back and forth.

Events elsewhere encouraged Belasyse to believe that he had the upper hand. On March 21st Prince Rupert relieved the siege of Newark on Trent, took the surrender of a large parliamentary army, and set free some royalists regiments from duty to the south. These regiments hurried north to assist Belasyse, under the command of General George Porter. Thus reinforced, Belasyse launched a large-scale advance against Bradford, where Lambert was stationed.

The attack took place on March 25th 1644. Although the sources are confusing, in that they reflect different viewpoints both of those taking part and those who received news of the action, the fighting at Bradford falls into four clear stages. The royalists attacked a town heavily defended by Lambert and his men, who fought off several assaults until their ammunition began to run low. The parliamentarians then attempted to escape from Bradford, and took the royalist cavalry under George Porter by surprise. Porter's men were scattered, and Lambert, instead of retreating, turned at bay. Porter's failure caused the main royalist army to draw back from the town, and Lambert immediately entered it again and assumed defensive positions. Belasyse's army withdrew towards Leeds, and the attack on Bradford was called off.

At this point, events conspired against the royalists in no uncertain terms. General Porter, who had disgraced himself outside Bradford, retreated into Nottinghamshire where he sat idle. Belasyse sent him orders to return to the main army, but Porter protested that his troops had been badly mauled and needed a rest. Although he did eventually set off northwards, he did not arrive in time to prevent a catastrophe overtaking the royalist army at Selby.

In the wake of the defeat of the royalists at Bradford, Lord Fairfax left Hull and joined his forces with those of his son, Sir Thomas, freshly arrived from Cheshire, at Ferrybridge. The parliamentary troops had instructions from London to move north to assist the Scots, and Belasyse clearly knew of this. He therefore waited at Selby from March 26th until April 11th to block any such move, anxiously awaiting news of the arrival of George Porter's men. At Selby, the royalist army of Yorkshire fought its last pitched battle, when the Fairfaxes and Lambert launched a fierce attack on April 11th.

The battle of Selby was a terrible defeat for the royalists. Their entire infantry were either killed or captured, and John Belasyse himself was wounded in hand to hand fighting before being taken prisoner. York was defenceless, and the parliamentarian domination of the West Riding was absolute. As a result of the action at Selby, the royalists fighting the Scots had to give up their campaign and retreat to defend York. The victorious parliamentary troops from the battle of Selby linked up with the Scots and laid siege to the royalist city, receiving reinforcements from the army of parliament's Eastern Association. In June 1644 Prince Rupert raised the siege of York, but was then decisively beaten in battle on Marston Moor on July 2nd. Henceforth, although there was still to be fighting in the county, and on occasion the parliamentary forces were to get the worst of it, Yorkshire fell into the ambit of parliament's territory. Bradford, which had witnessed no fewer than five encounters of rival armies between October 1642 and March 1644, now settled back into a kind of normality.

CHRONOLOGY

1642
Oct. 23rd   Royalist attack on Bradford beaten off.
Dec. 18th   Royalist forces under the command of Sir William Saville attack Bradford but are beaten off. *(Rider of the White Horse* account).

1643
June 30th   Battle of Adwalton Moor.
               Royalist forces under the command of the Earl of Newcastle defeat the Parliamentarian forces under the command of Lord Fairfax.
               Bradford occupied by Royalist forces.

1644
March 3rd   Parliamentary forces under the command of Major General John Lambert drive Royalist garrison out of Bradford.
March 25th   Royalist forces under the command of John Belasyse attack Bradford. Lambert's Parliamentary forces beat off the attack.

SOURCES USED

Much of the text is based upon the present writer's 1978 University of York D.Phil thesis, *The Royalist Armies in the North of England*, and upon his article 'The Defeat of John Belasyse: Civil War in Yorkshire January to April 1644', *Yorkshire Archaeological Journal*, Volume 52, 1980.

As well as the sources quoted extensively in those works, the present writer has used again *The Rider of the White Horse*, reproduced here; T. Wright ed. *Autobiography of Joseph Lister*, 1842; and 'Memoirs of Captain Hogson', *Bradford Antiquary*, N.S., Pt. XII, July 1908.

FOR FURTHER READING, the following are recommended:

Parsons, D., ed.   *The Diary of Sir Henry Slingsby.* 1836.
Firth, C.H., ed.   *Memoirs of the Life of Colonel Hutchinson, Governor of Nottingham, by his Widow Lucy.* 1906 edn.
Firth C.H., ed.   *Memoirs of William Cavendish, Duke of Newcastle, and Margaret, his Wife.* 1906.
Gatty, A., ed.   *Joseph Hunter's Hallamshire.* 1869.
Vicars, J.,   *Parliamentary Chronicles,* II. 1644.
Bell, R., ed.   *Memorials of the Civil War* (Fairfax Correspondence) Vol. I. 1849.
Holroyd, A. ed.   *Collectanea Bradfordiana, a collection of papers on the history of Bradford.* (Contains original and secondary sources). 1873.
Dewhirst, Ian.   *Pity Poor Bradford* (a 20th century illustrated account of the Civil War in Bradford) in *Yorkshire Ridings* magazine, vol. 6, no. 10, October 1969, pages 16-18.

NOTE ON THE AUTHOR

Dr. P. R. Newman, BA, DPhil, FRHistS, is the author of:
The Battle of Marston Moor, 1644. 1981.
Royal Officers in England and Wales, 1642 to 1660, a biographical dictionary. 1981, and
An Atlas of the English Civil War. 1985.

OPPOSITE

Facsimile reproduction of a rare pamphlet in the possession of Bradford Libraries and Information Service.

(The account relating to Leeds and Wakefield is *not* reproduced).

Note

Sir Thomas Fairfax was called *The Rider of the White Horse* because he rode upon an animal of that colour.

THE
RIDER OF THE WHITE HORSE

And His Army, Their late good
Succeſſe in YORRE-SHIERE.

OR

A true and faithfull Relation of that famous
and wonderfull victory at *Bradford*, obtained by
the Club-men there, with all the circum-
ſtances thereof.

And of the taking of *Leeds* and *Wakefield* by the ſame men
under the command of Sir *Thomas Fairfax*, with the manner and circumſtances thereof from good hands.

Serioully commended to the High Court of PARLIAMENT, and
all that are of GODs ſide for their incouragement.

LONDON,
Printed for *Thomas Underhill*, 1643.

1

BRADFORDS
Deliverance.

Fter the Lord *Fairfax* his Excellency had retired from *Tadcaſter*, the Lord of *New-caſtle* poſſeſſed himſelfe of *Pontefract*, ſo making himſelfe Maſter of our Weſterne parts, block't up all paſſages betweene us and our ſtrength, and then manifeſted his reſolutions to ſeſſe the whole County, but to exact extraordinary ſummes of thoſe who had ſubſcribed the Parliaments Propoſitions. We could expect nothing now, but that thoſe Townes ſhould firſt ſuffer, who had bin moſt forward to aſſiſt the Parliament; *Leeds*, *Bradford* and *Halifax* were principally aimed at. In *Leeds* the malignant humour being predominant, eaſily converted the Towne into their temper. *Bradford* was the next place in their way, the Towne moſt unable to reſiſt them; and indeed who ever conſiders their dangers, weakneſſe and diſcouragements, muſt judge their attempt as worthy admiration as their ſucceſſe. The maine body of the Popiſh Army was within a dayes march of *Bradford*, ſome amongſt them grievouſly exaſperated by a diſhonourable repulſe from this Towne not long before. So farre were we from expecting help from the Lord *Fairfax*, as we thought it ſcarce poſſible to ſeeke it : Our malignant ſpirits before charmed, now appeared, breathing forth nothing but threatnings againſt thoſe who had bin moſt active for the Parliament: and their apparition was ſo terrible, as it affrighted many of the beſt affected perſons out of the Towne ; and thereupon, out goes our Royaliſts to bring in the Kings Catholick Army. Some religious perſons in the Pariſh, conſidering what danger might reſult both to their conſciences and Country from ſuch cowardize and treachery (inſtigated by feare of perjury, if they ſhould contribute any aſſiſtance againſt the Parliament, and care of their lives and Eſtates, evidently endangered by a bare refuſall without reſiſtance) reſolved to ſtand upon their guard, invited all the well affected in the Pariſh to aſſiſt them, and entied the Towne. When out Malignants were returned with a Letter from Sir *William Savile*, wherein he manifeſted an intention to burne and plunder, if we did not contribute to the maintenance of the Popiſh Army. To which no other anſwer was return'd, then the apprehenſion of thoſe who brought it, and had ſubſcribed it ; All couragious attempts, yea deſperate in the account of many, who ſaw neither wiſedome nor ſtrength ſufficient to manage them ; There wanted both the head, body and ſinewes of warre, we had never a Gentleman in the Pariſh to command us, nor would any ſtranger be perſwaded to undertake the charge. All our trained Souldiers with their Armes, were with the Lord *Fairfax*, and the moſt of thoſe who were fitted for ſervice as voluntiers. Nor could it be expected, that the well affected

of

of our poore Parish, could pay a Garrison any long time, and none would tarry one day without pay. Our neighbours perceived this, and therefore judging our attempt desperate (as in the eye of reason it was) and fearing the issue would be our ruine, refused to helpe us, least they should perish with us. Nor wanted we discouragements from our own men, to instance in no more ; the very night before the Enemy assaulted us, the greatest part of them left us. This was on Saturday, *Decemb:* 17. The next morning about 9 of the Clock, the Enemy was discovered, approaching the East end of the Towne : They were marshall in two Bodies, the Van was commanded by Collonel *Evers* (eldest Sonne to the Lord *Evers*) wherein were 3 Troopes of Horse, 2 Companies of Dragooners, 100 Foot, 20 Pyoni rs, 2 Drakes, the traine of Artillery, commanded by Major *Carew* a Dutch man. The Rere was commanded by Sir *Francis Howard*, wherein were his own and Captaine *Hiliards* Troops, 6 Companies of Collonel *Eddringtons* Dragooners, and a 100 Foote. Collonel *Goring* came along with them, and some say the Earle of *Newport* ; but whether they had any charge or no in this expedition I heare not. All these our *York-shiere* Gentlemen had procured of the Lord of *New castle*, as though Sir *William Savils* Regiment, Sir *Marmaduke Langdale*, Sir *Thomas Gleman* and Sir *Iohn Gothericks* Troopes, Sir *Ingram Hopton*, Captain *Nevill*, Captaine *Batt*, Captaine *Bins* Companies had not bin sufficient to have swallowed our despicable Towne : I should now shew how our men were marshald, but *t*is a hard matter to marshall those who had neither Commanders, Collours, nor distinct Companies. The night before, we had borrowed a Commander of *Hallifax*, wee had neere upon 40 Musquets and Calievers, in Towne about 30 Fowling, Birding and smaller Peeces, and well nigh twice as many Club men. These our Captaine disposed in severall parts of the Towne, 10 or 12 of our best marks men upon the Steeple, and some in the Church ; Who being next the Enemy, awaited not their warning peece, but at the first sight gave fire upon them bravely. The Enemy who expected a surrender, rather then resistance, being herewith something daunted ; and perceiving how advantagious the Steeple was to us, presently possest themselves of some Houses not farre from the Church, very convenient for the shelter of their men, and planting of their Ordnance, and from thence sent out Sir *Iohn Gothericks* Troope, who partly to divert us from hindring them planting their Canon, and partly to hinder the Parish from comming in to our aid, past through some Parish villages on the one side of the Towne, robbed a Woman, most cowardly slew two naked Men, and so came within sight of our Sentinell at the West end of the Towne, Our Musquetiers there discharged at them, shot 2 or 3 Horses, whereof one of them lightly wcunded was brought into Towne ; and in a short space (partly by our shot, partly by the approach of some Club-men from *Bingley*) they were forced to retire back to their strength. In the meane time their Canons were planted in places most convenient for battering the Steeple, (which did most annoy them) and scowring of *Kirkgate*, downe which, our men must upon necessity march to resist them ; This done, Major *Carew* draws down some Foot, and therewith takes two Houses within 30 yards of the Church, and this he did without any other impeachment then from the Steeple ; Wee having not any strength to sally out upon them, from these Houses they plaid upon the Church very hotly, and the Church upon them : Our Steeple made a notable advantage of them, which our Musquitiers there especially improved against them, for when any Buffe or skarlet Coat appeared, they laid 2 or 3 of their Peeces in one hole, and discharged at once upon them with good successe, and thereby deterred the rest from relieving their men in the Houses,

A 2   and

and thus they continued till high-noone, about which time there came to our aid from Hallifax some Fire-men and many Clubbs, such of these as came to fight, were forthwith drawne downe to service, some of them were placed in the Church, others in Lanes neare the fore-said Houses; The Church and Lanes kept the Houses in play, and the Steeple hindred the Enemy from relieving the Houses. But this was not the way to repell the Enemy. The largenesse of the Church windowes, and smalnesse of the Houses, made their assault secure, and our defence dangerous, which our men perceiving, resolved to win or lose all at once; watching an opportunity betwixt the discharge and charge of the Enemy, they sallyed out of the Church, and being seconded by those in the Lanes, rushed in upon the Houses, burst open the doores, slew those that resisted, tooke those who yeelded; the rest fled into the next Field, whither some few of ours followed, (the greatest part being employed in conveying the Men and Munition which the Enemy had left behind them:) and in the Field the skirmish was hotter then ever; Our men were too eager to keepe Ranke or File, though they had knowne how to keepe it, and indeed their disorder was an advantage to us, for mixing themselves with the Enemy, they fought securely in the mouth of the Enemies Canon, and in the eye of one Body of their Forces, both placed in the Field above them; the Enemy not daring to discharge, least with them they should slay their own Men, (otherwise, they having 10 Fire-men for one, might have cut us off in an instant) nor could ours use their Muskets otherwise then as Clubbs. To speake ingeniously, their Commanders exasperated by the cowardize of their common Souldiers, manifested great courage, but they smarted for it; our Sythes and Clubbs now and then reaching them, and none else did they aime at: One amongst the rest in a Scarlet Coate, our Club-men had got hold of (and he in all probability, as some credible reports give us occasion to beleeve, was Collonel Goring) and were spoiling him: Their Horse fearing the losse of such a Man, became more couragious then they intended, leaped over the hedge, and rode full upon our Men, forcing them to give a little ground; too Much (alas that they had known him) to lose such a Man, but they quickly recovered the ground 'tho they lost the Man; doubled their courage, would neither give nor take quarter; (nor was this their cruelty, as the Enemy complaines, but their ignorance) and in the end forced both Man and Horse to leave the Field; and yet could not we keepe it, for we being separated from theirs, the Musketiers had liberty to play upon us; and indeed they rained such a showre of lead amongst our Men, as forced them to retreat for shelter to the next hedge, and so hindred them from pursuing, till they had removed their Canons. Their Ordnance all this time played upon us, one of them ranged an 8 pound Bullet; yet see the Lords mercy to us: that which was planted against the Steeple never hit it; another intended for the skouring of Kirkgate, 'tho planted in as advantagious a place as they desired, 'tho the Street was continually crowded with people; yea, though many of their Bullets hit the Houses, and some the Street, yet was no body at all hurt therewith; they bored indeed 3 or 4 Houses, yet (which is observable) did most harme to a Malignants; and thus the terror of the Lord, and of us falling upon them, sending their Foot and Artillery formost, away they went. (using their feet better then they used their hands) and about 50 of our Clubbs and Muskets after them; Which courage in ours, did most of all astonish the Enemy; who say, no 50 Men in the world, except they were madd or drunke, would have pursued a Thousand: Our men indeed, shot as they were madd, and the Enemy fell as they were drunke, and so we will devide it. Some discharged 10 some 12 times in the pursuit; and having the whole Body of of the Enemy for their butt, it may eafily be imagined what good execution they did in a miles march (for fo farre they purfued them) even to the Moore, where fearing to be environed by their Horfe, they retired, fome of them fo wearied with this 8 houres hot fervice, as they could fcarce returne to the Towne, One thing I cannot omit, a hearty Round-head left by his comrades, environed with the Enemies Horfe, difchar-ged his Musket upon one, ftrooke downe anothers Horfe with the thick end of it, broke a thirds Sword, beating it backe to his throat, and put them all to flight ; which (though as the reft wonderfull) I dare pawne my credit to be true. And thus ended our skirmifh ; wherein there was

Slaine of theirs, Sir *Iohn Harper*, (as one *Savile* taken at *Halifax* confeffeth,) Captaine *Wray* (in whofe pocket was found good ftore of gold, and a Commiffion directed to Major *Williams*, which made us thinke him to be the Man) and Captaine *Bins* (whom they carried to *Leeds* fcarce dead, and buried two daies after) and many common Souldiers, more I am perfwaded then we fhall ever know of. Of ours, I can-not heare of two that perifhed by the Enemy in the fight.

Sir *Iohn Gothericke* got a baftinado, had his Horfe killed with a Syth, and about a 100 common Souldiers were wounded, as we are informed from *Leeds* where they are Billeted : Of ours, about 12. all curable except one or two.

Taken of theirs, Serjant Major *Carew*, (a Man of great account, borne in the Low-Countries of Englifh Parents) 26 Common Souldiers, about 10 Horfes, 180 weight of Pouder, and about 40 Muskets ; and thus God fupplied our wants out of their ftore, giving us as many more Muskets as we had, and well-nigh as much Pouder as we fpent.

This was the iffue of the fight, wherein nothing can be feene but God, and the won-derfull effects of his glorious Attributes : Let us and our Enemies both fee it, that they may feare and fhame, that we may truft and praife our God, who hath manifefted him-felfe to be the Lord of Hofts.

A 3   A

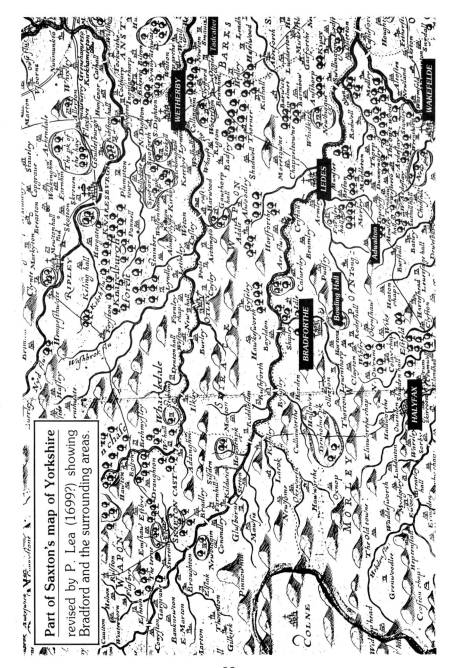

Part of Saxton's map of Yorkshire revised by P. Lea (1699?) showing Bradford and the surrounding areas.

THE RIDER OF THE WHITE HORSE — 1643

(A present-day version by Andrew Parkes)

Bradford's Deliverance

After his Excellency Lord Fairfax had retreated from Tadcaster, the Lord of Newcastle captured Pontefract. In order to make himself master of our western regions (of Yorkshire), he blocked all routes between us and our main forces, demonstrating his intention to sieze the whole county in order to exploit those who had supported the aims of Parliament.

We could expect from this, that the first towns to suffer would be those who had been most forthcoming in their support of Parliament; hence, Leeds, Bradford and Halifax became the principal targets. In Leeds however, Royalist sympathies were predominant and the town was easily brought into line. Bradford was the next place in their way, the town least able to resist them. Indeed when one considers Bradford's weaknesses and the dangers and discouragements, the town's act of resistance must be considered very worthy of admiration for its successful defence against the Royalists.

The main force of the Papist army was within one day's march of Bradford, amongst them were many, who had been incensed by their dishonourable retreat from the town not long before. We had been expecting help from Lord Fairfax, however we realised there was little possibility of us receiving it now.

Formerly our enemies had tried to placate us, but now came nothing but threats against those who had been the most active in their support of Parliament. The fear created by their threats was so great that many of the more high-ranking people fled out of the town — out went our Royalists to bring in the King's Catholic army. Some of the religious people in the parish, considering the dangers that might befall them (as regards their county and their consciences) from such cowardice and duplicity (which was instigated by the threat of perjury if they put up any resistance to the Parliamentary forces in the commandeering of their livelihoods and estates), decided to act positively. They invited all the remaining wealthy people in the parish to assist them and entered the town.

Our deserters were returned with a letter from Sir William Saville, in which he stated his intention to burn and plunder Bradford, if we did not contribute to the maintenance of the Papist army. To this we returned no answer other than in the impressions of those who had delivered it. Our stand was seen as a courageous attempt, desperate in the eyes of many who saw neither experience in our forces, nor sufficient capability to organise them — the mind,

33

body and constitution for war were deficient, we had no man in the parish to command us, nor would any stranger be persuaded to undertake the task. All our trained soldiers and their troops were with Lord Fairfax, together with most of those who were capable of service as volunteers. It could not be expected that the prominent people of our poor parish could pay a garrison for any length of time and no such garrison would remain more than one day without pay.

Our neighbours realised this and therefore judging our attempt at resistance (futile as it was, in the eyes of reason) and fearing that the result would be our downfall, they refused to help us, in case they should perish with us. In this respect we were not lacking setbacks from our own allies, as it was on the very night before the enemy's assault that the greater part of them deserted us. This was on Saturday December 17th.

The next morning at about 9 o'clock, the enemy was sighted approaching the eastern end of the town, they comprised of two groups. The forward group was commanded by Colonel Evers (the eldest son of Lord Evers) and included three troops of horsemen, two companies of dragoons, 100 foot soldiers, 20 pioneers[1] and two drakes[2], the train of artillery being commanded by the Dutchman Major Carew. The rear group was commanded by Sir Francis Howard and included (in addition to his own men) Captain Hilliard's troops, six companies of Colonel Eddington's dragoons, and 100 soldiers. Colonel Goring came with them and according to some, the Earl of Newport, but whether they had any command in the expedition I cannot say. All of these were Yorkshiremen who had been procured from the Lord of Newcastle in the same way as Sir William Saville's regiment.

Sir Marmaduke Langdale, Sir Thomas Glemnan and Sir John Gotherick's troops, Sir Ingram Hopton, Captain Nevill, Captain Batt and Captain Binn's companies had not been enough to overwhelm our lowly town.

I shall now describe how our men were arranged. It is a difficult task to organise men who have neither commanders, colours, nor distinct companies. The night previously we had borrowed a commander from Halifax who had almost 40 muskets and cavalry in the town, about 30 fowling[3], birding[4] and smaller pieces together with almost twice as many club-men[5]. Our Captain positioned these in several parts of the town, 10-12 of our best marksmen in the church tower and some inside the church. The latter did not wait for the warning sound from the enemy when they came in close proximity, but defiantly opened fire on them at the first sighting.

The enemy, who were expecting a surrender rather than resistance, were somewhat surprised. Realising how advantageous the tower was to us, they captured some houses not far from the church which were convenient for sheltering their men and siting their artillery. From this point they sent out Sir John Goodrick's troop, who passed through some of the parish villages on one side of the town robbing a woman and cowardly killing two unarmed men (this was partly to divert our fire from where they were positioning their cannon,

34

and partly to prevent the rest of the parish coming to our aid). Eventually they came within sight of the western end of the town. Our musketeers there fired at them, shooting two or three of their horses — a lightly wounded one of which was brought into the town. A short while later they were forced to retreat back to their main force (this was due to our shots and to the approach of some club-men from Bingley).

Meanwhile their cannon had been conveniently positioned for bombarding the tower (which was causing great annoyance to them) and for shelling Kirkgate, down which our men had to march in order to engage the enemy.

This accomplished, Major Carew led out some foot soldiers, with whom he captured two houses within thirty yards of the church. He did this without any interference from us other than from the steeple. We did not have sufficient strength to advance upon this group, and from the houses they fired at the church with considerable ferocity, as did the church upon them. Our steeple was a notable advantage to us, from where our musketeers could contain the enemy, as when any buff or scarlet coat appeared they put two or three of their weapons in one opening and fired upon instantly, with considerable success, thereby deterring the rest of their forces from relieving their men in the houses. This continued until noon, at which time some fire-men[6] and many clubs came to our assistance from Halifax. These were promptly pressed into service, some were placed in the church and others in the lanes near the previously mentioned houses. The church and lanes kept the houses in the battle and prevented the enemy from relieving their men.

However this was not the way to repel the enemy: the large size of the church windows and the small size of the houses made their advance secure and our defence dangerous. Realising this, our men decided to force the result of the battle. Watching for an opportunity between the firing and loading of the enemy, they advanced out of the church, and on being reinforced by those troops in the lanes stormed the houses. They burst open the doors, killed those who resisted and captured those who surrendered, the remainder fled into the adjoining field where a few of our men followed (most were involved in removing the men and munitions that the enemy had left behind). In the field the battle became more heated than before.

Our men were too enthusiastic to keep rank and file, despite the fact that they knew how to. However, their disorder was an advantage, where in mixing themselves with the enemy, they could fight before the mouths of the enemy's cannon and in front of the eyes of one other group of their forces which were both located in the over-looking field. The enemy did not dare to fire for fear of hitting their own men, (otherwise, having ten fire-men to our one, they could have cut us down instantly, especially since our men could now only use their muskets as clubs). To be fair to the enemy's commanders, who were exasperated by the cowardice of their ordinary soldiers, they demonstrated great courage, but suffered for it, our scythes and clubs being aimed directly at them. Our club-men had got hold of one of them who was wearing a scarlet coat (he was in all probability Colonel Goring, if we are to believe several credible reports) and were beating him. The Royalist cavalry fearing the loss of such a man renewed their efforts and jumped over the hedge towards our men, forcing them to give a little ground. Our men however quickly recovered this ground but despite losing the man, fought with renewed vigour and without mercy (they were not barbaric as the enemy states, but merely ignorant of the rules of war).

In the end they forced both the foot and mounted soldiers to leave the field. However we could not keep it, because once we were separated from the Royalist troops, their overlooking muskets had the opportunity to fire on us. In fact they created such a hail of lead that our men were forced to retreat to the nearest hedge for shelter and prevented from pursuing the enemy.

Throughout this time the Royalist artillery had been bombarding the town, one of the guns was firing eight pound balls, yet — thanks to the mercy of the Lord —, the one that was aimed at the tower never hit its target. Another which was intended for the bombardment of Kirkgate (despite being situated in the best possible position, and the fact that the street was continually crowded with people) did not manage to hurt anybody, although many of its shells hit the houses and the street itself. The enemy hit three or four houses, but unfortunately for them did the most harm to one of their own sympathiser's houses.

Thus with the wrath of the Lord and of us falling upon them, away the enemy went, sending their foot soldiers and artillery first (using their feet better than they had used their hands), and after them went about 50 of our own clubs and musketeers. The courage of our men greatly astonished the enemy, who believed that no 50 men in the world would dare to take on a thousand unless they were either drunk or mad. Our men did indeed fire as if they were mad, and the enemy fell as if they were drunk. Some of our men fired 10 to 12 times during the chase, and having the entire force of the enemy to aim at, the severe toll that they inflicted on the enemy during the mile's march (that was as far as they pursued them) can easily be imagined. At the moor our troops retreated, fearing the threat of being surrounded by the enemy's cavalry. Some of them, who were exhausted from eight hours continuous fighting, could barely return to the town.

One thing I cannot omit is the tale of one hearty roundhead, who, separated from his comrades and surrounded by the Royalist cavalry, fired his musket at one, cut down another's horse with the butt end of it, broke a third's sword, pushing it back towards his throat and saw all of them off. A story, the truth of which I would stake my life on.

Now the battle was over. Amongst the dead of the enemy were: Sir John Harper (according to the confession of a Saville who was captured at Halifax), Captain Wray (a large amount of gold was found in his pocket, together with a commission to Major Williams, which at first led us to be believe that the man was in fact Major Williams), Captain Binns (who the enemy carried to Leeds and buried two days later), and many ordinary soldiers who we shall never know of. Of our own forces, I have not heard of even two that were killed by the enemy during the battle.

Of the injured, on the royalist side, Sir John Gotherick got a beating, his horse was killed with a scythe and about 100 ordinary soldiers were wounded (according to our information from Leeds where they were billeted). Of our troops, about 12 were wounded and all except one or two were curable.

From the enemy we captured; Major Carew (a man of great distinction, born in the low countries of English parents), 26 ordinary soldiers, about 100 horses, 180 weight[7] of powder, and about 40 muskets. God had supplied our needs out of the enemy's store, giving us many more muskets than we had before and nearly as much powder as we had used up.

This was the result of the battle where nothing can be seen more clearly than the wondrous glory and power of God, let both us and our enemies see it, so that they may be shamed and awed, and that we may trust and praise our God, who has proved himself to be the Lord of Hosts.

FOOTNOTES

[1]Pioneers — Infantry soldiers, especially those trained in elementary engineering.
[2]Drakes — A form of small field gun/artillery.
[3]Fowling — Fowling pieces, muskets used to kill game birds.
[4]Birding — Similar to [3].
[5]Club-men — Men armed only with clubs or similar primitive weapons.
[6]Fire-men — Men armed with firearms.
[7]Weight — Hundredweight.

17th Century Room set up as a Bedroom

Bolling Hall, Bradford

38

BOLLING HALL

Bolling Hall is one of the very few buildings in Bradford which have definite connections with the Civil War. It was at that time the home of a Royalist, and was situated safely out of and above the town; for a few days it was the local Royalist Headquarters.

The manor of Bolling is first recorded in the Domesday Book of 1086, when it was held by Ilbert de Laci, Lord of the Manor of Pontefract. By 1316 it was held by a William Bolling, and it remained in Bolling hands until 1497. In that year Rosamund Bolling was married to Richard Tempest of Bracewell, and received the house and adjacent lands as her dowry. We do not know anything about the early buildings on the site, but the oldest part of the present Hall, the tower at the main entrance, was almost certainly built before 1500 and thus dates from Rosamund's time.

The young couple settled at Bolling. Their descendants lived there too, and by the time of the Civil War the owner was Richard Tempest, Rosamund's great-great-grandson. At the beginning of the war he fought for the King, and the Earl of Newcastle stayed in the house during the short seige of Bradford in 1643. Although Tempest submitted to the parliamentarians a year later he was fined £1,056. He was later fined a further £1,748 for being involved in the 1648 rising. This placed him in financial difficulties and in 1649 he sold the manor to Henry Savile of Thornhill Lees.

The Hall was sold again in 1668 to Francis Lindley of Hull; he died less than a year later and his widow managed the estates until their son, also Francis, came of age. His only son, Walter, was of unsound mind, so his mother and sisters managed the estate for him. After his death it went to a cousin, Thomas Pigott, and then to Mrs. Pigott's cousin Captain Charles Wood of Barnsley. Captain and Mrs. Wood employed the famous architect John Carr of York to redesign the east wing, but Captain Wood probably never saw it as he died of wounds in 1782.

The Woods' eldest son, Sir Francis Lindley Wood, leased the coal and mineral rights in the area to the Bowling Iron Company. The nearness of this heavy industry drove him out of the Hall, and in 1816 he made over the building too. It was owned in turn by two of the partners, but was let to tenants; by 1912 it was divided into several parts and was falling into disrepair. The owner, Mr. G. A. Paley, presented it to the City of Bradford, and in 1915 it was opened as a period house and museum of local history.

39